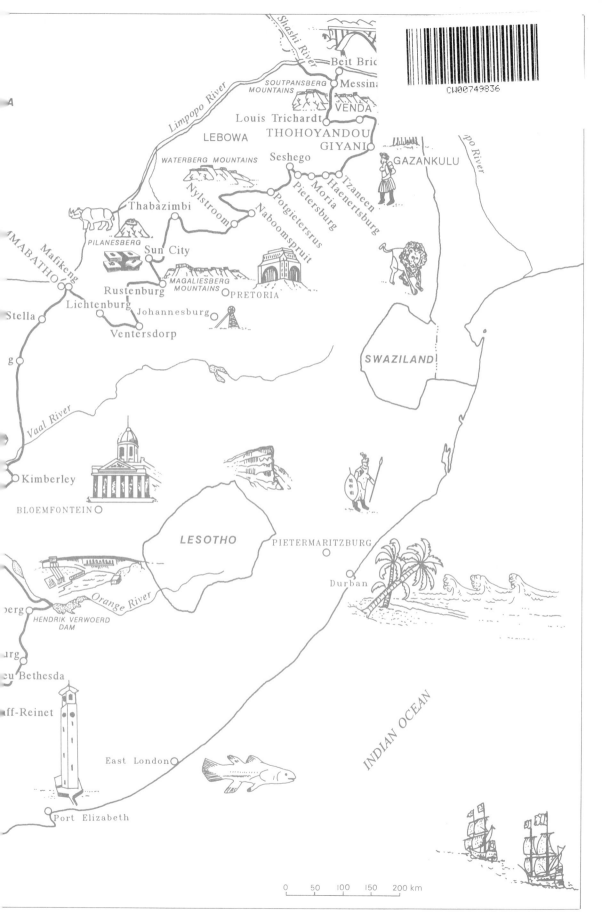

DRIVING SOUTH

To Denis,
for your birthday
26 April 1993.
I hope the places you
know so well will
come alive once more.
love,
Googles.

DRIVING SOUTH

DAVID ROBBINS

SOUTHERN
BOOK PUBLISHERS

ISBN 1 86812 467 3

First edition, first impression 1993

Published by
Southern Book Publishers (Pty) Ltd
PO Box 3103, Halfway House, 1685

Cover design by Insight Graphics
Cover photograph by Obie Oberholzer
Map by Ingrid Booysen
Set in 12 on 13 point Garamond
by Kohler Carton & Print (Natal)
Printed and bound by
Kohler Carton & Print (Natal)

Acknowledgements

Valuable material assistance from Barlow Rand Limited helped immeasurably in the research required for the making of this book. Others who provided special assistance and advice were Professor K D Gordon-Gray, Clive Lawrance, and Robert Lawson. My extensive debt to the many historians, biographers, and other writers upon whose work I have drawn is also acknowledged.

For

HOWARD DALTON

10 July 1952 – 13 November 1992

Contents

INTIMATIONS

I STOOD on pale rocks at the southern edge of Africa and watched the waves roll in from ice. The oceans stretched away for thousands of kilometres into the frozen places at the bottom of the world. Behind me lay roads and tracks and highways which had borne me for thousands of kilometres through the continent's most southern land. I had begun on a bridge; I had traversed South Africa's gaunt and complex heart; and now cold waves crashed against the rocks of journey's end.

Agulhas: these rocks, a bank of white pebbles, a low horizon, a lighthouse beneath a bleak and windswept sky. No inkling of what lay to the north and north-east from here. No presage of mountains and rivers and great space; no clue to the clamour and vehemence of the voices I had heard. Yet I carried my experience of these things as a burden in my memory now.

I remembered dust and soldiers and the grip of desolate landscapes. I saw again a bearded man with his arms outstretched like God, and in another place the presence of a multitude of people on their hands and knees in sand. I had witnessed caves of death and the beginnings of human life, and the marks of a beast standing upright at the door of sanctuary. Sheba's breasts were contained within my experience; so too the bitterness of defeat and the strapping on of weapons once again. I had passed through the glittering spires and the tortured failures of ethnic engineering, land bruised with claim and counter-claim; and through the thirst and the stampede for survival induced by drought. I had glimpsed the arrogance of power, the delirium of hope, the mire of despair, and the slithering persuasiveness of myth raised up to bolster the sore longing for a home. I had witnessed, too, something of the inner landscapes and contradictions carved out in humankind by the impact of great plains and of mountain and valley alike; and also the rage of youth and the bleakness of burial grounds. I remembered wind and billowing dust. But above all I remembered the sun as it burned down upon the land, a relentless force all through my journey; and then the sudden rain of winter; and now this bleak place where the waves rolled in from ice.

I felt that in accumulating this burden of experience, built up by plan and chance and what the turning of the road revealed, I had lost something of my innocence. And as I stood on those final Agulhas rocks, I felt my burden as an unwieldy weight upon me. What was I to make of it? Could I find an inner form or logic to a country where the shouting was so strident and opposed? Was there a deeper reality, even a shimmering of one, which hovered underneath a surface of such turmoil and transition?

But the experience itself must define the answers. The journey must unfold. So I turned my attention to the bridge and to the relative freedom of my innocence then. At Agulhas, meanwhile, the weather closed about me and the rain lashed fiercely down.

1

ON THE BORDER

THERE WERE no longer any machine guns under the bridge which spanned the wide bed of the Limpopo River. I could not see this, standing as I was upon the bridge itself, but the Major told me. He said the days of open aggression were over, and that now in the 1990s the army had moved into a more co-operative role.

Yet the river still formed a boundary, with Zimbabwe on the northern side. The far bank wavered slightly in the heat of a searing day, and the mounds and rippled expanses of sand in the river itself glared white. No water to speak of, except in a narrow and meandering channel. A little way upstream, a large tree trunk lay bleached and beached to one side, half concealed in an expanse of reeds. And on the southern bank, the stark and unconcealed straightness of the electric fence: two parallel netting barriers from which all vegetation had been cleared, and between them rolls of razor wire lay heaped up, a formidable obstacle made doubly so by the electricity threaded through the middle.

"At 220 volts it gives a nasty kick," the Major said, his eyes following the upstream march of the fence. "At 3 000 volts it's lethal. In both cases, we can see in the operations room exactly where it's happened."

A neat and compact man, this Major: carefully trimmed beard and moustache, blue eyes alert beneath his sloping beret. He tapped his cane briefly against the metal side of the bridge and shook his head.

1

"Very few people have died on the fence. Only a handful. Less than five in the last two years."

But through most of the 1980s, this northernmost border of South Africa had bristled with tension and guns. I did not ask the Major how many insurgents had died on the fence during those hostile years, nor for that matter how many civilians had been blown up by land mines planted in the sandy farm roads of the Northern Transvaal. Such things were of an era now passed, an era of rigidity and isolation, of soldiers under the bridge and little traffic upon it. Now, however, the country appeared to have turned clumsily onto a different course, and the immediate manifestation of this was the constant vibration of the bridge under the weight of the vehicles crossing in both directions.

The volume of traffic now posed a serious problem, the Major told me. The Colonel would shortly be arriving to inspect the emergency arrangements which the army, in its more co-operative role, had made. He pointed with his cane to a large area of bare earth scoured out of the bush on the South African side, the wheels of heavy vehicles lifting thick dust, a few soldiers directing the traffic. "Now that sanctions have gone, the congestion is terrific. Some of the lorries wait fourteen hours to clear customs. Before we organised the parking, they blocked the roads. They still make a two kilometre queue on the Messina road, waiting to come north."

I had a sense of a gateway having been opened. Huge articulated trucks growled on the bridge. Many had stickers on their doors: Zimbabwe Food Relief. Driving north laden with maize; returning empty for another load. "They get priority at customs," the Major told me. And the vehicles of trade and commerce also thronging the steel gateway; a long train sharing the same structure over the river; pedestrians with bundles passing to and fro. "Six hundred of them coming south on one Saturday alone," the Major said. The gate stood open, and it made a contradiction of the electric fence, grimly exposed down there in the grey-green bush of the southern bank.

I had stood with the Major in his operations room earlier that day. On a big map with blinking lights, he had pointed to the curve of the Limpopo, Beit Bridge close to the apex. "The fence runs from here," he said, indicating a point east of the bridge, "right through to the Vembe Gap in the west. On this side," he went on, his cane outlining the border as it ran towards Mozambique, "we have sisal, a thick barrier of it you can only get through by hacking a pathway which is easy to see. And here's the Vembe Gap, near the confluence of the Limpopo and the Shashi. It allows for the migration of game. There's only a foot-and-mouth fence there to keep cattle out." He spoke briskly and confidently to me, showing the position of some of the army's quick-react units which, once the alarm had been raised, could race in their Casspirs to any point along the border in no more than 20 minutes.

I asked: "But since we seem to be at peace with everyone these days, is the fence all that necessary?"

"Definitely," he said, nodding in his compact way. "There is no longer insurgency; the big problem now is illegal immigrants."

He showed me figures: thousands of arrests since the turn of the decade, the figures increasing sharply each year. People from as far north as Ethiopia, the Major said, from Zimbabwe, Zambia, East Africa, Zaire. Over 60 Mozambicans arrested outside Messina only the other day, walking all the way from the top end of the Kruger National Park, over 100 kilometres into South Africa, hiding by day, moving at night, running from starvation.

And I thought – as I stood with the Major on the bridge, that open gateway now – of those unable to make legitimate use of it, instead sawing through the sisal, digging under the fence, thin bodies freezing in the headlights of the Casspirs. The big Zimbabwe Food Relief lorries rumbled on the bridge. The sun glared down. Another African drought, its wretchedness brushing against me, and the prospect of famine came like a vague stench on the humid air.

As we walked from the bridge, I saw above dense mopane trees the pale blue clock tower and terracotta tiles of the customs and immigration complex, a limp South African flag, and the line of vehicles edging down the low hill towards the river. The Major greeted his soldiers working in the newly cleared parking area with an irate, "no no no". The vehicles were not being parked in neat rows. "They're all over the place," he said, marching purposefully about; "all you're making is another traffic jam." One young soldier, his expression slightly impish, explained that they had allowed the vehicles to drive all over the place to compact the earth, but now they would introduce neat rows. The Major grunted. But when the Colonel arrived, the Major explained about the need to compact the earth before a more orderly system of parking could be introduced. The Colonel laughed, undeceived.

He was a young man for so high a rank; his body seemed simultaneously stout and athletic; his face showed openness and intelligence. I had asked him for permission to visit an archaeological site

which lay on military land to the west of the bridge. He now drew
me a map and gave me the name of a contact. His English was fluent,
his manner relaxed. Later, I heard him talking in similar style to two
civilians about conditions in Zimbabwe: the drought, the shortages,
maize farmers turning for financial reasons to tobacco ("But who
will it feed?"), transportation in a state of collapse. "Only the quality
of management marks the difference between this side of the river
and the other," the Colonel said; "you will notice I have no other
discrimination." The two civilians smiled.

I stood to one side with the Major. I asked him if he enjoyed
working in the Northern Transvaal. "I like it," he replied. "I have
my family with me." He told me he had spent some years in Namibia.
"Up on the border there. And in Angola." I could imagine this
compact man, a career soldier, standing neatly to attention with his
service ribbons pinned to his chest.

"Yes, I like it here, even though I am from the Cape. So I think
wherever the army sends me next, I could not get further from my
home."

I told him that when I left the Limpopo I was planning to drive
to the south-west Cape, but by a circuitous route.

"All the way, hey," he said with a smile.

THE SANDY farm roads of the far north. I did not know whether
the one on which I drove, the Weipe road, had ever been planted
with land mines. I saw, however, that it cut through harsh bush and
then circled into a lush wet plain of ploughed fields, green crops, the
silver mist of irrigation systems lending a softness to the long view.
In a road sign, a bullet hole; in the fields, many black people stooping
as they worked. The wetness of things was a surprise, but I knew
that all these farms had as their northern boundary the Limpopo. I
was on my way to see Hansie, one of the riverside farmers, and I
stopped at a shop to ask for directions.

Waterplaas Cash Store, a rectangular building with a veranda running along its length, and in front of that a sandy yard, two donkey
carts under a tree, a dilapidated bakkie, bicycles, groups of black
people. A tight crowd of shoppers jostled inside the store, chattering
loudly. Two women appeared to be talking about someone from
Zambia. Young black men behind the counter deftly handled money
and change, and swept merchandise (most of which had to be
fetched from behind bars or wire) with some panache towards the
waiting hands: packets of sugar or flour skidding on the polished

timber of the counter, disappearing into carrier bags; boxes of cigarettes sprinting close to the outer edge, but never falling. I asked three youths on the veranda about the way to Hansie's farm. They would not look into my eyes. A hand jerked perfunctorily in a direction. As I drove away, I saw them smiling and nudging among themselves. But perhaps they did not find me particularly funny; perhaps it was the name of the farm which would always raise some amusement among them.

Vasbyt Boerdery. Part of it the jargon of young white South African conscripts serving on the various borders or other unpleasant places. Vasbyt: hang on tenaciously. Vasbyt farming. The tenacious farmers on the Limpopo, facing the uncertainty of the tumult of Africa with which the youths at the cash store doubtlessly identified. There seemed to me to be another insight implied in the farm's name. Vasbyt, min dae: a favourite conscript combination so frequently used that the two elements had become inseparable. Hang on tenaciously, not long to go. But there were no min dae for Hansie, I discovered. He told me quite adamantly he would never move again.

Yet at first he seemed a little ill at ease with me, standing out there on his lands in his khaki shirt and shorts and his strong brown boots. A middle-aged man, clean shaven, watchful eyes, polite but guarded. He left me for nearly 30 minutes while he followed a tractor engaged, it seemed to me, in some sort of insecticide experiment. The tractor grew small as it moved at walking pace between young citrus trees planted in perspective-converging rows across a big flat field.

Vasbyt Boerdery was extensive and well-equipped. This I had seen as I drove in: irrigated lands stretching away on either side of the gravel road, and then an airstrip, a yellow biplane parked at one end. Another aircraft of more modern design standing in the large workshops where several white men busied themselves with tractors and various pieces of agricultural machinery. A young man, unshaven and wiping grease from his hands on a piece of waste, came out to greet me with a friendly smile. He said Hansie was on the lands. He went into an office off the workshop; a two-way radio crackled. I saw a woman sitting at the keyboard of a computer. Long rows of tools adorned the back wall of the workshop: a hundred spanners hung in order from the smallest to the largest, scores of wrenches, screwdrivers, hammers, similarly displayed. The young man drove me in an open Land Rover onto the wide spaces of the farm. I glimpsed the farmhouse and outbuildings embedded in trees closer to the river. To the south, the husbanded lands stretched out. We passed a large metal structure which the young man said contained a cotton gin. Hansie had bought it in the American Deep South, had disassembled it there and shipped over the pieces. The white tufted cotton lay ripening in the fields. A big-business operation, this farm on the Limpopo.

I stood in the middle of it, waiting for Hansie. To one side, a field of lush-looking tomato plants in flower. And over there a big tractor dragging a piece of equipment over bare earth, raking it smooth, dust blowing out from behind. A flock of crows – black and white plumage and yellow legs – stood or flew short distances through the dust, waiting to see what the process might uncover. Closer at hand, a group of black women worked among the young citrus trees. And here was Hansie coming back, sitting on the front bumper of the tractor, while behind walked two labourers spraying liquid from a tank attached to the back. The liquid fell upon the long rows of citrus leaves so that they shone and glittered in the fierce sunlight.

"Not insecticide," he said after he had given instructions to the tractor driver and turned his attention to me. "Fertilizer. Absorbed through the leaves. For the moment," he went on, indicating the women crouched along the rows of young trees, "they're my insecticide: they pull off the caterpillars and eggs by hand."

We clambered into another Land Rover. A small fox terrier jumped in after us and stood on the back ledge of the cab, its front paws on Hansie's shoulder as he drove. He did so in silence for a moment, and then said in his guarded way: "Ask me any questions you want."

So I inquired about the big tractor raising dust – we were driving through a cloud of it – as it raked the area of bare earth, the crows circling now. He told me that more citrus would be planted there. "We're spending some money now, levelling it out, because once the trees are in, there'll be no chance. And we'll need to get vehicles in and out between the rows."

I said I had thought only cotton was farmed along the Limpopo. I said it had surprised me to see citrus and also tomatoes.

"The cotton market is low at the moment. It's hardly economic. Even if that wasn't the case, it makes sense to diversify. Maybe we'll try some mangoes later."

He stopped the Land Rover to speak to some men who were laying bricks behind the gin. I looked towards the river, unseen behind trees, and it seemed like a slightly sinister presence then, a mark of termination and potential danger. The sun beat down, burning the skin. In the silence – of that type which drums against the ears – I could hear Hansie's authoritative voice, issuing instructions. When he returned, the small dog trotting at his heels, I asked what conditions had been like during the insurgency years.

He hesitated, as if weighing me against his own guardedness. He started the engine and drove in the direction of the workshop. He said: "The uncertainty was the worst."

The vehicle rattled suddenly and sinews showed in Hansie's brown hands, gripping the wheel, as he negotiated a rougher section of the road. I grasped a handle which protruded from the dashboard.

"No, I didn't farm with a rifle by me, although others did. But the uncertainty... worrying about the wife and children in the house..." He glanced at me with a slight smile. "But we were used to it."

I raised my eyebrows.

"Zimbabwe," he said, "that's where we come from."

He had been born there, he told me, of Afrikaner parents. He had farmed there. By the late 1960s, he and his partner owned 16 farms, for which they had been offered 2,5 million Rhodesian dollars. They lived through the bush war. When independence came, black families settled on three of the farms. "There was nothing I could do. I saw everyone. One official at last admitted to me that he had given the farms away. Finally we sold out to the state for half a million dollars and came south. So it was not too bad here. We were used to worse."

At the workshop – the young man who had driven me earlier offered a wave – Hansie took me into an office and showed me aerial photographs of the farm. "This was in 1980. You can see there was no development. Just riverside bush. It had been a game farm. Then the government started to subsidize the price of farms. They wanted people in here for security reasons. But the subsidy had the effect of pushing up prices. Anyway, we bought. Four thousand five hundred hectares in total now."

More recent photographs showed a highly developed farm, the fields neatly laid out, clusters of buildings, a network of roads, the river curving gently along the northern edge. I remarked that it was an impressive transformation for not much more than a decade's work. Hansie agreed. He fetched a jug of orange juice from a refrigerator in one corner of the office, and we sat down at a table to talk. He seemed freer with me now, and he spoke without obvious reserve.

"Of course, with the subsidy on land came development: tarred roads, electricity, telephones. And then when the incursions started, more subsidies were offered for security fencing around the houses, for mine-proofing vehicles, and cheap loans for two-way radios. Even so, a lot of farmers couldn't make it, especially the smaller ones. Not for security reasons, but economic ones. They had no experience in extracting water from the sand in the river. We ourselves can do it now, but we paid a lot of school fees learning how. No, I don't think anyone moved for security reasons."

He offered more orange juice, refilled his own glass and drank. I heard the roaring of an engine from the workshop. When it had died down, I asked him to tell me more about the insurgency years. He shrugged.

"We still used to walk across the river to have braais with the farmers on the other side. The army tried to plant a sisal barrier, but it wasn't much use. It grew only in patches; the climate was too dry; the baboons ate the sisal or pulled up the young plants. Then in 1987 they put up the electric fence. That was a good move, although it put an end to the braais. It stopped a lot of petty theft from across the river: batteries and other movable equipment. It also had some impact on insurgency: the insurgents had to go round, or through the Vembe Gap, but that made it difficult for them to get out again.

"Mind you, its been a lot easier since the insurgency stopped. But now of course it's illegal immigrants running from the drought and economic collapse. Never mind apartheid; there's food here, the possibility of money. People from all over Africa. Not that this is anything new. It's been traditional for young men in Southern Africa to want to come south, work on the mines for a few years, then go back home. Now, people are coming south for food. People from the north have often offered to work here on the farm for nothing in exchange for food. It's strange – or isn't it? – this notion of the south being a haven in Africa. For whites and blacks. All whites in Africa knew, and still know, that when things become impossible they can always move south."

A man came into the office, nodding in our direction. He fetched a gun in its holster which had been lying on top of the refrigerator, and went out again. Hansie was looking across the table at me. I asked about his experiences in the Deep South when he had been dismantling his cotton gin.

He laughed. "They don't play down there," he said. "They call a nigger a nigger. The farmers I bought the gin from told me how once their Negro employees had wanted to join a trade union. The farmers had taken a few of them outside. And that was that. No trade union. Not even any Negro employees after that."

His face became thoughtful. He said, as if he felt the assertion necessary at that point: "I'm not a racist – I think some blacks are very clever – but there are differences."

"What are they?"

"I can put it this way," he said, regarding me with his watchful eyes. "The European developed in a cold climate: he had to think ahead or freeze to death. This is not so in Africa, not generally at any rate. Here you can eat a banana or kill a buck at any time. There's been no need to think ahead. They're clever people, don't get me wrong; they have a finely tuned memory, never having relied on reading. But the African style is different to our own, and we are the ones who are going to have to adapt. I personally am willing to adjust. I am forced to. I've got millions invested here. I'll never move again. I'm here to stay."

He accompanied me to my car. He said that although the uncertainty had sometimes been killing, he felt a guarded optimism. "Communism seems to be on the way out. Socialism has proved to be an economic failure. Multi-party democracy and free enterprise are trying to grow in Africa. This gives me some confidence. But even if things get worse again, I'm not moving."

We stood in the harsh sunlight together for a moment, the rasp and clatter of the workshop enhancing his sense of purpose. "And anyway," he said, "I like it here. I've become interested in the history. A man did his doctoral thesis near here recently, digging down. I think the black man's history is very fascinating."

I told him I had obtained permission from the army to visit Mapungubwe. Did he know of it? The archaeological discoveries? He nodded. We shook hands. I left him standing in the sandy yard. Then I saw him turn and stride once more towards the workshop, the small terrier at his heels.

HARDLY A dozen years before, the neat farmlands of Weipe had been a wilderness of bush and game. Now, only a few hints of this reality remained. On Hansie's farm, for example, black women were employed to camp among the ripening crops. They built crude shelters against the sun, sitting all day in the fields, keeping watch for baboons, banging metal against tin if the animals emerged to maraud among the harvests. And the gun on the refrigerator, taken for protection perhaps against the crocodiles which must still frequent the tangled bush and undergrowth down by the river where the farmers pumped their water from the sand.

Driving by the river in the Vembe Gap, not much further west, the full wildness of these northern places enclosed the mind. Large trees hung with vines; the white sand of the river between them; vervet monkeys swinging above the foot-and-mouth fence; baboons ducking beneath it, unconcerned by its electricity. And on the rough track, a glimpse of dark-haired bush buck, some impala leaping suddenly across, a warthog charging into undergrowth, and the pale fever trees rearing above the lower thicket of the bush. I was driving with an army warrant-officer, Serfontein, the contact the Colonel had given me at the bridge. Serfontein: a man whose whitening hair was cut short so that it bristled somewhat; about to go on pension, he told me, after spending all his working life in the army; a slightly pinched smile which revealed only his upper front teeth; a compulsive talker, yet without fluency in either English or Afrikaans, as if he suspected his listener would in any case doubt most of what he said. But for the moment he occupied only the periphery of my attention which was focused on the wildness of the country through which we drove.

Once away from the thickness of vegetation by the river, the country showed a harsh and broken face, abrupt cliff-sided hills between which lay a labyrinth of narrow valleys, water courses from a primeval time and littered with huge boulders which had not been washed away. A primitive landscape; a sense of slow evolution; a knowledge that *Homo sapiens* had trod the valleys and climbed these hills of rock at the confluence of the Shashi and Limpopo rivers for hundreds of millennia; a vision of sloping foreheads and hairy limbs and that look of puzzlement which I imagined must have haunted the eyes of those men and women who had helped to launch us on the great confusions and hopes of the human adventure. Stone Age overlaid by Iron Age on the banks of the Limpopo, and then the golden artifacts of Mapungubwe.

Serfontein was telling me how he had listened to the land mines exploding and how he had rushed out to kill insurgents creeping through the Vembe Gap.

The hill called Mapungubwe, shaped like a loaf of bread with slightly convex cliffs on every side, seemed impenetrable. We had stopped at the hill's south-western side. Before me, in the foreground as I contemplated Mapungubwe, stood a natural rock monolith three storeys high; and close by was ancient stonework, largely broken down, which made of the monolith a gateway. Perhaps this had once been the only entrance to the high places of their demi-god king. I passed through the gateway and ascended in a direction which Serfontein pointed out. He said he was too old to climb. At the base of the convex cliffs, I discovered a narrow gully, and a rope hanging down which archaeologists no doubt had left. I went into the gully and climbed, hauling myself up the steep cleavage in the rock.

The summit was seared and without shade. The view was of the summits of similar hills, standing like castles on either side of the river. The Limpopo could not be seen, but in the distance the Shashi swept in from the north-west, swollen with sand. Closer at hand, from one corner of the roughly rectangular summit of Mapungubwe, a large black bird sat watching me. A sense of the immense silence of past ages came upon me. The sun burned against my face and arms. Through binoculars, I could see the bird's unblinking yellow eye, the hooked beak; an image of royalty; not inappropriate, I thought, standing as I was on the site of the royal dwellings of one of Southern Africa's first cities.

The Shashi-Limpopo basin had been full of their development in medieval times. I thought of the gradual replacement here of the ebb and flow of old African chiefdoms by the relative permanence of kingdoms. Generations of royalty had presided over the Shashi-Limpopo city states, of which Mapungubwe was the most significant. Kingdoms based on tribute to the king, the tribute made possible by surplus production, the surplus production made desirable by external trade (controlled no doubt by the king) with Arab merchants whose ships used the trade winds around the shores of the Indian Ocean to bring the two continents within touching distance. Indian-made glass beads dug up by the million at Mapungubwe. And Mapungubwe gold (mined far to the north by tributary tribes, but worked into artifacts here), and ivory, and the work of craftsmen making articles from bone, and woven cloth, much of it almost certainly carried in the Arab ships to India and the Middle East.

But all was silence now. Mapungubwe's summit had been roughened by the archaeologists' digging, and the desolate surface was littered with potsherds, some of them perhaps a thousand years old.

I looked over the edge and saw Serfontein, a bare-headed khaki-clad figure, standing by the truck. From my vantage point the valley in which he waited had broadened into a small plain. In the distance a herd of buck moved slowly, heads bowed in the heat. It was on this plain, in the tenth and eleventh centuries, that the city of Mapungubwe had thrived. I became aware that Serfontein was looking up at me. We both waved, and then I turned towards the rope.

There were no longer any royal dwellings on the summit, no longer any stone-built walls and passageways. But I wondered what I had looked like from down there with the afternoon sun at my back. A king, a demi-god, a secluded and mysterious being, at once protector and lord? The majesty of hills, of being higher than the general level. How human it was to crave a lord, to seek his protection, even to welcome the imposition of his order and his will. And how powerful and willing to govern a hereditary king must feel, how permanent in his lineage. But the Mapungubwe plain was empty now, save for the slow-moving buck, as was the summit of the hill, save for the yellow eye and hooked beak of the watching eagle.

Serfontein greeted me with a smile which revealed only his top teeth. We drove slowly on towards the military camp where he was stationed, one of those quick-react units marked on the big map in the Major's operations room. Serfontein was talking about all the changes he had seen since he had joined the army in 1946. Better food for the infantry now; and the old foot days giving way to this modern idea of mobility, the lighter weapons, the Casspirs and the Buffels. We saw the Casspirs, rear doors open in readiness, as we drove into the camp – tents, sandbags, a long aerial protruding from a bungalow – huddled in a narrow valley in the broken, rock-strewn country. A sign at the entrance said in Afrikaans: "make weapons safe". Black soldiers, some of them clad only in shorts, watched as we drove in. I heard the repetitive beat of township jive coming from one of the tents. Black troops, white officers, Serfontein said. For a while, after he had parked the truck, he stood talking to me about all the special missions he had gone on during his career, staying away for weeks, and how dirty he would become, and how when he returned no one would come near him until he had bathed. I asked where these special missions had taken him. "I can't reveal that," he said, showing me his upper teeth.

In the evening, I climbed a hill to the north of the camp and looked down at the meeting of the Limpopo and the Shashi rivers, and at the flatness of the bush country to the north. Serfontein had told me that water to a depth of 20 metres seeped downstream beneath the sand of the rivers. To extract it: this was the technology which Hansie and his partner had paid a lot of school fees to learn.

In slow meanderings, the whitish scar of the Shashi came out of the darkening distance. The sun had set. The huge vista of northern bush turned blue-grey. Small birds noised in thorn trees close by. Above the camp, a black and white football spun into golden sunset air. I heard a soldier's strong laugh. And to the south, the land was broken, filled with boulder hills, falling away suddenly to narrow plains, like the plain at the foot of Mapungubwe, the medieval city-state which was no more. In the golden light I had a vision of the king, adorned with gold and ivory, standing on his mountain while the people kneeled beyond the monolith and the gate. I saw them kneeling in the harsh landscape. I felt their homage and their gratitude as I stood among the warm rocks of the Limpopo valley, looking south, seeing how the land rose slowly in jagged browns and greys to higher ground and darkness now.

Mosquitoes began to whine about my face, and a sudden hyena shriek ripped at the evening air, a sense in me of torn flesh as if somehow the sound had got into my bloodstream.

THE ROAD south from Beit Bridge and the border runs through interminable mopane bush studded with those most anguished and defiant of trees, the baobabs. Gnarled and twisting branches; hardly sufficient foliage to sustain so large a living structure; trunks half-collapsed sometimes under the weight and spread of the tree; and also a sense of reaching upwards in torment, the perfect visual representation of a blind and determined will to survive. They can live to great ages, these trees, sometimes measured in thousands of years, and then when they die they crumble away quickly into a softness of pulp and dust.

On the road south, when I finally turned in that direction, the traffic was dominated by big trucks, coming quickly out of the distance, black smoke pulsing from vertical exhausts, then roaring past with their invisible but buffeting slipstreams. I passed a convoy of 14 trucks, each one marked: Zimbabwe Food Relief.

The baobabs and the trucks, these glimpses of the concern with survival on the Great North Road, and the Great North Road itself, brought me to my purpose in driving south. I remembered the neat and compact Major from Cape Town as I drove. Cape Town: where this road began, and where I was going, or thereabouts. As the Major had said: all the way. But I would not travel the Great North Road for long. It seemed too direct; I had preoccupations to pursue other than simply getting there. Yet the road would act as touchstone sometimes as my broader purpose swung me to and fro across its route.

A direct route, perhaps, but the traffic upon it was not unstoppable. Outside Messina, which lies hardly 16 kilometres from the bridge, rows of vehicles waited in silence while a small train of cocopans clattered from a copper mine on the right of this important road to a processing plant on the left. Not much else to stop for in Messina though. A hot town which hardly interrupted the spreading of the bush, but with a dogleg at the northern end of the main street which forced the heavier vehicles to change down. To the right of the main street, the railway, a glimpse of smoking diesels crawling north. To the left, the shops: a few bottle stores, a jumbo discount centre, an ice cream bar, a few banks and filling stations; a few cars in the side streets, a few pedestrians, most of them black, some of them illegal immigrants perhaps.

But what of my broader purpose? I pondered this as I sat in an eating place in Messina that evening. The Restaurant Kremetart. Appropriate enough, since kremetart was Afrikaans for baobab; and the piped music and soft rushing of a bank of air conditioners not loud enough to silence the harsh-throated blast of decelerating trucks on the darkened road outside. Survival in all its varied forms; to see it manifested here, in my country, this southern haven as Hansie had intimated, this tumultuous place behind the electric fence, this ancient landscape filled with the marks of much humanity gone back to dust, filled also with strength and grief, and the arms of the living clawing out and up like the branches of baobabs.

To see it manifested here in the Restaurant Kremetart: dark red carpets, velvet curtains, upholstered chairs; and on the farther wall the incongruity of mirrors, thatched alcoves housing brandy advertisements, and an area of wood panelling in knotted pine. A big black waiter moved with an easy deference between the tables, small bowtie attached to the front of his short-sleeved shirt. Seven men in shorts, long socks and rough leather shoes came in and ordered steaks. A young couple held hands and gazed together into the flame of the candle on their table. A diamond sparkled on her left hand. A white waitress in a frilly dress always delivered the food to the tables, I noticed. Conversations droned and rippled. The girl with the diamond turned sideways to kiss her fiancé who had the name of his company printed on his shirt pocket. He paid the bill. They came close to my table on their way out, and I saw that the girl's eyes were molten with love, that stirring antithesis of fire and deep liquid. He held her to him as they walked, as if to save her from swooning away. The seven men, drinking beer, laughed while they waited for their steaks. I had climbed Mapungubwe with a rope, and had seen the black eagle up there, the eagle as sentinel, oblivious witness to the onrush and continuum, the old confusions and even older hope, of the human adventure.

I had written some of these things down on a slip of paper as I ate. But then the waitress startled me. Her frilly dress was at my elbow. Her face, as I looked up, seemed oddly square, no fire and liquid here. Did I need anything further, she asked, or would I prefer to look and write some more? Ons gee nie om nie – her tone was slightly tart – we don't mind. Surely she could never know how clearly, in her slightly outraged sense of invasion, she had read my deepest purpose.

2

FRONTIERSMEN

THE ROAD from Messina to Louis Trichardt switchbacked south through the ancient hills of the Limpopo valley, but all the while ascending to reveal at last a panorama of rolling bush country which ended only at the Soutpansberg. The bush showed grey in the light of early morning, with hundreds of greener baobabs rearing out of it, arms flung to the sky. The mountains formed a smooth east-west barrier stretched out across my path. As I approached, however, they began to show depth, revealing ridge after ridge, fold after fold, and the summits were shrouded in cloud. A dense whiteness tumbled down the northern sides towards me, as if spilling over from some great reservoir, but even as it did so it melted into wisps and then to nothing in the dry rain-shadow air. The road ran down towards the base of the mountains, through a narrow cliff-sided gap gouged by a river, and then ascended, climbing round big bald shoulders with massive bulks of rock and earth towering above. Then over a neck between two summits and into a markedly different world.

A misty lightness; overcast sky; northbound vehicles with their lights on; lusher vegetation at the roadside now; a fine spray of moisture gathering on the windscreen. Indigenous forests, huge trees looming in the mist. Further down, commercial plantations of wattle and eucalyptus reaching up the lower slopes of the range. Monkeys loping into trees. And then the spires of the churches of Louis Trichardt, the town's iron roofs gathered loosely together at the southern

16

foot of the Soutpansberg. An aspect of greenness under a clouded sky; and a publicity brochure referring to Louis Trichardt as the "gateway to Africa".

Stone Age artists have left their marks all over the Soutpansberg. After them came Iron Age people who, by AD 270, were living in the mountains. Although Europeans had visited the area for more than a century, it was only in the 1830s, during the Great Trek away from British rule at the Cape, that a substantial number of them settled here. A party of Voortrekkers established a town which was ultimately known as Schoemansdal, but in 1867 Schoemansdal was evacuated and partially burned down by Venda tribesmen whose stronghold was the mountains. For the next 30 years, the Vendas' occupation of the Soutpansberg could not convincingly be challenged. In 1898, however, Boer commandos finally smashed the Venda autonomy, and the town of Louis Trichardt (named after one of the original trekker leaders) began to develop. Beyond the mountains lay uncharted hunting grounds and the great malaria-infested valley of the Limpopo River. No wonder the town became known as the gateway to Africa. The epithet, and that sense of the frontier which underlies it, has remained.

The largely empty streets of Louis Trichardt on a Sunday morning: a modest gathering of cars outside the Church of the Vow, originally erected in thanks to God for the Venda defeat; one car with a bumper sticker which stated baldly, "proud to be white"; and in the middle of town a modern shopping complex – the Noor Centre – which occupied the better part of an entire block.

The Great North Road bypasses Louis Trichardt these days. It runs towards the Soutpansberg on the eastern fringes of the town, and on its farther side is Eltivillas and the Oriental Plaza. In common with most Northern Transvaal towns, Louis Trichardt has always had a small Indian population, Muslim traders who ran shops in town and lived in their dwellings close by. But the Group Areas Act, designed to separate urban people by race, changed all that. So Eltivillas stands apart, and the Oriental Plaza (where the Indians have traded since being pushed out of town in the early 1970s) comprises a central parking area surrounded on three sides by shops: among them A V Mahomed & Sons, Cassims, the Venus Trading Company and Solly's Discount World, its windows crammed with radios and television sets, hi-fi and photographic equipment, and household appliances.

A generous acquaintance had opened her Louis Trichardt home to me while I explored the Soutpansberg; and it was this acquaintance

who told me of the linkage which existed between the modern shopping complex called Noor and Solly's Discount World in the Oriental
Plaza. Solly Noor, she said, was one of the most successful business-
men in the far Northern Transvaal.

But there were more immediate preoccupations. In spite of the
misting on my windshield as I descended the mountain, Louis Trichardt was a town in the grip of drought. Only six to eight months'
supply of water left in the dams; people bemoaning the state of their
gardens; plantation fires, a winter hazard, already upon the Soutpansberg even though summer had hardly begun to fade; theories
about the drying out of Africa.

On that first Sunday in Louis Trichardt, as I drove west along the
foot of the Soutpansberg, going to see a man who ran a game farm
and hunting lodge high up in the mountains, I came across a large
bakkie which had slithered off the road, the windscreen smashed,
radiator grille buckled inward. Two other vehicles had drawn up
close by. I nevertheless stopped and asked if I could help. A man
came across to me, smoking a cigarette. "No problem," he said in
Afrikaans, "the police have been called." I asked what had happened.
"A kudu ran into me. The poor buggers are looking for something
to drink." There was no sign of the kudu now, but a big woman in
a sleeveless dress, perhaps the driver's wife, stood quietly by the open
door of the bakkie, bleeding from the face and upper arms.

TO GET to Tony's farm, I drove straight up the side of the Soutpansberg. In these more western parts, the mountains were steep-
sided, a succession of huge bulges and volcanic mounds and great
walls of greyish rock extending for kilometres. With the sun on them
and with mist still clearing from their heights, they presented a landscape of magic and dreams, as if anything might happen there. My
road was no more than a track cut in a zigzag into the mountain,
the gradients tortuous, the bends acute. The rear wheels of the car
spewed out stones and dust sometimes as I ascended.

I sat with Tony on the patio of his gracious hunting lodge, looking
out through trees over the wildness of those high mountain places.
No trace of agriculture anywhere; only the rocks and grass and trees
of the summit. I had seen a few animals on the way, and it was about
hunting them that we now spoke.

He said that overseas hunters paid a great deal of money for a 14-
day hunt. There were prices on the animals they wanted to kill:
leopards, for example, in which he specialized, carried a shooting fee

of thousands. Add the cost of accommodation, taxidermy and airfares, and hunters were paying up to R40 000 to bag a trophy in this wild part of Africa.

"We take only overseas hunters," he said in his diffident way, "and only four or five each winter. This is to conserve the game."

I asked him what sort of men these hunters were.

He looked away into the distance of the high places, his pale eyes absent, slightly pained by my presence. He shrugged his shoulders. "All walks of life. From plumbers to managing directors. And all ages. Sometimes men in their sixties. Americans, Swiss. Also a Chinese income tax expert from Singapore. Some of these men save for years to come to Africa and hunt."

A middle-aged woman emerged from the house at this point. Tony introduced her as his wife. She said that the telephone was giving trouble again, and that she would drive out to see if she could discover the problem. Tony said to me: "It's the giraffes. They rub their necks against the poles and tangle the wires. Quite a nuisance."

I judged Tony to be in his late fifties, but with a lean body which sat awkwardly in the wire patio chair; his eyes reserved, his skin, where it was not concealed by a grey-brown beard, severely weathered, with occasional patches of pale pink showing on the darker surface of his forehead, temples and cheeks.

He found my eyes upon him, and he looked at me for a moment and then said: "I have a friend who wants to get into his vehicle with the best bottle of whisky he can find. Then drive north until he has a good view of Mount Kilimanjaro. Then stop and drink the whisky." He smiled, but I saw that his eyes had deepened. Had he shared something of himself with me? His own attachment to Africa perhaps? This English-speaking African with the battered skin: his private perceptions of a landscape of dream and magic, the animals and the wildness, and the consuming quality of his solitude here. I asked him why he thought people liked to hunt the animals.

He said: "Mankind has killed for the pot for tens of thousands of years."

"But for trophies?"

"It's the adventure of the chase, I suppose. The excitement of being in Africa. If we couldn't hunt here, the place wouldn't exist. We are taking a yield out of the country and at the same time conserving it. But it's an extremely difficult way to earn a living. Our only real income is from hunting, although we make a small amount from our nature and wildlife trails."

He went into the house and brought out a few overseas hunting magazines: advertisements for rifles, specially designed jackets, boots, headgear, knives, and other hunting paraphernalia. The magazines also contained photographs of privately owned trophy rooms, slightly bizarre crowds and collections of stuffed animals, each no doubt with its own story. Tony told me that Spaniards, especially, loved to come out and hunt in groups of up to six men. "We don't take them. We take a maximum of two at a time. Because these groups turn the whole thing into something of a competition. They like to kill, they get hooked on killing rather than on hunting."

And then he said a revealing thing: "But the trouble with tapping into the tourist trade, even to the extent that we do, is that one is back to people, the need to socialise and be polite. I don't enjoy it."

We nevertheless spoke about the hunting. Tony's son, it turned out, had a professional hunter's licence, acquired only after much study and a three-hour written examination. They would not have been allowed to operate without such a licence. Then Tony told me how the leopards of the mountains were hunted. Bait, in the form of an impala, was hung in a tree. A leopard would be allowed to feed off the buck for several days, then a hide would be built about 50 metres away and the hunter would wait inside it.

"It's not as easy as it sounds," Tony said. When I offered no comment, he went on. "We shoot only males. But they're clever. They're individual. There are no rules, no standard patterns of leopard behaviour."

I asked if hunters wanting to shoot a leopard ever went away disappointed.

"Often. Our success rate is around sixty per cent. That's higher than most places. But it's never a certainty."

He showed me briefly over the hunting lodge, built partly of the warm terracotta stone with which the mountain was littered. The large and tastefully furnished lounge and dining room; the self-contained rooms built as a wing off the main house. Dark-tiled floors, small carpets and rugs; appropriate pictures on the walls, but no hunting scenes and no horns, everything much more tasteful and subtle than that; and the gun racks a standard feature in all the built-in cupboards.

In the dining room he directed my attention to a place in the ceiling where one of his clients had accidentally blasted a hole while cleaning his rifle. It had not been repaired, but remained as a warning to those succeeding hunters who passed through the lodge each winter. Those excited Africa-hungry men in their hunting jackets and northern hemisphere complexions, jetting in for a kill.

Tony was telling me how one evening he had watched, through the big windows at the front of the lodge, a leopard take a buck hardly 40 metres from the house. He described the screams, his sense of the terror. And how the baboons would take a bush buck and tear it to pieces and begin to devour it while the agonized buck was still alive.

"The natural world is tough and savage and highly organised," he said, looking out of those same windows now. "It is the only world I respect and admire."

"We come out of that world," I remarked.

"Yes, but we've come too far. We are hammering away and messing everything up. One wanders where it's all going to end. I can't help feeling that even this drought is partly man-made."

He walked with me to my car. He was a tall figure, slightly stooped, perhaps with his age, but perhaps more surely through his reserve and shyness with people. A solitary figure, living on the wildness of Africa, it seemed to me, both physically and spiritually. Was there such a thing as the aesthetics of savagery? This lure reflected in the diffident eyes, this need to find in the constancy of mountain and bush some refuge from humanity's great onrush. He told me, as I stood with my door open, that his long attraction to the wild places had extracted a price. He had not long ago had quantities of cancerous skin cut out of his face and arms.

ON THE way back to town I had my first sight of a phenomenon which would soon dominate my travels for many hundreds of kilometres. The grass and thorn trees which stretched away on the flat plain to the south of the Soutpansberg gave way in places to areas of dense human settlement where the vegetation had been used up. The areas were reddish in colour, studded with dwellings, a few fields of stunted maize; and animals everywhere, cattle grazing on what they could find, goats standing upright to browse the leaves off bushes and low trees; and not infrequently women in single file, bundles of wood balanced elegantly on their heads. And always the houses stretching away, a few iron roofs and cars flashing briefly as they reflected the sun. Homeland places. In this case, a few small pieces of the Venda homeland, "independent" since 1979, and supposedly a separate country.

I would go later to the main piece of Venda, still tucked into the eastern Soutpansberg; I would go to the self-governing states of Gazankulu and Lebowa, and finally to another "independent" country, Bophuthatswana, much further to the south. And I would see the same denseness of settlement, the same sparseness of vegetation, nearly everywhere.

The creation of the homelands had been motivated by the same concern for separation of the races as the Group Areas Act. But in terms of social engineering it was more ambitious. It had resulted in the formation of whole countries, none of them economically viable, meant to absorb unwanted urban labour, to house the families of such labour as was needed in the cities, and to provide black Africans in general with a political voice, but only in these rural backwaters where the ruling elites were in any case propped up by funds from central South African coffers.

In almost every sphere, the homeland system had failed, and much of the apparatus required to keep it in place had been abandoned. Yet the homelands themselves remained. I saw the reddish colour of them as I returned to Louis Trichardt. I saw a hundred boys playing football on a field with branches for goalposts, and heard all the dusty laughter and shouting of the game. To the right the steep Soutpansberg looked proud and unconcerned in the light of afternoon.

In Louis Trichardt, the slate spire of the Church of the Vow stood against a background of the plantations and forests covering the mountain even to its summit. The God-given victory over the powerful Venda tribe leading to the Venda homeland, and now finally to Venda protest. White men, I had heard, whipping Venda youths with sjamboks in these quiet streets some time before my visit.

I turned at last in the direction of my acquaintance's home, a rambling and silent house set in trees some way up the southern side of the mountain. My acquaintance was away on business, so it was a reception of dogs' wet muzzles and friendly tails, as if they had been told that sooner or later I would turn up, of the richness of bookshelves and collected things, and of the unquestioning comfort of deep chairs and thick carpets. I sat for a long time thinking of the white men of Louis Trichardt whose predecessors had been frontiersmen, nearly always with hunting rifles clutched in their rough and ready hands.

AT THE town headquarters of the Schoemansdal museum, I met a man named Sidney, the archaeologist who had excavated the old frontier town. His office was filled with artifacts from the various digs spread out on tables around his cluttered desk. Hundreds of bits of glass and metal; fragments of old tableware; tobacco pipes in porcelain and clay and soapstone; some weapons; a few tools and tin boxes.

The first thing he said to me was: "We live very close to history here. Do you know that even in the 1930s, the land between the Soutpansberg and the Limpopo was used as open winter grazing, and for hunting expeditions, little different from Schoemansdal days?"

In spite of his name, Sidney was an Afrikaner. After we had made our initial exchanges in his language, however, he spoke to me in English. He was in his late thirties, slightly overweight, with dark hair and trimmed beard, a coarse and sun-ravaged skin, but with thoughtful eyes which seemed unhardened by certitude and absolutes.

I said I was interested in learning more about Schoemansdal. He began by providing me with a brief chronology. Louis Tregardt and another trekker leader named Van Rensburg, aware of the environmental richness of the Soutpansberg, arrived with their followers in 1836. Both these men ultimately died in the low disease-infested eastern areas of the subcontinent, but there were by then sufficient trekkers under the leadership of Andries Potgieter for the town to be laid out in 1848. By 1855, the year Pretoria was founded far to the south, Schoemansdal boasted a population of over 1 500 frontiersmen and adventurers. The economy was based on what they could take off the land: ivory and skins, and timber from the indigenous forests. Yellowwood planks up to 30 metres long were on offer, much of it going to Natal. But ivory was the main export, over 200 tons being exported to England alone in 1855. One source records that more than 1 000 elephants were shot in less than three months.

But the town soon faced problems. The frontiersmen had begun to use the Venda, even though a Schoemansdal law forbade it, to do their hunting for them. Tension mounted as the natural resources were used up and as Schoemansdal realized there were over 100 elephant rifles in the mountains with the Venda. In 1867 Paul Kruger, later to become the President of the Transvaal Republic, arrived with a commando but decided in favour of withdrawal rather than to fight. The frontiersmen themselves demolished the houses to take the materials south. The Vendas burned the church and the parsonage, more a celebration perhaps than a sacking. As one Venda chief put it at the time: "These people are the locusts who will eat up our country."

Sidney showed me a collection of old photographs from the time of the 1898 revenge. "Until then, the Venda had never pitted themselves in force against the whites," he said; "they were too full of schemes and intrigue for that." But in 1898 they had little choice. For the first time, exploding shells were used against blacks in South Africa. The photographs showed something of the destruction. One shell had shattered a large stone monolith in the chief's royal enclosure. After the battle, a piece of the broken rock had been brought down the hill on a gun carriage to serve as the foundation stone of the original Church of the Vow.

Sidney drove me to Schoemansdal. The town had been built on the same flat country south of the mountains upon which I had glimpsed those pieces of the Venda homeland. Indeed, Sidney told me that the land had been given to these local tribes because they had helped the 1898 commandos by showing them a way into the mountains to mount an effective attack on the rear of the real Venda enemy further to the east.

The country shimmered with heat as we arrived, thorn trees in the distance seeming to dance, as in a mirage. Before us stood a collection of thatch and mud structures, obviously recently built, and to one side, not far from a dry river, earth mounded into a square, the original redoubt, Sidney told me as we walked among the low and crooked buildings.

"This is where the people lived temporarily, while Schoemansdal was being laid out," he explained. "We have tried in this reconstruction to be as authentic as possible, not to romanticize these Voortrekkers. They were hard people, not very clean, and with no altruistic intentions at all. They came to the area to exploit it, to survive. For their first buildings they used what was available, making a response very similar to blacks. Most of them were also illiterate, and their investment was counted in cattle and sheep."

We went into some of the houses: mud floors and walls, branches holding up the roof, low beams and lintels, small unglazed windows. "A family of nine or ten might have lived in these two rooms." These crude buildings of the frontier provided a sense of primitive living – indeed, of primitive people – but also a sense of ingenuity and determination. They had flown a flag here which was almost identical to the diagonally-crossed emblem of the American confederacy, and they had taken slaves under the name of "apprentices", usually young children, from the surrounding African homesteads.

"And, of course, out there," Sidney said, indicating the flat country as it lapped against the base of the mountains, "was the game. There would have been very few trees in those days. It would have been pure savannah, long grass, herds of buck, elephants, giraffes, all plainly visible. A hunter's paradise."

Schoemansdal proper had been laid out a few hundred metres away, but there was little to see now. Sidney told me we were standing in the main street, and it is true that a vague outline did appear then. The vegetation seemed substantially lower along the thoroughfare, and the remains of building foundations running along its edges could sometimes be seen among the weeds and thorns. But there was not a single structure left standing.

Sidney said: "It's always incredible to me: the age of the land, of human experience on it. Under here, there's Stone Age stuff at least a hundred thousand years old, probably older. In the mountains are San paintings. Then there's the Iron Age, from early to late. And black art and rain-making symbols. And all the stone-wall stuff which began at Mapungubwe, and found its way down here, some of it via Great Zimbabwe. And overlaying all that is Schoemansdal."

Under his guidance, the town returned. It had been laid out in the classic Dutch grid, and he knew the names of all the streets. He showed me the foundations of a 30-metre-long brick house, the largest in Schoemansdal, where General Potgieter had lived and died. He showed me gnarled keiapple bushes, planted as hedging and still surviving after nearly 150 years. And stunted pomegranate trees in a row. And here the fort had stood, brick-built on a stone foundation, 50 metres square, with bastions on two corners, and a cobbled place for horses.

"I don't know whether they ever used it. I believe that the prag-matism of the frontier would have encouraged a symbiotic relation-ship with the indigenous people. The water supply came from the mountains in that furrow over there. If the two sides were hostile, it would have been easy enough for the Vendas to have stopped the water. Here's a story for you about the sort of relationship which must have existed, at least for a time. A woman from Schoemansdal, Dina Fourie, walked with her family and some other people to Sofala – that's Beira now – and on the return trip she lost her husband and children. Black people found her and brought her back to Schoemansdal."

Of the 50 hectares on which the town had stood, Sidney had excavated one and a half. The only town in South Africa, he said, that was frozen in this time warp of 20 years, then left; nothing changed, nothing altered or added on. He spoke about the use of recycled material, stones from a nearby Stone Age site used in the foundations of the fort; and, look here, even a hollowed-out grinding stone, doubtless from the same site. He picked up a piece of glass which glinted in the sun. A piece of an English gin bottle. Sidney had found bottles everywhere. A rowdy frontier town with plenty of drunkenness and merriment and noise. Yet here was church and parsonage, the latter boasting the only timber floor in Schoemansdal. And over there, facing onto the market square, had been a row of shops, one of them owned by Cassimier Simoneon, a trader from the Indian province of Goa. Solly Noor's forerunner, I thought.

At the end of our visit, Sidney fell silent. We returned in this way along Schoeman Street. He stood by the car, his door open, but lingering a moment. The thorn trees endured in a silent yet pressing throng.

"All the voices of the people," he said, looking across the site of the old frontier town, "they're here. They're still here. When you work here a lot, you really do begin to hear the voices." His eyes were thoughtful, yet alive with an abiding interest.

SOLLY NOOR said: "It's been very turbulent, very difficult. There were over 100 laws to prevent Indian traders from succeeding. They wanted us to go back. Indians for India, they used to say. My grand-father came to this country, to Pretoria, in 1895. At one stage he was a close neighbour of Paul Kruger. If Oom Paul knew what the laws would do to us, my grandfather used to say, he'd come out of his grave fighting.

"My father was thirteen when the family immigrated. They came from Ranavav in south India. I've been in many parts of the world. I go to the east – Japan and Hong Kong – nearly every year. But I've never been to India. Yes, I have a yearning to see it.

"Just after I was born in 1948, my Dad moved here to Louis Trichardt. But in the early 1960s he took ill. I had just finished standard six. There was no more schooling available here, and no money to go anywhere else. So I was right in the deep end of the river at fourteen. My Dad was a jeweller by trade, but that wasn't my piece of cake. As a youngster I loved music, so I started with a little record store. I bought a cheap record player for the shop. Some-one wanted to buy it. I bought a better one, and again sold at a profit. That's how I got into the hi-fi business. Once I went to the Victoria

Falls for a holiday. I couldn't find a small camera anywhere in Louis Trichardt. I ordered a cheap Instamatic from a supplier. It took beautiful photos. So I ordered a few more for sale. That's how I got into photographic equipment. Then, in 1972, when we were forced to move, I wanted some kitchen equipment for the new house here in Eltivillas. The supplier said he could help, but only if I stocked his range. I agreed. And that's how I got into kitchen appliances. Today, with the grace of God, we have thirty-nine companies under our umbrella, all based in Louis Trichardt.

"The Noor Centre? There was an old hotel on that site. I bought it under the nominee system, you know, because Indians weren't supposed to own land in a white group area. It was a big chance, a big risk, but I was quite open about it. The result was we had a massive backlash against us. Anyway, we went ahead and built the centre. But we had to live with a wave of human aggression, as well as all the restricting legislation. But I was determined to do it. We had a huge opening – I wanted to prove my point – with dignitaries from far and wide. It was the first time in history that the opening of a shopping centre was covered live on national radio.

"But we endured a silent war here. On the day of the opening – it was in 1988 – we had a bomb scare while we were having lunch. Since then, the centre has been vandalised five times: anti-Indian graffiti, smashing ceilings in the walkways. The irony is that the people who do it are all my customers. It shows the hypocrisy of the situation: the ideology and the politics have nothing in the end to do with economics.

"Recently a white South African now living in Zimbabwe criticised Mugabe for his proposed land appropriation. 'As a civilised man, I can't agree with this,' he said. I blasted him. 'He's doing to you exactly what you did to us,' I told him; 'I'm not condoning land appropriation, but don't talk civilised behaviour to me.' We were forced out. My shop was in the main street of Louis Trichardt. We lived there. Our compensation was ridiculous. It was very much like theft.

"But I mustn't get indignant. The amazing thing is I've fought the system all my life, but I've never felt any bitterness. In the 1960s I had to get a permit just to travel to Natal. We've been chucked out of resorts for being Indians. The usual thing. Slowly but surely we are winning the day though, even with the ultra-right. It's all economics, and they are seeing the light. In the end they will see it is possible to live together. In their hearts they already know it is possible.

"I've never felt more optimistic in my life. There are years of turbulence ahead, sure. But I feel real optimism. Even when things were bad, I've never thought of emigration. This is home. Our love for this country is as much, perhaps more, than that of some of the more vocal political people who talk about 'our country'. I think," Solly Noor concluded, "that I would like to die here."

AT THE taxidermist's showroom: catalogues filled with hunting equipment similar to the advertisements in Tony's magazines. Were all these jackets and knives (and a smart-looking waistcoat with loops for cartridges) popular among the hunters of Louis Trichardt?

The taxidermist chuckled. "People here would laugh if you dressed like that. South Africans don't bother too much about what they wear. Khaki shorts and a bush hat is good enough. Hunting here is an extension of their lives; it's part of a tradition reaching back to Schoemansdal and beyond. Hunting for the pot, collecting biltong for the winter."

A pleasant enough young man, the taxidermist, looking at me through gold-rimmed spectacles. He had long hair, as the earlier frontiersmen would have had. I asked him if he himself shot wild animals.

"There's a big difference between shooting and hunting," he said.

"What is it?"

"Have you heard of a Kalahari gunship? That's ten men on the back of a bakkie shooting everything that moves. Hunting is done on foot, stalking the animal, pitting your wits against the animal's. The gunship thing isn't ethical. It's like Australian underhand bowling. It really isn't cricket," he added, pleased with his analogy.

Then he said in his pleasant way: "You have to enjoy nature to hunt. I like to hunt, yes. It is enjoyable."

"Is there a lot of poaching here?"

"There is some, yes."

I had paged through back issues of the local newspaper and found regular stories of court cases where a considerable percentage of the accused were white men. Poaching game at night, and also cattle. I had begun to think that every man I saw in Louis Trichardt must be a hunter. The men behind the wheels of cars and bakkies: often overweight, khaki fabric straining against bellies and thighs, invariably smoking cigarettes, big meat eaters and beer drinkers, swapping stories around their braaivleis fires, stories of the hunt, perhaps, or of the Kalahari gunships, and almost certainly of that climactic moment, finger poised on trigger.

The taxidermist, by contrast, was markedly thin, and he wore an apron. He told me that he supposed taxidermy could be called an art form. In his workshop behind the showroom, black men and women, and two white men even younger than the taxidermist himself, were busy with the various stages of the taxidermy process. First, the scouring of the wet skins to deflesh them, then the treating of the skins, then placing them over the polystyrene forms with the eyes and mouth pinned into position – a particularly unsightly stage – and left for up to six weeks to dry. Then the touching up, the art form part, putting in the plastic teeth and marble eyes. The workshop smelled vaguely unpleasant. The taxidermist said they did no work for museums; all their creations ended up in South African and overseas private collections.

I found it difficult to grasp the deeper rationale. Perhaps it was a perverted rationale now. The original: shooting to survive, even the shooting of thousands of elephants out of Schoemansdal for economic gain, tearing out the tusks and leaving the carcasses to satiated vultures and hyenas. Now the hunter pays to kill. He pays some more for taxidermy. Then he lives in close proximity to the image of his victim, a mark of his triumph, a mark more surely, I suspected, of a hard-eyed machismo pacing restlessly in suburbia now.

Could these things fairly be suggested to describe the big Afrikaner men of the Northern Transvaal? Manly, they certainly were, displaying that scarcely-hidden aggression that goes with the male consciousness of gender. I spoke to Sidney about these things. He laughed at me with his thoughtful eyes. Was there a link, I asked, between that kind of manliness – giving no quarter to man or beast – and political conservatism?

But Sidney thought that the very heart of the conservative response was made of myth, rather than the realities of the frontier. It was only during the first 30 years of the 20th century, he said, that the rapidly urbanising Afrikaans speakers, smashed and impoverished by the Anglo-Boer War, had struggled towards the concept of Afrikaner nationhood. And much of this struggle had been built on 19th Century mythology, a distorting of their own history. The myth of the Voortrekkers as Israelites looking for the promised land, for example; the myth that the Afrikaner nation had been forged in pioneering, urged on by an exclusive covenant with God. It was that mythical nation which they saw as under threat again now, betrayed by their own intellectuals who had dispelled the historical myths and were now moving towards a new reality.

"But you must speak to them yourself," he said.

PIETER F turned out to be an eloquent talker. Not so surprising perhaps, since he was a Louis Trichardt lawyer and town councillor. Sidney had told him that I wanted to learn something of his views. Obligingly, he invited us both to lunch. He had a prosperous look about him: clean-shaven, hair carefully styled, a pale grey suit, an easy and confident chuckle.

He spoke about the Soutpansberg, its beauty, its uniqueness. He said once you had drunk the water of the mountains you would always be drawn to return. He also said that the Soutpansberg could be considered a gateway.

I suggested that it might be more like a melting pot, a meeting place of different peoples through the ages.

Yes, he said, the melting pot idea was good: the Soutpansberg as a microcosm of Africa. Then he began to talk about what he called the meta-political development of societies. The struggling upward of mankind to the idea of a social order headed by an all-powerful monarch. Europe, however, had moved through that ceiling to the concept of a house of lords, a partially representative support group for the monarch; and that in turn had led to ideas of wider repre-sentation and to a house of commons, and from there all the way through to multi-party democracy. That was in Europe. But not in Africa. In Africa, people had never broken through that ceiling, never got beyond the idea of an all-powerful monarch. In Africa, therefore, it was dog eat dog, one monarch swallowing up another monarch. When the men had nothing better to do they went and made war on their neighbours, stealing their neighbours' grain and women. Nevertheless, Pieter F said he loved and respected black people. It was simply that they needed guidance from the white man.

I said jocularly that I would prefer to hear him base his claim in Africa on right of conquest, rather than on some vague moral and intellectual superiority.

But he persisted with his own line of thought, developing it from this idea of guidance to that of a catalyst which brings something to life and to its full potential.

I asked him if I could use my notebook. He agreed.

"This is what the whites will be," he said, "the catalyst to lift Africa out of its current stage of development. Africa is like a bull-dozer in low gear. You cannot make it go any faster, but you can't make it stop either. It will go on in its own way. But it needs that catalyst to rise and become great."

He was silent a moment, chewing, but I could see he had warmed to his subject. It surprised me somewhat, therefore, that his next comment seemed to change it.

"I suppose you've heard about the sjambok incident in Louis Trichardt?" he said. "It was after the African National Congress was unbanned. They wanted to march through town. Permission was denied them. The army and the police were called in. No marchers appeared. That was on a Saturday morning. Then late that afternoon, taxis bussed in a lot of juveniles looking for trouble and a few Louis Trichardt men took action with sjamboks. How many of the men were charged?" he asked, looking at Sidney.

"Four," Sidney said, "but three were acquitted."

"And that's what the press said was Louis Trichardt sjambokking children on a Sunday school picnic," Pieter F said indignantly. "Rubbish. And the overseas press calling us neo-Nazis. Utter rubbish!"

He looked at me with a sternly set jaw. "The biggest injustice done to Africa is this idea, very prevalent overseas, that white and black are enemies. Not true. They are God-given friends. Bushman and Venda kings – I sat on their laps as a child. I know their history. And," he added, his eyes glinting as he steered himself back to his subject, "I know that they need us."

He mopped at his mouth with his napkin. "I heard something on the news once which made me laugh. Something had gone wrong in an African country and the news item quoted the Minister of National Disasters." He chuckled. "But that's Africa. Where has it gone right? Nothing changes anything in Africa. The east coast traders, the Arabians, the Portuguese – what did they leave? The African bulldozer flattened it. Then the colonial powers left. Look at the results. Failure after failure. The point is they need us. We have our God-given purpose: Africa will be great and we will be the catalyst. I am part of the covenant, part of God's purpose for Africa."

I asked if he was not a republican seeking an exclusive republic. But Pieter F swept this aside.

"I am a monarchist," he said. "We lost our monarchs in Europe. We were chased out because we were Protestant. We came to another continent and forged a new nation. God is our monarch. Through our monarch we have achieved democracy and we have been given our mission. We are a special creation of God, and we have been created to help God with Africa. Africa is God's problem-child continent. That's why He has placed us here. Only if we bow to the forces of evil, will we not succeed.

"But we will not bow. We are His covenant nation," he said, and a note of something exalted had entered his voice. "Our covenant church. Our covenant town, the gateway to Africa for Christianity, and for the purpose of making Africa great. But we cannot be this catalyst without a home. We are African ourselves; we have a special mission here; therefore we must have our own home here. Perhaps the Northern Transvaal. But perhaps there will be white cantons in other parts of the country, looking to the Northern Transvaal as their spiritual home, and perhaps looking to us for practical help in times of need."

Then Pieter F sat back with a smile and rested his case.

I WAS taken to dinner that evening by Solly Noor. We went to the best restaurant in Louis Trichardt, and the manager, filled with courtesy and smiles, assured us that the service would be perfect. Solly was accompanied by his wife and young son, and they sat comfortably together.

He seemed to me in some ways to be an ingenuous man, his strong features relaxed with an easy mixture of confidence and modesty; a man pleased by simplicity and therefore capable of genuine pleasure. His wife looked at him often, a look of admiration and friendship.

Now Solly apologised to me for having brought a tiny radio into the restaurant. He held it close to his ear for a moment. "Cricket," he said. "I hope you don't mind my rudeness. South Africa against the West Indies. I think they're giving us a hiding."

We spoke about the World Cup which had been played in Australia that summer. "You know, always before I had wanted the South Africans to lose. All those unofficial tours. Now, for the first time, I was cheering. It was our team."

At the shop, his secretary had sometimes interrupted us with papers needing Solly's immediate attention. He had held them close to his face to read, his head tilted to one side. He did so again now with the menu. This time I asked why. His wife responded: "We've tried everything. Even doctors in America." Solly smiled at her. "It's not so bad," he said. When I looked at him, I had a sense that his left eye was opaque. Meanwhile, they had ordered vegetarian food.

I said to Solly that I had been surprised by the huge amounts of stock contained in his shop. His reply was simple: "My market is large. The whole of the Northern Transvaal, Botswana and Zimbabwe." He spoke more generally about the shop, how his staff – Indians, whites and blacks – worked well together. Then he smiled, remembering an anecdote.

"There was a big thing with unions in Louis Trichardt recently. The union organisers came to visit me, demanding a specific minimum wage. I called in my staff. I told the organisers that our minimum was about double what they were demanding. I said I was willing to drop my minimum, but could the union make up the balance? No answer. The funny thing was that one of the organisers came back the next day and asked for a job."

Over the meal, he told me that his family was deeply involved in what he called social activities. "We have a bursary fund for promising students, largely black, but white and Indian students have also benefited. We are also putting boreholes into rural areas to ensure a water supply for people, especially now in the drought."

But his mind had wandered to another anecdote. When Eltivillas was first built, he told me, the main road went through the middle of Louis Trichardt. The bypass came just after the Indians had started trading in the Oriental Plaza. "We couldn't believe our luck," he said with some relish. Far from being forced into a trading backwater, the Indians found themselves sitting right next to the Great North Road itself, while the white town became the backwater. "The white council was furious. Do you know they wanted to build a high wall between our shops and the new road? For our safety, they said. Of course, we resisted that." His wife looked at him in her friendly way while he talked.

With his next anecdote, he returned to that optimism of which he had spoken in the shop. The executive of a major German electronics company had come out to do business with Solly, and to stay in his home. "One evening," he said, "we got talking about various things. He said that his wish was to see, in his lifetime, a unified Germany. I said that mine, in my lifetime, was to see the demise of apartheid." His weak eyes smiled as he paused, waiting for me to ask the inevitable question. "Yes, we have telephoned each other. When the President spoke in February of 1990; when Germany was unified. We have been crying together on the telephone," he said simply.

I had a sudden sense of intransigence transcended, of things immutable mutating to dust; and a look of genuine excitement coming through the slight opacity of his eyes, and his wife smiling warmly up at him.

After the meal, we drove in Solly's big car through the centre of Louis Trichardt. "We lived right there," he said, pointing. "And around the corner was my shop." We passed the Noor Centre, but he did not even glance in its direction. His attention was on the old things. "I grew up in these streets. They were full of life then. The café's were open until late." He paused, remembering, then said: But look at it now. It's dead." Beyond the electrically operated windows I saw only a few night-watchmen sauntering on darkened and empty pavements. "People are everything," Solly Noor said. "Without people, nothing happens."

ON MY last afternoon in Louis Trichardt, I accompanied Sidney and a young woman named Karen to see an elderly man who lived on the northern side of the mountain. Tapping into the oral tradition, Sidney said. He hoped to tape record his conversation, and then to move on with the man, Petrus Uijs, to other old people of the area. In the end, I had only a brief glimpse of Petrus Uijs, but the afternoon offered other rewards.

We drove in the heat of the day up and over the mountain, its faces of rock glaring in at us, and down to the arid side where even the hardy bush seemed wilted. Eddies of dust swirled sometimes along the verges of the road.

Suddenly Karen said: "That's him. We've just passed Petrus in his bakkie."

Sidney put his foot on the brake. The bakkie had also stopped, and the two vehicles reversed towards each other. I saw a lean man, all sinew and muscle, wearing khaki and a military beret. There had been an accident, he said. On the back of the bakkie sat a black woman with her son, an anguished looking boy who had fallen off a roof into some wire. Petrus told her to open the blanket in which the boy was wrapped. The inside of one knee had been ripped away from the bone. The boy's eyes were drenched with pain. Sidney and Petrus spoke together in Afrikaans: while Petrus took the boy to a hospital in nearby Venda, we were to proceed to his house and wait for him there. It was the last we saw of him.

As we drove towards his house, Sidney and Karen gave me some inkling of what Petrus must be like. In his early seventies now; a veteran of the Second World War; an expert in tracking and bush craft; living alone in a house which should be made into a museum; a frontier survivor with a lively mind, vast stores of knowledge on many subjects and a passion for collecting.

"Collecting what?" I asked.

"Wait and see," they said with knowing smiles.

Sidney hooted at a gate which was chained and padlocked. The old house stood under trees, and the entire farmyard was sturdily fenced, with coiled razor wire running along the top. I wondered if the boy with the damaged knee had fallen onto the fence. Then a black woman opened the gate and we drove in.

We sauntered into his workshop, a large shed with a sandy floor, and discovered at least a score of tractors, some of them ancient, and ploughs and other farming equipment spilling out beyond the shelter of the roof, red-hot to the touch and rusting in harsh sunlight. Most of the machinery had been raided for parts; it looked undone, dishevelled, sometimes with wires and pipes hanging down. "People come to Petrus from all over Southern Africa for spares," Sidney said.

The interior of the house was, quite simply, an astonishment. Curtains had been closed against the heat, but there was sufficient light to see what the various rooms contained. A passion for collecting, Sidney and Karen had said. But I think old Petrus Uijs' passion had become insatiable mania. He collected everything. His house was a combination of a personal museum, a score of general dealers' warehouses from the various decades of the century, and at least a dozen antique shops.

Karen's face showed a sort of pleased amusement as she watched for my reactions. Sidney smiled: "Incredible, isn't it?" I saw collections of old radios, telephones, flags, typewriters, leopard traps, electrical meters, porcelain plates mounted on one wall, ammunition boxes on another, tools of every description, geological specimens, Stone Age implements, military artifacts, musical instruments, and a locked cabinet containing "the finest collection of beads in the country", according to Sidney. The range and the detail, the sheer quantity of objects, threatened to overwhelm in one hot and airless room after another.

Sidney had brought a bottle of brandy to share with the old man while they talked, and he now poured some into a glass, added something cold and fizzing, and drank. Then the three of us walked in silence about the house.

Tortoise shells, Venda drums, a box of military thunder flashes. And on one wall an old oval-framed portrait of a young woman in dark clothes, a cameo brooch at the stern throat. Gun safes, a small display of Venetian glass beads found at Mapungubwe, model steam locomotives, Iron Age hoes, old Afrikaner candle moulds looking like a battery of missiles, stuffed birds of prey in dusty glass cases, thousands upon thousands of books and magazines. And on another wall, photographs of black men in western clothes; personal friends probably, Sidney offered. We spent perhaps three hours in the house.

Several times as we waited, the telephone rang and either Sidney or Karen would answer. Then they went to the kitchen door and called. Once the woman who had opened the gate for us came through and spoke rapidly in the Venda language. Another time a younger woman took the call. She was tall and slender, very black, and quite graceful in her movements and the way she stood, one hip thrust out.

Our talking had become desultory as we waited. Sidney poured another brandy, then another. Karen languished in a huge easy chair. I could feel perspiration running down my temples. The house oppressed me, this monument to a remarkable mixture of tastes, to an idiosyncratic and lonely life. Why draw all these objects so closely around one? A characteristic of living in wild places, perhaps, a drawing together of every available resource until the place of refuge became the life it shielded. I looked at some of the books: a complete set of Scott's Waverly novels in proximity to heaps of *Popular Mechanics* magazines; dozens of books on military matters, on geography, on politics, on the Homelands, on ethnography, the list seemed endless; and a copy of Eugene Marais' collected works. I sat on a huge settee and thought of Marais briefly: another lonely life, morphine-addicted, and yet the brilliance of this Afrikaner poet and naturalist managing at times to shine through. A clock ticked from another room. Sidney was staring into his drink. Karen's eyes were closed.

"Let's go," he said, rising abruptly.

"Will you leave the brandy for Petrus?" Karen asked.

"No."

She glanced at the bottle. "Shall I drive?" He passed her the keys.

As we returned to Louis Trichardt through the long shadows of the lingering afternoon, Sidney said: "The thing with archaeology is that it brings you close to something underneath the old civilisations. It is this. There is a clock of the human race. I hear the clock. Everyone is so different, yet so much the same. The clock ticks to many different rhythms, but the mechanism inside is the same.

"Civilisations rise and fall," he went on, "and I think we're living in another decline. We're reliving the decline of Schoemansdal on a massive scale. Within twenty years we'll see levelled cities again, not so much for political reasons, but simply because the resources have been used up. The European culture in Africa is in decline for this reason. It's like Schoemansdal: the resources have been squandered."

Dust and fine sand billowed up from a big truck driving with its left wheels on the verge. Karen swung the truck around and took us up and over the mountain into a slightly greener dusk.

"Africa will reassert itself," Sidney said. "It's the bell tolling. The Congo – that's when the bell started tolling for whites in Africa – Kenya, Zambia, Mozambique, Zimbabwe, Namibia. Now here."

I asked him if he felt anxious about the future.

"No," he replied. "Because I'm an African. I won't be a lesser person by living under a black government. People will have to use their knowledge and skills to influence their own lives." I heard an echo here of what Hansie, the farmer on the Limpopo, had told me: this need to adapt to what was perceived as Africa's muddle.

When we arrived at the house where I was staying, I suggested to Sidney and Karen that they come in for a drink. We stood on the grass in front of the veranda, looking out over a denseness of trees, and down towards the town. The air was still hot. Suddenly we heard footsteps. A man went running past on the road beyond the garden. There was a fire in the plantations, he shouted. In a moment a vehicle with headlights already blazing drove in the same direction.

Sidney looked at me with slightly bloodshot eyes. "Let them burn," he said, his tone slightly sarcastic. "The plantations shouldn't be there in the first place, sucking the mountain dry of water at two-hundred litres of water a day per tree. It's the start of the disintegration."

We stood in the half light in silence, poised for something to happen. But we smelled no smoke, nor saw the violence of flames.

3

IN THE HOMELANDS

FROM THE streets of Thohoyandou, Venda's capital town, the abrupt volcanic peak of Lwamondo mountain can often be seen. Part of the eastern Soutpansberg, yet standing tall and separate from the general range, the cliff-ridden protrusion is home to the sacred baboons of Lwamondo. Sacred, because it is believed by many local people that the spirits of Venda ancestors have invaded the bodies of these animals and live permanently within them. An immediate reminder that Venda is, as the literature says, a land of mystery and legends.

It is also a land of witchcraft and ritual, quite sinister at times. Strange to think of this in the main Thohoyandou shopping complex, a crowd of taxis in the unpaved carparks churning up the terracotta dust. I had read in the local newspaper about a case of a number of youths accused of murdering a 50-year-old man because they believed him to be a wizard. I knew this to be one of hundreds of similar cases which had burgeoned in Venda since 1989. At one stage in 1990, the fenced grounds of the main police station in Thohoyandou was filled with people who had been accused of witchcraft and therefore feared for their lives. The accusation and the sentence had become directly linked, with no intervening mechanism of proof. Wizards and witches were stoned or beaten with sticks, then tied up and burnt in their own huts.

The dust from the car-parks lay in drifts across the paved walkways inside the complex. Apart from the mini-bus taxis, the car-parks contained clusters of informal stalls, crowds of people, the smell of cooking meat: a dusty Third World mishmash set against the facades of more formal enterprise, the huge names and bright colours of furniture and clothing shops, music blasting from their doorways, fast-food places, supermarkets, and a conglomeration of smaller stores, some of them Indian-owned. This long trading association between the two continents made manifest here in the pale eyes and hooked noses of shopkeepers, and the wail of Eastern music distorting from a radio tied to the ramshackle grating protecting a till. A throng of black pedestrians surged outside the shops; Venda women in pale checked gingham skirts, bias-binding sewn in to stiffen the bottom third; black youths in T-shirts and Bermuda shorts. One of them asked me for money. I said I had none to spare. He stared at me in an accusatory way, hovering for a moment. The faces – sometimes glancing in surprise at my whiteness – were unsmiling, inscrutable, suspicious perhaps, and they seemed to me to be caught between the old ways and some new idea of African modernity.

Dederon, my contact in Thohoyandou, told me: "Venda is the most untouched part of South Africa. It was hardly impinged upon by colonialism at all. It is therefore the most authentically African part of the country. Everything here is better preserved: the music, the art and pottery, the religion and ritual. But it's all going fast, yes?"

Thohoyandou itself was part of the going. Laid out on a sloping plain directly below the older Sibasa in the foothills of the Eastern Soutpansberg, the new capital was a homeland creation, filled with homeland architecture, slightly pretentious and overbearing public buildings, none of which were more than 15 years old. Some probably had been erected for the 1979 launching of this "independent" state, others have been erected since. It was also filled with Western produce and amenities, and, to quote Dederon again, "that great leveller of individuality, the constant blast of bubblegum music".

The politicisation of the people, however partial, was another part of the going: tribal and village concerns slowly being overlaid with national preoccupations like people's democracy, the desirability of a unitary state, and the rejection of tribalism and old-fashioned customs. Perhaps one of the main reasons for the terror of the witch hunts was a desire, often expressed by bands of outwardly politicised youth, to encourage modernisation by eradicating superstitious practices. The African National Congress seemed firmly entrenched in Thohoyandou, its initials often repeated, and not opposed, in the graffiti lately sprung up on walls and concrete fences about the untidy town.

The University of Venda, not surprisingly, manifested both the homeland architecture of the town and signs of its political awareness. The buildings were modern, blue pillars being a recurring theme of the ornate facades, with plenty of face-brick, concrete and areas of glass. A boycott of classes was in progress: it pertained to the University's exclusion rules and the great debate surrounding the maintenance of academic standards versus the right to tertiary education for all, or at least as many as possible, regardless of performance. I saw two students, one armed with a staple gun, putting up hand-made posters which advertised a mass meeting for the morning. "All comrades please attend" had been scrawled across the bottom.

In the university library, I came across a model of a stone-built site called Mapakoni: a labyrinth of stone-sided walkways leading, on substantially higher ground, to the royal residences. Similar to Mapungubwe: the king inaccessible, guarded from the common throng who lived below. I remembered Pieter F's comments regarding one of the fundamental problems in Africa: that people had never got beyond the concept of the all-powerful monarch.

I remembered, too, that I had suggested to him that the Soutpansberg was a melting pot. Mapakoni had been excavated high up in the mountains. The stone building expertise had drifted east from Mapungubwe, or perhaps had been developed in the mountains at roughly the same time. It had also drifted north to Great Zimbabwe. But long before the southward migration from a collapsing Zimbabwe of the Singos, who now formed the Venda ruling class, the Sotho cultures of the south and the Shona stone builders of the north, had met and mingled in the Soutpansberg. The two distinctive pottery styles, the Sotho and the Shona, had merged into an authentic Venda style, called Letaba by archaeologists, and it is probable that a fused Shona/Sotho language (that spoken in Venda today) existed at least a century before the subjugating Singos swept south in the last quarter of the 17th Century. Indeed, the Singos had gradually adopted the language of their subjects.

I fancied that the complexity of Venda history revealed itself in the facial expressions of many of the people: the slight sullenness, the sliding secrecy of their eyes, the sense of intrigue when in their presence. "The secrecy," said Dederon, "is obsessive. It's part of the culture here. Maybe it's a result of their subjugation by the Singos, motived by fear and a certain cowardice. The Vendas rarely fight;

they'd rather make a plan. Even in their first contacts with the white settlement at Schoemansdal, they made schemes not war."

Dederon came to see me in my small bungalow which I had hired from Venda Tourism at a place called Acacia Park. He flew in on a motorcycle, long blond hair fluttering beneath his helmet. He had originally studied archaeology and art history in his native Belgium, and there his imagination had initially been enthralled by the idea of Great Zimbabwe. As he studied further, however, his craving was for Venda. "Not this banana republic of a homeland," he said pleasantly. "My abiding interest has been the real Venda region, which includes parts of southern Zimbabwe, the north-western Transvaal, and reaching into Botswana." So he had come to South Africa in the 1970s to do a post-graduate degree in social anthropology, and shortly thereafter had moved to the University of Venda to teach.

We drove in my car through the teeming streets of Thohoyandou, and up the hill towards Sibasa. On the way he showed me the enclave where white government officials, usually seconded from Pretoria to help with the administration of the independent state, had set up home. The locals, Dederon told me, called the area Sowhito, a deliberate play on Soweto, Johannesburg's complex of explosive black townships. Bougainvillaea bloomed profusely in Sowhito, a place lush with ample vegetation to soften the high walls, a glimpse of luxurious houses and lawns, a secluded place where the officials and their families could enjoy Africa without the insistent nuisance of Africans. To one side of Sowhito stood the imposing South African Embassy, the only embassy in town.

Dederon had been called in there once, accused of encouraging communism by the way he taught. He was offered a house in Sowhito or in Louis Trichardt, 70 kilometres to the west, plus a subsidised car. He had refused these overtures. As an anthropologist, he wanted to live with the indigenous people. He had done so. In the end, he had married a Venda woman. All part of this European's adventure in Africa; and, to judge by his enthusiasm, an adventure still.

He had lived through much of Venda's recent history: homeland independence; the death of President Mphephu in the late 1980s which marked the beginning of a period of instability and lawlessness (including the rise of witch burning) and student and worker action in and around Thohoyandou; and the military coup of April 1991. "Since then, things have quieted down a lot, and both witch burning and medicine murder are now being severely punished."

We drove into the mountains behind Sibasa. For some time, the slopes were covered in plantations of bright green tea. Dederon pointed out the dam from which the plantations were watered, now only 20 per cent full. "It's good drinking water," he said. "It's a disgrace that it should be wasted on the growing of tea. More than eighty of Venda's two hundred settlements are now dependent on transported water."

Beyond the tea, the high places were filled with sweeping plantations of pine, some indigenous forest, and then all at once we descended into rain shadow. A narrow valley, dun-coloured and dusty, inside the Soutpansberg; a Singo stronghold in the old days, with their stone city built on the ruins of an earlier settlement at Dzata.

But we did not linger in the valley. He wanted to show me a pre-Singo stone-built site high in the mountains to the north. We drove on rough stone roads, passing women queueing at a communal tap, school children playing on a denuded and stony field, and then up into wild places void of signs of development and modernity, but redolent with signs of the drought. Vegetation eaten away; the mountains all boulders and red eddies of dust whipped up by wind. As we travelled, I asked Dederon to explain the difference between the witch hunts and the ritual killings.

He spoke at length about the witch burnings. He said that the youth had often worn political T-shirts and even carried political flags and banners, but he did not believe that political organisations were directly involved. It had more to do with the social instability of the time, an instability which had encouraged the emergence of old personal enmities and jealousies. "All you had to do was make the accusation, and the politicized – " he used his fingers here to denote inverted commas " – youngsters would do the rest."

Medicine murder was something else entirely: it concerned the collection of body parts for use in witchdoctor medicine or ritual. But it too had thrived under conditions of social instability and manifest government corruption. A cabinet minister was removed from office after allegations of medicine murder had been levelled against him. "But the point is this: if you want to get rid of a political opponent, why not simply mutilate his body after you have killed him, so that people will say: ah, another medicine murder. The thing is always more complicated than it first appears, yes? But medicine murder does occur. There was a case not so long ago of a man who murdered his own pregnant wife to sell the foetus to someone in Johannesburg."

We drove on a rough track just below the summits of the mountains, surrounded by pale red earth, dusty thorn trees, a proliferation of stones and boulders with cliffs above. The settlements lay to either side, the dwellings built of patterned mud, the courtyards demarcated by smooth low walls, so that each area had its specific use, and people must walk only in the passageways to get through. Small replicas, it seemed to me, of the way their ancestors built with stone.

Dederon was talking about the rituals of the Domba School, which had to do with initiation into adulthood, circumcision for males and females, and which included the python dance where young Venda women, naked to the waist, formed a long line of sinuous bodies to emulate the movements of a reptile which had become a potent symbol of fertility.

"Famous among tourists," Dederon said, "but not to be toyed with. I saw a European tourist try to move an elderly Venda woman to one side so as to get a better video shot. The woman turned and clouted the tourist heavily across the face."

But the Dombas needed medicine, Dederon went on, his voice lowered and perhaps unconsciously conspiritorial. Human parts, especially the genitals and foetuses; and this still gave rise to murders and mutilations of the most gruesome kind. And, of course, high prices were paid.

Anyway, Dederon said, there had been a young woman named Alice whose sister was crippled and confined to a wheelchair. Men came to her, speaking softly, saying it would be a blessing if the cripple died, and it could be useful to the sacred rite of initiation. Coerced perhaps by her own fear, Alice agreed. They took the sisters to a secret place in the mountains where they tied Alice to a tree. They then cut her sister's throat, not to kill, because the belief is that parts cut from a living body have more potency, but simply to weaken and silence. So while the crippled sister slowly bled to death, the required parts were amputated. Then she died. This was the evidence in the Supreme Court. When two years later a dog unearthed her sister's remains, police came to question Alice. She was almost paralysed with fear because some of the policemen carried cameras. She went with them to the place of the killing where she told them everything, thinking that in any case the cameras would show the police what had happened.

Dederon, while he spoke, had lost his way somewhat on the mountain tracks. He asked walking women on the road. "See the chief," they said, avoiding his eyes. He asked a man with a wheelbarrow, who ignored us as if he were deaf. Then we found a roadside shop, built into rocks at the top of a steep slope. We climbed through goats and chickens towards it. "Do you want to take snapshots?" the woman behind the counter asked suspiciously in Afrikaans. When Dederon said we merely wanted to look at the stones, she said: "See the chief". The shop was poorly stocked, many of the shelves bare. A group of children stared at us. In a room to one side, a strange-looking young man – huge eyes, locks of hair hanging partially over them – was being served with food and drink while writing something in a hard-covered note book.

Meanwhile, the woman had directed us to the chief's homestead. As we approached the group of huts, an old man came out to us, asked our business, then told us to wait. We stood in the hot sun, the dry wind ruffling Dederon's hair. In a few moments, a woman emerged and beckoned us nearer. We walked in among the huts, into the smooth courtyards, and again were told to wait. Children ducked down behind walls, peering at us occasionally from behind them. The courtyards were earthy, smelling vaguely of dung, and immaculately clean save for small drifts of leaves which the wind had brought in. I noticed water stored in two large drums, carefully covered.

Then a stoutish woman appeared, regarding us quizzically from a little distance away. "What do you want?" she said, "I am the chief."

Dederon greeted her and requested an audience with her, saying he was from the university. She demurred for a moment, then told us to sit. We did so on a smooth mud ledge built into the wall of one of the huts. I saw the eyes of children peering at us over the courtyard walls; a toddler, too young to be abashed, climbed onto the seat beside me, gazing up at my face with unfathomable eyes.

The chief, meanwhile, had installed herself on a similar ledge on the far side of the hut's door. Dederon spoke to her across the doorway; he spoke for some time; the chief at last said: "This request is a great nuisance to me, but I will take you."

She sat in the back of the car with a companion while we drove further along the top of the mountains. When we could drive no longer, we walked. We trudged up steeply rising ground and there, at the summit, the stone walls began. The chief sat down with her companion, while Dederon and I entered through a gateway of stone. The place was much overgrown, the various enclosures and walkways presenting a thicket of thorny scrub, the roots of ancient trees snaking among stonework which, in places, had collapsed. "Fourteenth or fifteenth Century," Dederon said.

I began to think about the long sweep of the human adventure as I wandered about the site. The walls were sometimes gracefully curved, always with the individual stones interlocking in a solid fit. A craft which, by the 14th Century, was already hundreds of years old in this part of Africa. It came to me quite forcibly then, how diverse the continuum of human endeavour had become: the Venda chief (she was out of sight but I could hear her voice intoning), defensive of her power now perhaps, yet confident in her setting; and Dederon, the fair-haired European, confident in his knowledge, yet honest enough to be humbled by these historic walls. I watched as he stooped to photograph some detail in the stonework. His camera clicked, but it could not, as Alice had thought, reveal what had taken place within these walls. What anxieties made manifest, what actions based on hope or some searching for significance, and what rituals, in themselves savage, had emanated from these profoundly human concerns? I stood at the entrance to the stones, listening to the wind, and to the insistent crowing of a rooster somewhere in the valley below.

As we returned to the car, Dederon asked the chief whether she would like to live among the walls. "Certainly not," she replied. Not really surprising, Dederon told me later; it would be a bit like living in a graveyard, although he thought they did use the site for religious purposes sometimes, propitiating to their ancestors there. Children came running down to see the car as we returned the chief to her homestead. She stood in the sun, looking at us. She said it had been an arduous task for her, taking us to see the stones. Dederon gave her a R20 note for her trouble. She looked down thoughtfully at it lying in her open palm, saying it had been so hot, and had taken so much time and trouble. I gave an extra note. She turned towards her homestead without a word and walked away.

While we were still in the mountains, Dederon took me to see a potter named Rebecca Matibe. We arrived at her village in the late afternoon, driving on sandy thoroughfares which bore no trace of tyre treads. By contrast to most of my encounters with Venda people, Rebecca seemed pleased to see us. She was a large rounded woman full of smiles. She washed clay off her hands in a drum of water. She took my hand in both hers, a wet and generous greeting. She laughed with Dederon, showing her new work: pots painted in brilliant colours, giraffes and other animals similarly treated, some guinea fowl in natural clay with wings of graphite, all arranged on the floor of an unfurnished hut. She disappeared into her house for a moment. Dederon told me she had learned the craft from her husband's first wife. And here was her smiling face again, showing us her photograph in a lavish book on South African ceramics, and again in the catalogue of a major art exhibition. Children looked up at us as we talked in slanting sunshine which cascaded into her walled courtyard. Rebecca's easy laughter was warm and generous, and suffused with a simplicity which was close to joy.

And then I saw her in her setting, her village, her neighbours; and I looked out beyond her garden and saw people sitting in their lovely courtyards all over the village, the air filled with a quiet murmuring of voices, a sound of contentment and pleasure, with no sign of wrenching transition here, no sign of chanting comrades on a witch hunt, only the murmuring of people and the smell of clay and beer; the murmuring and the dust of the village like a patina over everything, even over the people in that ancient homeland village, over their hair and eyebrows especially, like a slow wave of peace. But what darknesses of times past, of ritual or intrigue, of a spirituality which could burn in a dark eye, lay beneath that placid surface? And how soon would it be shattered and tormented by the grinding mills of change?

In the tree-filled Acacia park that evening, I heard a sudden commotion in the bungalow next to mine. I went onto my patio, and heard black voices welling up in anger. A curtain was torn down while it was being drawn, the rail forced back at an angle. The voices shouted out. One of them said in English: "You're fucking drunk, man, what's the point of trying to hold a meeting?" A political meeting? Or one in which revenge or murder would be planned perhaps? In a moment, doors slammed, and a car drove away, the interior light left on, and after that in the darkness the silence returned and the undisturbed screeching of insects went on.

A DOCTOR working in a major hospital in the self-governing but not independent homeland of Gazankulu spoke to me about malnutrition. An ageing Swiss with clear and intelligent eyes, the doctor had worked in this part of South Africa for decades, and he had witnessed the coming and going of droughts long before the one which gripped the country now.

"We saw a huge increase in malnutrition during the drought of the mid-1960s," the doctor said. "The whole region operated almost entirely on a subsistence economy in those days, so when people could no longer scrape enough food from the ground, they died. But the economy has largely switched from subsistence to cash now. There is a great deal more money coming in from migrant labour; there is also the thriving informal economy which operates within the region itself, and at much higher levels than before. These factors will offer some protection against starvation, for a time at least."

I asked about the more general health problems facing the people of Gazankulu. The doctor shrugged. "Measles, of course, we have, but there have been major immunization drives, and the disease is under control compared to fifteen years ago. AIDS is still very much in its infancy, with an HIV positivity rate of one per cent. And tuberculosis: we always have a lot of that."

I suggested that the link between high incidences of tuberculosis, a so-called indicator disease, and poverty was inevitable.

The doctor said: "The only thing inevitable about it is that it is always said." He looked at me steadily, his clear eyes slightly amused. "Poverty, yes. But among other things. Do you want to say that the state is to blame? For some things, yes. But not for everything."

Not perhaps for the hopeless overstocking of a homeland like Gazankulu. The doctor himself had told me that the disregard for the carrying capacity of the land was "a big problem". He also told me that during the drought which had culminated in 1983, 150 000 head of cattle had died in Gazankulu.

My friend Angus, an educationist now working in the homeland, provided a depressing glimpse of the current picture. "There are more than two hundred thousand cattle here on land which can sustain only ninety thousand," he told me. "As a result, sixty per cent of all calves die in the first three months."

It has been suggested that one of the reasons, but not necessarily a primary one, for the disintegration of Great Zimbabwe was over-grazing. The accumulation of capital and power by the ruling elite tended to be expressed in larger and larger herds which finally de-graded the surrounding country to such an extent that it became impossible to hold the kingdom together. In Gazankulu today, not a few senior government officials do roughly the same thing. Even in lean times, these men cling to their herds, preferring loss through starvation to profit through timely selling. Cattle seen as prestige, not as an economic commodity. And cattle for socio-religious use rather than an agricultural one. An example: I read somewhere that 95 per cent of all Gazankulu marriages are still concluded with the transfer of gifts, sometimes in the form of cattle; and cattle, even today but in declining numbers, as the animal of sacrifice.

Since Gazankulu land was mainly pastoral, with only 15 per cent suitable for the growing of crops, the agricultural picture which emerges is one of hopeless under-utilisation of available resources. Many thousands of small herds roaming the Transvaal lowveld, waiting for marriage or sacrifice to become socially useful, while agriculture contributed less than 5 per cent to the national income. And this in a homeland where urbanisation has hardly taken hold. An essentially rural people, these Shangaans and Tsongas of Gazankulu, nearly three-quarters of a million of them, living in settlements where the cattle enclosure is invariably the central focus, and all of this set in a landscape of vegetation worn thin, the earth often collapsed into canyons of erosion and waste.

Yet from a distance, fair to look at as I drove down from the mountains and into the low country lying to the south-east. Malaria country in the bad old days, but no longer; now an expanse of flat bush, with little grass between, and nearly always the sound of cowbells tinkering with a powerful silence. In the principal town of Giyani (hardly 75 kilometres on the tarred road from Thohoyandou) the buses and taxis gathered in a crowd of litter and loitering about three suburban-style shopping centres built in close proximity. Youths lay on a worn patch of grass, smoking cigarettes, part of the urbanised minority. The slogan on a T-shirt: "Viva Saddam Hussein, I support you", and on another, worn by a well-endowed young woman: "Spiritual Healing Crusade". Queues stretching away from money-dispensing machines outside a bank. A grimy shop called Fish and Chix which sold fried fish and chicken, a popular low-cost meal being the feet and heads of poultry, known locally as "walkie talkies". The women in their bustle-skirts and broad sashes at the waist, brilliantly coloured blouses, and scarves wound about the head like a turban; those elegant heads, and the whiteness of their smiles. As in Thohoyandou, music blared from nearly every shop, but I thought there was more laughter in Giyani. Certainly a smaller town, and I felt it to be more relaxed and open.

Angus and his wife Bridget lived in Kremetart, Giyani's version of Thohoyandou's Sowhito. But Kremetart was fenced; and once the Chief Minister, Hudson Ntsanwisi, had publicly remarked that he was not sure whether the fence was meant to keep his people out or the white officials who lived there in. Many of the houses in Kremetart were prefabricated, and the one in which Angus and Bridget lived – in Marula Avenue – had been eaten by termites. Holes in the skirting dribbled little piles of sand onto the plastic tiling of the floors.

Bridget said they had given up the garden: it seemed immoral to water it when there were people in Gazankulu who were really feeling the effects of the drought. Brown grass in consequence, dying shrubbery, but the few trees soldiered on, and the hibiscus near the veranda was in bloom.

Angus drove me in the late afternoon to a place called Mangombe Hill, and from its slopes we could look down over parts of the spread-out town, and over the country beyond as it stretched in a huge plain towards the haze of the Soutpansberg to the north.

"Isn't it magnificent?" Angus remarked. The subtle lure of Africa's landscapes had come upon him. "This is where Satan tempted Jesus. You can have it all, Satan said. It must have been a sore temptation."

I had known Angus for years, but in another place. A big man in his late sixties now, cheerful, slightly tired, yet as expansive of gesture and precise of expression as I had known him before. I asked him, as we stood on the hill, whether he had been changed by living in Gazankulu.

"Profoundly," he said. "For some reason I've come to realise here that the West – its plunder and its urge for productivity and growth – is wrong. I feel it in my gut. But I suppose it's too late. The desertification of the planet is accelerating all the time."

I heard a cowbell on the plain, and when we drove down onto it I saw cowbells at the throats of thin cattle. We went to a half-empty dam – named after the Chief Minister – which supplied Giyani (but not Bridget's garden) with water. The sun had begun to set. Angus waved to a youth lounging against a gate post. "That's the sad thing about these places," he said to me. "The number of young people standing about doing absolutely nothing. There's nothing for them to do. And it'll be like that all their lives." He had parked the car under spreading thorn trees and we now walked to the water's edge, the sun in flames upon the surface as it sank into low black country on the farther side. While we stood with the last of the sun on our faces, Angus began to speak to me about education in the homeland.

He had come to Gazankulu in 1988 to launch a college of education. He occupied the position of Rector. "One of the first independent colleges of education in the country," he said, "and it's working well. But the tragedy is that we're now at a standstill. The college was planned to take two thousand students, which would

have meant an annual output of around five hundred qualified teachers. We're stuck on a maximum of six hundred students. Our original
building grant has run out thanks to hesitation coupled with inflation,
and also to downright bungling and dubious political agendas."

His face showed concern and irritation as he spoke about these
things. "Look at the reality," he went on, "just over a hundred high
schools in Gazankulu served by three thousand teachers, most of
them unqualified or under-qualified. If we could have produced the
planned five hundred a year, we could have replaced those existing
teachers in six years. But of the first two hundred and fifty due to
finish their courses this year, only sixty per cent will pass. Now add
this: each year around seventy thousand children reach school-going
age. To cater for these children even at a pupil/teacher ratio of one
hundred to one, we need seven hundred new teachers every year. In
many ways it's a hopeless situation.

"And yet," he went on, "I have some remarkable people, especially
black people, who are making the most of the opportunities which
the college offers. We also have a really excellent student representative council, politically and emotionally mature, and I think far in
advance of many of their counterparts elsewhere."

A few donkeys had come down to the water to drink. Angus
watched them for a moment, then said with a characteristic bluffness:
"I'd like to own one of those animals. They're lovely creatures: so
vicious and bad-tempered."

Over dinner that evening, an air-conditioner rattling in one of the
side walls, Angus spoke of the corruption in the homelands: black
corruption; white corruption; the white-enclave mentality of the officials living in Kremetart, many of them politically right wing, not
a few of them hell-bent on manipulating the system for their own
immediate ends. Angus, the pragmatist, his voice ironic and appalled
by turns. Bridget, more an idealist, burning sometimes with indig-
nation. They told me of the Impala Hunting Club – not only for
Kremetart men but for the upper heirarchy generally, both black and
white – and how they had heard that initiates were obliged to kill
an impala and then swallow its testicles in a tumbler of brandy.
Bridget told me about the camps outside Giyani filled with people
who had fled from Mozambique; about philanthropic burn-out and
compassion fatigue in Africa; and about the Tsonga/Shangaan women,
revered because they had kept alive the traditions and language of a
defeated people now coming back into their own once more. "They
are the romantics of Africa," Bridget said, "with their music, their

poetry, their art." Angus talked of the youths in black berets and dark glasses who had stood on the roof of the college when the ANC's Nelson Mandela had used it as a venue once, and of a semi-secret Gazankulu organisation called Ximoko which appeared to be for a continuance of the homeland status quo and against the ANC. The complexities thickened. And the 1990 boycotts – "nine weeks of profound hope, unease, tension and talk of 'liberation'," as Angus described it – imprinting itself indelibly upon the minds of these urbane people as they lived in the midst of tumultuous days, and "Hudson's voice booming down from helicopters, like God, telling people to be calm and to go back to work".

The 1990 troubles began with discontent over taxi fares, a black teacher told me, and soon spread to an expression of educational grievances. It was as though a lid had been taken off, as indeed it was taken off in many parts of the country with the release of Mandela and the unbanning of political organisations, most importantly the ANC. Angus told me of some of the educational grievances – preferential bursaries, unsuitable promotions, the use of corporal punishment in schools, the quality of food in institutional cafetarias and dining halls – and how he and his staff had responded. "We were dealing with the grievances, many of them justified, as they affected the college. We were setting up problem-solving procedures. Everything was going marvellously, and then in three or four days the whole business had turned political."

The grievances were smothered by a new call: the reabsorption of Gazankulu into South Africa. How many people supported this call was unclear; what was clear was that they stayed away from work, and students away from lectures, and the whole homeland slithered to a smouldering and unstable halt. Cars were stoned, and sometimes screams had pierced the night. And when the boycott and the call for reabsorption at last petered out, at least on the surface, Hudson Ntsanwisi was there to stamp his authority once more upon his Tsongas and Shangaans.

The patient Tsongas and Shangaans, many times defeated into vassals, or forced to flee, in the rumbling aftermath of that great Southern African disturbance of the early 19th Century, the Mfecane. At its centre, Shaka's Zulu empire; and at the edges, a confusion of fleeing tribes, dispossessing and being dispossessed themselves in their scramble for land. The people of Gazankulu, first the Tsongas, then the Shangaans, had at last found a home in the Transvaal lowveld. "Coming back into their own once more," Bridget had said. In spite of the general failure of the separate development policy, perhaps it had at least given the Tsongas and Shangaans a sense of home more valuable to them than the idea of a unitary South Africa. Was that why the boycott had petered out? There were no clear answers.

I went walking one morning with Bridget as she exercised her dogs. We went down to a river called Little Letaba. Brown cattle stood in reeds next to a stagnant pool; a man on his haunches fished; the dogs charged into the water of a closer pool. "One of my favourite places," Bridget said, "there's always a bit of a breeze down here."

I asked whether she had been afraid or uneasy during the 1990 boycotts. What had she felt, this small woman with wisps of her hair shining in the sunlight on the river bank, this determined woman who devoted much of her time to working in the refugee camps, and who also talked of compassion fatigue?

She answered my question in thoughtful tones. "The boycotts marked the end of my complete confidence in people and place. We used to sleep with our doors open before. Afraid? Not at home. But distinctly uneasy while driving. A bus used to go down to Duiwelskloof and Tzaneen twice a week to fetch and return school children who are weekly boarders there. During the boycott, an armed parent would go in the bus, and another in a car behind, in case of ambush. I continued to go to church in Duiwelskloof, but with considerable unease."

We walked by the river in silence for a moment. She paused to look at a bird through her binoculars. Then she glanced up at me and said: "There are these two extremes in Africa. People underrate the African stoicism and generosity. I see it clearly, this nobility. But there's the obverse: the chaos, the indifference, the corruption. Is there some flaw in the DNA of black men especially that makes all this inevitable? These are the two extremes; I vacillate between them five times a day. I feel compassion and a genuine respect. I also feel angry, and sometimes threatened."

Bridget took me to the camps which spread out in a disorderly mess beyond the eastern edges of Giyani. Between 10 000 and 15 000 in one of the camps alone, named Hluphekani, the plural imperative of being deprived. Bridget told me that these people were not, strictly speaking, refugees but displaced people. In any event, all of them had come through an electric fence similar to that on the Limpopo, but this one dividing war-torn Mozambique from the Kruger National Park. So first it was the fence, if they could get there without being arrested or shot in their own country, then it was the game reserve where South African police could arrest them as illegal immigrants. But in self-governing Gazankulu, they were recognised as displaced people and allowed to stay. They were, after all, of a similar culture and language to their South African hosts; and not infrequently they were related, sharing a common clan or family name.

Two bulk containers stood at the entrance to the camp, one serving as office and workshop, the other as clinic. Two nurses emerged to talk with Bridget: one of them a local woman, the other a Frenchwoman with wide-set blue eyes and small gold earrings. I learned that the biggest influx had been two years previously, but that people were still making the crossing at a rate of about 20 each week.

We drove into the camp in the company of a young refugee, hardly more than a boy, by the name of Fernando, who came along to act as guide. "It's a terribly confusing place," Bridget said, "and I often get lost." Fernando sat in silence in the back.

The camp was a chaos of dust and dwellings which, for the most part, were little more than hovels. A sense of deprivation certainly, and visible evidence of a dearth of material resources. People coming across with small bundles of clothing and food perhaps, but with nothing with which to build. As a result, the houses were made out of anything that could be found once they had arrived: sticks and branches, grass, cardboard boxes, rusting pieces of tin, and black plastic which sagged under the weight of accumulated sand, some mud houses with untrimmed thatch, the occasional sight of newer corrugated iron roofs.

We passed a ramshackle shop with an elaborate wire aerial for a radio which blared; a house made entirely of cardboard and incongruously adorned with Christmas tinsel fluttering in the breeze; a small hut with a tiny courtyard swept clean in front. The litter seemed worse in some places than in others, with tin cans and fluttering plastic evident almost everywhere. The women went about their work of cooking over open fires or washing at a collection of communal taps; the men sat in groups, sullen sometimes, but usually prepared to acknowledge our presence. The women held their heads high; and the children presented a spectacle of innocence and smiles.

I asked Fernando, using Bridget as interpreter, whether he liked it better here than in Mozambique. He replied that he did. In Mozambique there were no jobs. He was also able to go to school in Gazankulu. He was in standard three. Bridget told me that he had come alone, leaving his parents in their village in rural Mozambique. Fernando showed us where he lived: a place made of cardboard and plastic, and a crooked front door. I turned to look at him as he explained about his house and his face seemed burdened. I tried to ascertain what his imperatives were, whether he had any beyond survival, but it was not possible to gauge his eyes.

I chatted to two Mozambican teachers working in the camp's school, a timber structure with half-walls of bamboo and a thatched roof so thin that sunlight filtered through in generous yellow rays. Domingo, dark-skinned and broad-nosed, 36 years old, who said: "Yes, I was frightened. Any time you can die. We walked by night and were hiding by day. Yes, some of them died. The crossing takes one week for women and children. For men only it is shorter." And Agnes, a pleasant round face with high cheekbones, who smiled but said little. The entrance to the schoolroom was crowded with children when we turned to go. A young boy did a handstand for us. The children laughed. Beyond them was sunlight vivid as teeth, and the colours of tall women passing in the dusty sand.

The romantics of Africa. Even in the meanness of the refugee camp, and certainly beyond. It was Bridget's phrase, and I thought of it often as I stayed in Giyani, but never more so than when, quite by chance, I met Jackson Hlungwani, a sculptor in wood who, several years before, had been discovered by the commercial galleries and generally extolled by the critics. A visionary, some of them had said.

Bridget had taken me to see some of the women's co-operatives which thrive in rural Gazankulu: arts and crafts places, a silk-screen-ing workshop, and then a co-operative which specialised in batik work, the smell of wax pervading the scrupulously clean building where the cloth was being stamped. Small children lay or rolled on the shining floor. Bridget, who had been talking outside to the women at the dyeing troughs, came in and said that Jackson lived not far away, and that she had found someone willing to take us there.

We drove through a slightly dishevelled settlement, and up rising ground to the place where the sculptor now lived: a cluster of build-ings on a narrow piece of land which fell away on three sides – a feeling of being on a peninsula – while on the fourth, a large round hill rose steeply. Our guide disappeared among the buildings, and in a moment Jackson came out to greet us, shaking our hands and looking at me with shining and impassioned eyes.

I said I would be interested to hear him talk about his work. He nodded, his eyes gazing away down the peninsula of his land. He said in a rattle of English words: "White people are Adam and Eve.

Cain is the devil. His brother not the problem. He the problem. Black people are dangerous. But I am like a fish. I am in the water."

I made no response. His tone was that of fervent preacher – a response seemed inappropriate – yet his eyes were friendly. He took us a little way down the peninsula of his land and pointed to a large carving: thick thighs parted, a powerful torso, the suggestion of a shield, a mask-like face of fierceness and brutality almost.

"Warrior," he said. "Men eat and drink, then go out to fight and kill. No more the time of men. Now is time of woman."

A small man, as if made compact and taut by his own exhausting energies; somewhere in his late sixties, I guessed; and wearing a maroon balaclava rolled clear of his bearded face. He told us now in his disjointed way that he could only work when the sun was shining. "No rain this year. I can call the rain. But I must work this year. I will be finished in December."

He kept referring to the galleries, to Soweto and Johannesburg, his voice reduced to a mumble sometimes, yet faintly distraught. He tapped at a pile of carved fishes. I gathered they were for the galleries. He flicked off small aggregates of sand which white ants had left on the surface of one of the fishes. Then suddenly, as if his mind had made a connection, he pulled up his right trouser leg to reveal a suppurating ulcer the size of a fist.

He rambled on, distracted, then he found two sticks and held them at right angles, drawing the one back against the other.

"Bow and arrow," I suggested.

"Yes, yes, arrow," he said. "The devil shot arrow. A snake. It has gone inside me. I cannot sleep." He allowed his trouser leg to fall back upon ancient shoes, the leather cracked and grey.

"Come and see God," he said, as if his mind had leapt suddenly forward. "I look for big wood. To show all nations."

The wood he had found was on a monumental scale: a piece of tree cut roughly into the shape of a cross, with a huge lump of knotted timber at the centre. I heard subsequently that he had persuaded a road construction company working not far from the village to bring it into his yard with their earth-moving equipment.

"This is God," he said. He walked between the truncated branches – almost as thick as he was tall – and placed his hand on the timber at the centre. "The face of God," he said, his eyes showing the depth of his obsession. He had already begun to work on the timber. He showed me the eyes, two pairs, "one to look up, one to look down", and a cross already outlined on the forehead. Further down, a V had

been cut into the thickest branch leading away from the central piece.
I asked him what it was. He seemed disappointed by my lack of
perception. "Beard," he said, tugging at his own.

I understood then that his image of God was lying on its back;
the thickest branch would be the torso, and the two cross pieces the
arms. "Yes, yes," he said in excitement. "Left hand: woman. Eva
and Maria. Right hand: man. Cain. Fighting and killing." And the
branch which grew from the top of the head? "Crown," Jackson said,
"crown for the head of God."

Then he stepped away from the timber and pointed towards the
big round hill at the top of his yard. "Jackson's church up there. My
Jerusalem." It suddenly occurred to me – I had seen photographs –
that he had lived on the hillside for many years, in old stone-built
ruins to which he had added his own ideas. "Jackson's church up
there. Down here, woman country. Canaan. See, here is woman's
church."

We walked a little way from the huge timber he would carve, to
a shallow depression in the ground. Here, three stones had been
arranged to accommodate a round boulder resting on top. Jackson
said it represented a pot, and that he would light a fire beneath it.
Then he turned.

And I turned. And in a shock of recognition I saw what he had
done. The exact alignment between his woman church down here,
through God (I could look straight up the torso with its spread-eagled
arms) to his Jerusalem on the hillside. Something almost heroic in
the unity of design; something almost palpable, like an unseen presence. Jackson spread out his arms, as if in anticipation of what his
great carving would look like when it was erected. He stood transfixed, his eyes caught with the fire of his obsession. He said: "Moses,
Elijah, John. Then Jackson. And after Jackson, nothing." Then he
relaxed. He smiled. He said to me, his eyes at once limpid and trou-
bled: "Where is peace? Peace is woman, Jackson think."

We sat for a while in the shade of one of his huts, and he showed
us, Bridget and I, a large book into which he had glued pictures
collected over many years. A radio was on somewhere: the complexity
of harmonising voices of the Ladysmith Black Mambazo. And in the
book: pictures of dragons (again raising his trouser leg to show where
they had entered); 19th Century visions of the afterlife, the shining
towers of heaven, and the serpents and lurid fires of the pit; pictures
of the crucifixion and of the ruins of Great Zimbabwe. Jackson had
an explanation for every image, his staccato English often giving way

to his own language now. He kept referring to the three levels: in the air, on the ground, and under the ground. When he came to a drawing of the Globe Theatre in London, he said immediately: "The first church." In his mind, it undoubtedly was. "Turn," he said to Bridget who had become guardian of the pages. Photographs of a collection of English literary figures appeared. "The white rulers, the gods," Jackson said, although he was quick to point out the single woman represented, Christina Rossetti. "Turn." And here was Lord Mountbatten in all his braid and ribbons, seated at a table, signing something. It was the last picture in the book. "He is the king," Jackson said; "he is the father of George." I asked him what he thought the king was signing. He pondered for a moment. "My passport," he replied with an engaging smile. Then he said again, as if this must be the key to everything: "In the air, on the ground, and" – with a sweep of his hand low down – "under the ground."

"I am absolutely astonished," Bridget said when we were alone in the car.

I said that I felt the same. We drove in silence. I kept thinking of the strange mixing of influence, the fantastical cosmology drawn from Christianity, from colonialism, from things primeval, living in the old stone ruins, and from things temporal, pictures from magazines, music from the radio perhaps. And all this – the white rulers and the handsome father of the white king, the gentle strength of women, even his own ulcer – surging within him to form a unique vision: the world of women, the world of his Jerusalem, and the two exactly linked through the image of his four-eyed deity; maleness and aggression cast aside in a great quest for peace; but above all an obsession for grandeur, I thought, for God with contradictory arms outstretched, even as Jackson himself had stood, and for a moment had been transfigured.

LEBOWA, LARGEST homeland in the Northern Transvaal, is broken into several separate pieces, the two most sizeable of which almost enclose the town of Pietersburg, so-called capital of the north. I travelled down from Giyani through harsh lowveld country, the Gazankulu settlements built close to the road and stretching away. They had the look and colour of the earth, and the sheen of grass like hats upon the individual dwellings, or from a distance like tents pitched close together on the flat and thirsty land. Then the mountains – northernmost manifestation of the Drakensberg – barred my way westward to Lebowa and Pietersburg. But the road rose with them.

From Duiwelskloof, where Bridget worshipped, and from the cycads of Tzaneen, the road wound into hillside orchards all lush and tropical with mango, pawpaw, guava and banana growing in profusion, and then up into thickly wooded slopes, some cliffs above, the occasional sight of big dams below, and then on top to the surprise of the hamlet of Haenertsburg.

I ate sandwiches in a little restaurant where the candles had burned themselves into their holders the night before. Some art for sale on the wood-panelled walls, including a few photographs of wood carvings, made no doubt by a local carver, but in a sort of medieval style, appropriate perhaps in this steep little retirement village all hemmed about by forest.

A youngish woman with a slightly crooked smile talked to me about Lebowa. "Really laid-back people", she said. When she and her husband had first arrived, some sort of riots were in progress in Lebowa. "The school children had been told to stone passing cars. But they preferred to stand at the roadside to sing and dance. I went through twice – I had to get to Pietersburg – and there was only the occasional half-hearted stone." And, another thing: look at the discipline of the Zion Christian Church, with its massive following, the woman pointed out while I chewed another sandwich. "They have their Easter bash in Lebowa. A million people come to Moria – that's like their holy city – but there's never any trouble. Except for the traffic," she added with a crooked grimace.

On the western side of the mountains, Lebowa began. As I descended, I looked out upon a vista of broken country stretching west, and even from that distance I could see the regular flashing of sun on iron roofs otherwise too far away to see. I drove for nearly an hour through Lebowa. The Zion Church headquarters lay to the left of the road: women selling fruit at the entrance, a gathering of buildings, some of them impressive, at the foot of a hill upon the summit of which a cross and the words, Zion City Moria, had been fashioned from whitewashed stones. The settlements became more extensive as I approached Pietersburg, houses crowding upon the veld in a disorderly urban sprawl, little to see that could be construed as traditional, the houses rectangular, with iron windows and roofs. The country itself was littered with abrupt hills, all boulders and dark green vegetation, and littered also with grazing animals. A dual highway began, people dodging the traffic as they crossed it. I passed dead cattle on the central island, mutilated by the force of collision. And then over a rise and there was Pietersburg, its first suburbs set straight down on a long slope of yellowing grass and the dark of acacia trees.

The ANC offices in Pietersburg are not easy to find. They are not marked, and the organisation is not listed in the telephone directory. In the end, I called on the services of Jake, a black journalist who would later become my friend. He pointed out the building to me. I started on the ground floor. "Upstairs," a black woman told me. I went upstairs, and an unsmiling man in an office said: "Second floor." No indication on the landing, so I chose the left corridor. And there, at the end, a tiny ANC sticker and a big iron gate, which forced me to turn aside. I found myself in a reception area where the people were friendly. I asked to see the regional secretary. They asked me to wait. On the walls a few posters had been displayed: "Constituent Assembly now", some trade union stuff, "Welcome home, Oliver Tambo".

A small flag – black, green and yellow bands – stood on the regional secretary's desk, and a general air of wariness and suspicion pervaded his office. I made a comment about the seriousness of the drought: were the people in Lebowa having a hard time? But the response was noncommittal. What other questions did I wish to ask? I should write them down. I did so. The secretary said I should also write down my credentials. I did so. He looked at the piece of paper, then put it carefully to one side. "You can telephone in two days time to make an appointment to get the answers to your questions." I forgot to ask for his number, but fortunately Jake was able to assist me once more.

While I waited, I drove west from Pietersburg and into the other piece of Lebowa which crowded in upon the town. I went to Seshego, a small black city with some industry laid out to one side. Two million people in Lebowa, I had heard, and for the most part seeming more westernised than many in Gazankulu or Venda. The houses in Seshego, at any rate, were western in design. Small bungalows in one area, the gardens neatly kept, people sitting outside on boxes, stools, the occasional chair, children playing on small lawns, or out on the wide sandy verges of the roadways; informal trading being conducted under umbrellas at some of the intersections, certainly, but really for the first time since the Limpopo a thoroughly urban feel. Up-market houses in another area: individual designs; some workers laying a brick driveway in front of the double garage of an imposing house; a man in a floral shirt watering his rose bushes with a hose pipe. Black suburbia. But on the northern outskirts of Seshego, the classic signs of urbanisation: informal housing in a variety of materials, some mud huts, mounds of litter, children herding cattle at the roadside, a criss-crossing of paths on open spaces, stunted maize standing in ragged patches between the dwellings, a thriving mass of people and dilapidation going on for several kilometres before the open country began once more.

When I telephoned, I was granted an interview at the ANC offices, but not with the regional secretary. I spoke instead to a man named Norman, youngish, deliberate of movement, slightly guarded and slow to smile. He sat behind a desk, leaning backwards and blowing smoke towards the ceiling. He had a peppercorn beard, a thin moustache and a gold watch on his wrist.

He said, leaning far back in his chair: "The Northern Transvaal has borders with several Front-line States. When our insurgents came through, the first people to receive them were the Northern Transvalers. They played an important role, especially the youth and the women, the men all too often being away to work in the cities.

"Yes," he went on, "the people of this region have contributed effectively to the struggle. Especially so, when you consider the nature of the region: largely rural, dominated by the bantustans (his term for homelands), and by white political conservatism. So before 1990, the struggle was fundamentally against the bantustan system and the far right. There was also a lot of repression – by the army, the police, the bantustan police – against any form of democratic activity.

"But after the unbanning in 1990, it came sharper to peoples minds that this is what they had been fighting for. They came forward in their thousands to join the ANC. There was a lot of anti-ANC propaganda from the white conservative towns. But, being unbanned, we were able to speak for ourselves, and the people joined."

He lit another cigarette. He was sprawled out, his neck resting against the back of the chair. I asked him about the political struggles in the homelands themselves.

"In the bantustans," he said, "especially in Gazankulu, there has been a great deal of terror used against the ANC. The Ximoko Progressive Party in Gazankulu and the United Patriotic Front in Lebowa are actively against us. All public servants are forced to join these parties, and ANC members are persecuted at every level. But in Venda there is no pro-bantustan party. The people there accept the need for re-incorporation into a unitary South Africa.

"I am sure you know the ANC's stance to bantustans: that they are a perpetuation of apartheid, of ethnic groups and tribalism. The

ANC is non-racial, non-ethnic; this is what has caused us to grow. Federation? Not on ethnic lines. Some bantustan leaders are hoping for this because it will perpetuate their own power."

"Would you talk to me about the difficulties of setting up an office in a town like Pietersburg?"

He shrugged his shoulders. His eyes were half-closed, but watchful. "The usual things. Anonymous phone calls: the voice saying, is that the ANC? When we reply that it is, the voice saying, julle gaan kak, you are going to shit. But no breaking up of the office. Not yet."

He smiled a lazy half-smile. "The most reasonable towns have been Pietersburg and Tzaneen, but even these have been helped along by our consumer boycotts. In all the Northern Transvaal towns the boycotts have hurt the business people. So the business people are wanting to change, but the conservatives are saying: go to hell, we won't talk to the Satan."

He stifled a yawn with the back of one hand. He seemed to have subsided even further into his chair. "This is the ANC's challenge in the Northern Transvaal now: how are we going to change these attitudes? We must find a programme to do this. Some sort of dialogue. Now that we are able to speak for ourselves, this is possible. It is true that some whites are realising that we are also human beings. Others have a long way to go. But they must realise that we will not wait forever for them to change."

He had sunk so low behind the desk, that I saw very little of him, other than his face. Then he pulled himself forward, glanced quite briskly at his watch, and stood up. My time with him was at an end.

4

WHITE AND BLACK

WHILE IDLING away some hours in a Pietersburg museum one afternoon, I came across a portrait of Piet Joubert, the Boer Commandant-General who had finally, and with considerable ruthlessness, smashed the Venda independence in the Soutpansberg in 1898. I read in a document mounted near the painting that he had been entrusted with the foundation of Pietersburg years before in fulfilment of a promise, made by the National Council of the Transvaal after the evacuation of Schoemansdal, that a more permanent northern outpost be established.

There is also an imposing statue of him, I discovered, in the lavishly beautified gardens of the civic centre. He sits on his horse, his rifle hooked under his arm, while his wife Hendrina, on foot beside him, points forward to the redcoats she saw first in 1881 on Majuba Hill. Joubert won that round with the British, but he was too indecisive and finally too ill to change the course of the second War of Independence at the turn of the century. Indeed, he had to retire from his command in Natal after falling from his horse. Yet he looks solid enough here, in the Pietersburg gardens, his beard bristling fiercely from his face, his expression one of severity and unwavering purpose, while above him arched a sky slightly darkened by a few slow explosions of cumulus. Like the shells he had fired in the Soutpansberg, I thought, remembering how his men had brought a piece of shattered monolith on a gun carriage to serve as the foundation stone to the Church of the Vow.

Overburdened with statuary, this garden which had once been a dusty square for ox wagons. Enclaves of busts in the shrubbery: mayors, members of parliament, senators, civil servants, all gazing forward through the pierced pupils of their bronze eyes. Paul Kruger was there, looking tired and listing slightly to the left. He said once from this very square, according to a plaque: "Pietersburg is the bastion of the north." And here was the solemn face of Louis Tregardt staring out at me. It struck me how small a company of people the Voortrekkers must have been, and how small a company their ancestors still are. Someone told me, while I tarried in Pietersburg, that whites in the Northern Transvaal were outnumbered 33 to one. Outnumbered: the terminology of battlefields. The terminology also of survival. The statues were the icons of a religion whose object was to encourage survival through a sense of permanence.

I had religion on my mind. In a few days the Easter weekend would begin, and I wanted to see, if I could, what happened at Zion City Moria. Meanwhile, the abundance of statues in Pietersburg preoccupied me and I delved into the bustling town, trying to gain an understanding of the psyche behind the icons.

Was it suggested, here, in the big bright supermarkets, more black customers than white, or in the crowded streets filled sometimes to overflowing with LEB-registered cars, reminding me of the proximity of Lebowa both to the east and west? Or here, in the Great North Road Hotel, pseudo-Tudor facade with a Union Jack painted onto the sign over The London Club? Or in the shop in an arcade called The Bullet Hole, filled with gun safes and racks of firearms, a case filled with handguns, and zip-up rifle bags and shelves of cartridges, and a man in khaki stroking the butt of a pump-action shotgun, trying to decide whether or not to purchase? Or in a dimly lit steak house cooled by fans, where the white waiters and waitresses wore striped T-shirts and braces and into which, while I sipped my tea, walked two self-conscious young policemen, one of them carrying a sub-machine gun, muzzle pointed modestly towards the floor? I read in the library what are reputed to have been Piet Joubert's last words before he died in March 1900. "What," he asked, "is to become of our poor nation?"

"The whole history of the Afrikaner is one of conflict and struggle, largely against the British," Johann said. An Afrikaans-speaking academic, round-faced and cheerful. We sat in his study, desk piled with scores of books, and to one side a small computer, a printer and a novelty telephone which from time to time he answered.

"Then from around the middle of this century, a whole generation grew up adjusting to the new enemy: swart gevaar, the black danger. This is now ingrained, and perhaps it will take a whole generation again to unlearn that."

He smiled at me. I said I had been interested to see that Schoemansdal had flown a flag very similar to that of the American Confederacy. Was it far-fetched to see a linkage between the Northern Transvaal and the American South? They had also shared slavery and cotton, I said, remembering Hansie's cotton gin which he had dismantled somewhere in the Deep South. Johann looked thoughtful.

"There are parallels, yes, but there are also significant dissimilarities. But maybe we should think more of the Wild West than the Deep South. Or perhaps a combination of both. I think the parallels that there were, historically, arose as people on different continents responded to similar geographical and social circumstances – that of the frontier – at least to begin with. And that's still the essence of Pietersburg. It's a small city these days, but it's still by and large frontier. The frontier mentality is still strong."

I asked him to describe this mentality.

"Making use of what's available, wresting a living from the land, protecting yourself. That was to begin with. Then of course the Anglo-Boer War impoverished them. Then the added burden of the 1930s depression forced them into the cities. Those who remained were the toughest of the pioneers, the Northern Transvaal traditionalists, born here, used to a hard life, enjoying only limited contact with new ideas, dismayed by rapid changes and determined to hold onto what they've got. In a word: conservative."

I returned to the gardens and looked at the statues once again. They were the forefathers of a conservatism grown up through the rocks of the frontier, and nourished by conflict and struggle. And, I suddenly thought, by defeat. The sense of the past as an injury outlived, outlived in themselves and in their bronze, but with a profound sense of the enemy still, no longer a specific imperial power, but stylised now into potent myth: the Satan, as the ANC man had called it, or Pieter F's forces of evil. Not the black man himself so much, perhaps, as some abstracted sense of fresh defeat which the black man's aspirations could evoke.

As I strolled on the pathways in the civic centre gardens, I saw a flock of homing pigeons turn from black to silver as they circled far away beyond the heads of the statues and the surrounding trees.

WHEN I first met Jake, he was busy at his terminal in the small newspaper office, and he said immediately that he could only spare me half an hour. "I have a deadline," he explained. He struck me as being an intelligent man, talking seriously in English, his brow knit sometimes as he searched for a particular word. Yet he had a definite sense of humour, slightly cynical it seemed, and he laughed easily, a sort of quiet chuckle accompanied by a slight glinting of the eyes.

I said I would like to talk about the Zionist gathering at Moria. I asked how many people normally attended. "They say it's around a million," he answered, "but I don't know how they make that estimate. It's certainly hundreds of thousands though."

I said that I would like to attend. He laughed. "I would say that normally your chances would be nil. They're very private about what they do." He told of a year when he had tried to enter, going past the various check points by using someone's name; and then at about the fifth gate they said, "you are under arrest", and made him stand to one side with a guard. "I waited for a long time, until an acquaintance rescued me." But there was a possibility this year. Some big politicians had been invited to speak on the Sunday afternoon. This could mean that provision for media coverage had been arranged. "Will you let me know?" I asked. "Sure," Jake said.

I asked him what the Zionists believed. He shook his head. "I know very little about it." He nevertheless told me about the faith healing. "I think they go into trances," he said. "I've heard there's quite a lot of traditional African religion and healing wrapped up in Christianity. They're not supposed to smoke or drink. They don't in public. But in private . . ." His eyes glinted. "Look, if you're really interested, I can arrange for you to see someone." I said I was interested. Jake lifted his telephone.

In the streets of Pietersburg, there seemed to me to be an air of preparation. Perhaps it was a general prelude to the long weekend, but my eyes had become attuned to anything which spoke of Moria and the Zion Christian Church. Like the big lorry – I was on my way to speak to Jake's Zionist contact – filled with men in khaki, all with the ZCC star pinned to their tunics on a patch of dark green cloth, some wearing military-style peaked caps with the chin straps in place. The lorry had stopped at a filling station, and the men were standing up, stretching, as if they had travelled a long way. When the lorry pulled off, I noticed that a young white man in a powerful bakkie was obliged to wait. I saw his face above the bright stripes

painted down the side of his vehicle, a face of impatience and machismo, as if thinking: why must I wait for this lorry-load of rabble?
And I heard the rear tyres of his bakkie squeal slightly as he belatedly
pulled away.

Jake's contact turned out to be an imposing man in his fifties who
seemed to have a current of anger flowing just beneath his self-
consciously dignified surface. Hard eyes, a habit of talking with a
pencil in his hand, then sometimes tossing it up and letting it fall,
in the manner of bones perhaps, in any way it would. A gesture, I
thought, not of fatalism so much as fighting angrily against fate. I
noticed a ZCC star pinned to the jacket which hung on the wall
behind him. He had something to do with the administration of
education in Lebowa, Jake had told me. His office was unadorned,
yet cluttered with steel cupboards and cabinets. He said that under
no circumstances was I to use his real name. He gave me the titles
of two books which would give me an idea of what Zionism was,
and then he dismissed them both as superficial. All these things
combined to sharpen my interest in the man.

"Of course we are monotheistic," he said. "We are part Christianity, part Judaism. We believe in Christ. But we see no conflict in
this. The theological conflict between Jew and Christian – was Jesus
the Messiah or not? – is irrelevant to us. Christ said: I come to bring
new light, not to destroy the old law. So we believe in the old law,
and in Christ."

He looked at me with his hard eyes. "We practise the old law in
our daily lives. We do not accept divorce, for example. We rather
take another wife. I have two wives. My first wife, and her child
who is now thirty years old, are still taking my support. We are strong
believers in family responsibility. You cannot discard a wife or the
children from her. For us, this is very important. Not like Christians.
I had a white boss once, calling himself a Christian, but twice divorced, children all over the place. That was repugnant to me."

His look of repugnance was convincing: the hard eyes turned contemptuous, his upper lip curling, nostrils slightly dilated. I asked,
while he stared at me in this way, where the Judaism had come from.

"From the Bible," he said impatiently. "When we were able to
read the Old Testament in our own language we realised how thin
the missionary teachings had been, based only on the New Testament.
Nowhere in the Old Testament does it say people must not dance
and sing and clap their hands or partake in any ritual. Yet the missionaries said it was wrong. We must sit quietly in the pew. There

are also Jewish strains in Africa, as you know, and not only in Ethiopia."

Another example of the Zionists' adherence to the old law, he said, was their ruling that there should be no use of alcohol, tobacco or other drugs. "But we must put something in the place of booze and dagga. Every weekend, from Friday to Sunday evening, we put people with drinking problems into church. They worship and they work. There are over a thousand alcoholics in the Northern Transvaal who, thanks to the church, are now leading useful lives. All of the ten commandments apply to us," he added.

I said I knew Zionism to be a real force in many black communities. Taking all its variations and denominations into account, the movement could probably now claim more than ten million members. What was its appeal?

He looked at me in silence for a moment, but I could see that his anger was close to the surface. Then he sublimated it into scorn. "You don't know what it's like to be black," he said.

I agreed that I did not.

"Being an inferior nation –"

I shook my head. "By whose definition?"

"Wrong word," he said, sneering sarcastically at me. "Definitely the wrong word. Let me start again. Being a nation without rights, without a political voice – until now – we needed something to believe in, something to succour us in a situation which too often seemed, and was, completely hopeless. Something to believe in, in a world of mercantilism and progress."

Again the sneering tone; and then, surprisingly, a moment of real sincerity when he said: "We believe Zionism can play a role in helping the black man to live in modern society. We must have progress, too. For too long there has been no progress. Do you know why?"

I waited for him to tell me.

"Superstition," he said, tossing his pencil up in the air. "That is what has prevented progress. Superstition and all the ancestors and all that hocus pocus."

"But my understanding is that a revering of the ancestors is not at odds with Zionism, that it is accommodated."

"uMoya," he said. "The spirit. The holy spirit. That is the essence of Zionism."

It seemed to be his definitive statement, his body taut and leaning forward, nostrils flaring slightly, eyes hard, and – a new perception for me – somehow wounded. I said nothing. After a moment, he

leaned back in his chair and told me that he used to be a journalist,
but had given it up. I asked why. "I was being realistic," he said.
Why was giving up journalism being realistic? "Politics is a dirty
game. It was terrible."

I asked if it was possible to be a Zionist as well as a member of a
political organisation.

"Of course it is," he said. "Many church officials are also members
of the ANC."

"Could this lead to the politicisation of the church?" I asked.
"Perhaps like the Afrikaner churches had become politicised? Espousing and sanctifying Afrikaner political policy?"

He laughed in his scornful way. "Zionism is above politics. It is
built on a doctrinal principle. From a white man's point of view, it
might seem that the ANC has a following all through the country.
This isn't true. But Zionism has. It is here to build the black man
morally and theologically, not to play politics. The trouble with whites
– you included – is that you don't understand black people."

I asked him to help me to understand.

Again he laughed, but more a snort than any musical amusement.
"I would have to live ten years with the American Indian before I
even began to understand." He nevertheless gave me an example of
white misunderstanding. "When blacks laugh," he said, "whites think
they're happy. Not necessarily. Blacks laugh at nonsense or even at
death. To relieve the pain, the misery of it. The sadness. The difference between white and black is very great."

I said that we shared common roots. We were, after all, the same
species.

But he brushed this aside. He said: "I will give you one difference.
Here it is: being well off makes blacks lazy. There is great selfishness.
There are no Rotary or Lions clubs among blacks. Why? Because the
black man has spent thousands of years dependent on his wife. All
he did was fight every now and then, otherwise just sitting around
in his laziness and selfishness."

I asked if he could give another difference, but he said abruptly:
"No. I will give just that one. We could talk about this all day, but
I have work to do." But he could not resist giving me another difference anyway. "You whites live by the jumping jack principle: now
this man is your teacher, now another man. Our Bishop will be there
until he dies. That is the African way." Then he stood up, his big
fists resting on his papers.

As I prepared to go, I asked him if there was a special significance to Moria, the place.

"Absolutely," he answered. "It has been there for us since 1945 as Jerusalem is for Jews and Christians, as Mecca is for Muslims."

"What happened there to cause it to have this special significance?"

He seemed slightly nonplussed, but said in a tone of complete authority: "It's our headquarters. Our Bishop lives there. He is on the same level as the Pope."

Would it be possible for me to go to Moria on Sunday?

He shrugged his shoulders. "You can try. I know the correct procedures for gaining access."

"What are they?"

"No comment," he said smugly. "But if you get in you must wear a jacket. It is a service of worship."

I began to thank him for his time, but he brushed my thanks aside. "I will come down with you," he said. When we emerged from the building, he seemed suddenly anxious to detain me. He said, his hard eyes gazing down the busy Pietersburg street: "When I was at school, in standard eight, I had a nervous breakdown."

He paused, glancing at me, as if he longed to speak freely, this embittered and wounded man. I waited. In a moment he went on, but I doubted whether it was with the freedom he sought.

"I studied psychology through a relative who worked in the library, and I learned why I had broken down. I knew I had either to be a doctor, a journalist or a detective. Otherwise I would become the biggest criminal that ever lived."

I said I was glad he had not wasted his life.

"I have wasted it, man. I'm fifty-four."

"What would you have wanted to do?"

"Write history. Black history. Do you know what I mean? Tribal differences – why they are there."

"It's not too late."

He shook his head. "I've got no money."

I said that it probably did not help, still supporting his first wife and 30-year-old child.

"Exactly."

He stood looking at me for a long time, saying nothing. I offered my hand, and he shook it. I said perhaps I would see him at Moria on Sunday. He laughed a short laugh, as if to suppress his anger. "I doubt it," he said, turning away.

ON THE day before the Easter weekend I went to a holiday resort in the eastern piece of Lebowa, not far from Pietersburg. Cradled by mountains whose rock faces seemed, at that point, to plunge beneath the surface of the plains, the resort boasted an expanse of water and bungalows and a host of crocodiles contained within a labyrinth of concrete walls. Lebowa settlements stood beyond the perimeter fencing, low houses gathered together among grey-green trees, the occasional plume of dust which marked the passing of some vehicle through the bush. Within the resort: music wafting out of opened cars, three-legged pots simmering over slightly smoking ash, the smell of grilling meat, big white men at ease with their fishing rods and beers, some families, a loving couple pitching a tent. Up from the water, a swimming pool alive with black children, and beyond the pool, a bar filled with rows of chairs upon which young blacks sat to watch television. I saw a white man share some of his bait with a black fisherman. Here was an unconsciousness of race which might have brought a distinct unease to the eyes of the bronzed patriarchs. A launch with a roof of shadecloth ferried people across the water to see the crocodiles. A white teenage girl in the company of two young men, one showing a careful proprietorship, sitting on the launch with drinks in their hands, and surrounded by black girls with ribbon-bedecked hair. The crocodiles lay massed together in the sun; and beyond the concrete walls, a view of the resort: cars, umbrellas, white bodies down there oblivious of reptilian eyes blinking slowly, the open mouths showing those formidable teeth. Phatudi, the oldest male, lived alone in an enclosure with four females, explained a friendly black man with a child in his arms. "To venerate him," he said ingenuously. "A man with only one woman is not strong." I thought about the two million Pedi people of Lebowa then, and how someone in Pietersburg had said: "The Pedi are a cool people. Cool in the sense of being laid back. Impassive. They don't like to be swept along. Only twenty-five per cent of them are politically aware; and not more than five per cent are activist in any way." I saw a raucous black woman in a hat, smart trousers and a voluminous kaftan of brilliant red and orange florals, clamber aboard the launch. "Don't let them eat you," her friends called. The woman guffawed. "I think I will be too tough," she shouted. Her feet were encased in thick-soled running shoes. And now the shadows lengthened, and new wood-smoke and mellower tunes floated on the warm and placid air.

On the way back to Pietersburg, I stopped where the way to Moria branched off from the Great North Road. Long lines of vehicles were

already coming up from the south and turning for the last 40 kilometres of their pilgrimage. Traffic police had parked at the junction.
The traffic was punctuated by those big trucks, grinding up the slight
incline on their way north with food for drought-afflicted Zimbabwe.
And the vehicles turning off, cars and bakkies and mini-buses, all
loaded with passengers, a glimpse here and there of khaki, military-
style caps, the flash of a ZCC star; and roof-racks holding mounds
of luggage: food, bedding, camping equipment; an open bakkie bristling with passengers, a car with two drums strapped to the roof, and
not a few packed Mercedes Benzes pulling trailers. Darkness began
to fall. The lights were streaming over the hill from the south, and
a full moon stood clear of the horizon, and then the flashing blue
lights of a police car illumined the immediate gloom.

The same in the morning, except that now the cars and combis
had been joined by buses, at first a trickle of them, then followed by
a deluge, thousands of buses, and also lorries, those used for trans-
porting cattle with high horizontally-slatted sides, sometimes with a
tarpaulin stretched across the top to provide shade for those within.
I saw an accident on the dual-carriage road to Moria, not far from
the place where I had earlier seen the impact-mutilated cattle. A
twisted cattle lorry now, on its wheels on the central island but
battered, the high-slatted sides appearing caved in. Police cars; an
ambulance; the sound of another shrieking to the scene. A uniformed
white woman tending a gathering of bodies under blankets. People
lifting stretchers. Those passengers unhurt, sitting with their bundles
in the midst of blood and pain, the brown and greyness of the bundles,
and that sense of fervour ruined and of the profound stoicism of
Africa. I drove on. The dual-carriageway ended. And then, about six
kilometres from the Moria gate, the queue began, a long line of
stationary vehicles stretching up and over the hill in front. Some of
the vehicles had taken to the verges, and the dust drifted smoking
away over the veld. An astonishing spectacle, this manifestation of
the urge to worship on some hallowed ground; and equally astonishing was the dust and smoke of Moria, the place itself still out of
sight behind the shoulder of a hill, but those fumes rising in a dense
column to discolour the sky. Buses from the townships of the Witwatersrand, those places riven with violence, and these tens of thousands of people singing in their buses now, or waving to me – a lone
white civilian on the roadside – singing and clapping their hands with
joy and seeking a reprieve, seeking a miracle on their sacred ground.

Buses from Bophuthatswana, from Venda, from Swaziland, from Namibia, from Natal, from Lesotho and Transkei. I spoke to a young
man who said he was a teacher, his military-style cap held in his
hands. "People come to Moria to be healed," he said, "to be baptised,
and people come because they respect the Bishop." Meanwhile, the
queue of traffic grew longer.

    I sat that evening in the seediness of the bar of the Great North
Road Hotel. A few customers with listless eyes gazed into their drinks.
The barman had tousled black hair and a T-shirt depicting Marilyn
Monroe. He was dabbing at a flashy crash helmet with a felt-tipped
pen, shading in various areas of an elaborate and obviously homemade design. Sometimes he put it on and looked at himself in the
mirror behind the bottles. Two wild-looking young women came in.
The men brightened somewhat. They called the smaller girl skattie,
and bought them brandy and cokes. There was a moment of slow
banter. The barman said he was going to ride his motorbike that
night non-stop to Johannesburg and Hillbrow. "Ag, the kaffirs will
stamp you off the road," Skattie said. On the television above the
bottles, images of drought, cracked mud, thin cattle lying dead, "millions of Africans on the sub-continent facing starvation". Then a few
aerial shots of a crowded Moria, and a picture of the accident I had
seen, the voice saying "two dead". It was only for the rugby, however,
that the listless eyes were raised.

JAKE AND I drove to Moria on the media bus. The road near the
gate presented a chaos of stalls, and hundreds of lean-tos set up by
the traders to accommodate themselves and their families for the
weekend. As the bus crawled round the shoulder of the final hill,
Moria itself was revealed. From the stone cross on the summit of the
hill, down through a shallow river valley, and right up to the fence
by the roadside, the whole landscape was covered with people, shacks,
tents and tens of thousands of vehicles, all mixed into a thriving stew
over which the dust and smoke hung like a specific aroma. Automatic
film winders whirred at the windows of the bus as it turned in through
the main gate. Jake held his battered old camera on his lap, his
expression slightly pained, slightly amused, yet keenly attentive. He
caught my eyes on his face, and his eyes glinted with a brief smile.

    Now we were inside, the bus rolling slowly on an uneven road. I
saw serried tents, a male voice choir using their feet as they practised,
men in khaki sleeping against the wheels of parked buses. Then the
bus went down and crossed a dry river bed and lumbered up the

farther bank, grinding onto higher ground. I saw people swarming through trees between which the ground was like desert, all grass and undergrowth flattened into red dust in not much more than 48 hours. Dust and rubble. The dust billowed up from the feet of the people and then settled back, covering everything in drifts of fine red sand. The bus inched forward into a multitude. "Is this really the silent majority?" a journalist asked.

These panoramas of faces: men in green suits with yellow braid; the khaki-clad men with their stars on dark green cloth; women in blue dresses, more like tunics, with prominent buttons. And everywhere now, as the bus went between human walls, the smell of dust and the sound of singing, the sight of women applauding, the beginnings of ululation when they saw the bus with white people in it. The welcoming. The voice over the public address system droning instructions in several languages. The bus had stopped – "They are getting radio clearance for us to proceed," a man said, hanging onto the railing next to the driver – and the heat seeped in. Beads of perspiration stood on Jake's forehead.

The sea of faces stretching away from the bus, all looking towards it: impassive, amused, smiling, laughing, curious, but with no trace, in all those thousands of eyes, no trace at all of hostility or contempt. We were their honoured guests.

The long view: dust-laden cars, looking as if they had been there for months, abandoned there; a rocky outcrop, the summit crowded with human forms; many such crowds occupying whatever high ground they could find. Some permanent houses extending up the hillside towards the cross, each house marooned in a sea of humanity. And now the bus moved through up-turned faces, then through women in yellow, with green head-scarves, sitting in their thousands, watching us pass, sitting in such a way as to be clearly demarcated from those in blue. Tens of thousands of women sitting in the sun. Then we were told to alight. The journalists bustled out with their cameras and sound equipment, their cables and small lap-top computers, a brisk and confident crew. Jake, I noticed, stood to one side, and then in a moment he had melted away. The journalists arranged themselves in front of a large covered platform at the foot of the hill, and a podium which bristled with microphones.

Now a man in a maroon jacket occupied the podium and said: "The time has come. Open your ears so that you will hear what will be said. Please keep the roadway clear. Please stop dancing and settle down so that the cars can get through." To the tight group of media people he said: "I hope you will join with us in praising the Lord." Then he addressed a column of people who were passing across the open space in front of the platform: "These are our new members. They have just been baptised. They are holding up their blue cards. Men and women, young and old, joining the big family of the Zion Christian Church. A church of peace, sympathy, co-operation and love. Moria, a place of pilgrimage and renewal."

I turned and looked at the audience, those acres of seated men and women, and those on the hill to one side of the platform. Hundreds of thousands, with the dust blowing visibly off this huge assemblage, and all those women sitting with their legs stretched out before them covered with magazines, handkerchiefs, kitchen cloths and blankets. They would sit thus for several hours more. The stoicism and the endurance; people inured to discomfort, powerful in their fortitude and patience. And the sense of renewal, as if all at once I could see the spirit, uMoya, flowing in among them even as the dust billowed out.

The flash and flurry of the helicopters now, the big black cars; the clapping, the ululating, the waving hands, a forest of fluttering life above the heads of the multitude. The Zionists had invited major political leaders to address the congregation on the issue of peace in a land rent by violence and division. These illustrious men sharing a platform in that dusty place. And a strong sense came to me of men with the aura of power; individual men, controlling destinies, playing chess on a drought-ravaged board, or pulling the strings of a cast of millions. But in the end, perhaps, what they said tending to irrelevance in the face of the huge will for peace sitting out there in the sun, and for the chance to live, the chance for simplicity and joy perhaps. Jake came back at this point, his eyebrows pale with dust.

A band of green-clad musicians now marched into the open space before the platform, brass instruments flashing in their ranks, the music blaring above the huge resonance of the bass drum. Here were flags and banners: green, gold, blue, white. The band leader wore a kilt which swirled as he brought his cavalcade of sound and colour to a halt. And then the Bishop: I heard his presence in a hundred thousand throats. He wore a purple cloak and the gold chains of his office. A man of reverence and dignity, up there on the platform.

Up there. On the platform on the first slopes of the hillside? Up there. The unapproachable being, appearing only in a blaze of trumpets and colour? I thought of the king standing on Mapungubwe hill.

My king, my Bishop. Was this one part of the African consciousness embedded in the Zionist worship now? No wonder Africa had understood the Christian principle of Lord and Master so thoroughly. For there was no jumping jack principle here, rather a fidelity to leadership which strengthened the sense of communion, which in dispelling doubt brought peace, the warmth of uMoya flowing through them on this sacred ground.

But there was more. While the leaders were espousing peace from the podium, I read a leaflet which someone had thrust into my hands when I got off the bus. "The Western churches (I am summarising here) were founded by foreign missionaries who imposed their own culture via religion on Africans. The ZCC's founder, on the other hand, was African. The church thus assimilated Christianity into the African culture. Unlike the Western churches, the ZCC has never demanded that its members jettison African culture and belief as something heathen, but rather to adhere to it and accept it as a normal way of life, to be cherished and enjoyed and respected." The contradictions of acculturation assuaged here, in the heat and dust of Moria. The reality was that Zionism had become a haven in a sea of wretchedness and humiliation, as it was again now in a sea of bloody political incertitude. The combined idea of haven and unquestioned leadership: this brought the peace and dignity of uMoya fluttering within their grasp and, through the submersion of baptism, into their stoical hearts.

"The Lord holds in his hands the destiny of nations. Our destiny is not ours." The words leapt from loudspeaker to loudspeaker, each reproduction tumbling against the next. The Lord's grace was likened to oil, being poured onto the head, running down the beard, even to the corner of the garment, all that oil and grace. The Bishop's arms were raised, even as Jackson's image of God, and the multitude fell to its knees to pray.

On hands and knees in red dust, the heads sunk low, and the murmur of a million voices sounding like the transit of many trains as uMoya healed their wounds and gave them courage to face a destiny they could not control. And then the sudden silence as they rose.

The Bishop issued some instructions regarding safe driving and obeying the rules of the road. A great dispersal began, and we, Jake and I, were caught up in it. The people milled together, talking with contented voices, then spread out across the ravaged landscape, raising dust as they began a slowly growing scramble for home.

Most of the journalists had left early, cadging lifts and chasing deadlines, and not many had remained to board the bus. We entered it with some relief. But after less than a kilometre our journey took a wrong turning, and the bus became embedded in a welter of roadless traffic. We waited. It began to get dark. We saw the helicopters take off, pouring sheets of dust into the evening air. The cross on the top of the hill turned into a hazy neon beacon. The driver of the bus turned off the engine. We decided to walk to the road and try for a lift.

We walked. I tasted Moria as a burning in my throat and eyes. A few lights on timber poles came on. We walked into a morass of tents and shelters and dust-laden vehicles, and people packing up, and young men dancing, and people singing. We stumbled forward in the growing darkness, tripping on ropes, losing our direction. We asked; people answered; we moved forward, pressing through a throng. I smelled the stench of latrines and rotting refuse and dust and humanity and smoke and the cooking of food, but above all the dust. I saw Jake's teeth flash in the darkness. "This is the smell of Africa," he said; "this is what you white people miss so much when you're away." I laughed. I held onto his arm as we lurched forward. I felt suddenly grateful for his slightly cynical presence, the strength of his arm. We were going downhill towards the river. We stumbled. Unseen hands guided us. I could see lights at the bottom and going up the other side. We were pressed about by thousands of unseen people offering occasional shouts, some laughter and much joy and singing. The lights were the lights of vendors on the farther bank: small circles of illumination in which hands transacted coins for food. The smoke of fires mingling with the dust. A child's sudden scream in the darkness. Jake's hand on my shoulder, my arm bringing him forward. And now we were at a fence, groping for the wires. But suddenly unseen hands took hold of my elbows and lifted me bodily across. I could not see the men who had helped me. Then Jake was lifted across. We moved forward again, stumbling together, clasping each other, laughing out loud. We could see the lights on the main road to Pietersburg. I turned and looked back at Moria, the chaos of illumined dust and headlights and the burning cross, and I thought with a stinging clarity: this is what Africa is like, Africa's fortitude, Africa's faith, Africa's jumbled failure.

Our feet had come to smoother ground. Jake's eyes glinted at me in the light of the traffic snarled and stationary on the Pietersburg road. "What a business," he said with some feeling; and then, slapping my shoulder: "You know, I'm going to miss you when you go."

5

THE FIRST CRY

POTGIETERSRUS LAY hardly 60 kilometres to the south-east of Pietersburg, yet in higher country which gave a sense if not a direct sight of mountains all around: to the west the Waterberg range; closer at hand in the north-east the Ysterberg and the Makapan-Strydpoort escarpment. I would go into the steep hills and valleys of this escarpment, seeking primeval things. I would also, later, go into the Waterberg. But for the moment the modest town of Potgietersrus claimed my attention.

The main street named Voortrekker, with the big North Road trucks blasting from traffic light to traffic light; the sight of church spires and spreading jacaranda trees; boys in purple shirts and white collars and with socks around their ankles trailing home from rugby; black vendors active on the pavements at the top end of town. Potgietersrus stood at the southern end of the corridor between the two large pieces of Lebowa, but it seemed blacker than Pietersburg, perhaps because it was considerably smaller, perhaps because it was the afternoon of a public holiday when I arrived. LEB vehicles from Lebowa cruised the streets, for the most part filled with young men swilling beer from cans, young men without shirts sometimes, sweating, grinning, listening to loud music, trying to pick up women on the wide pavements of the street called Voortrekker.

I drove straight through the town to a place, not far south, called Moorddrif. In so doing, my mind was lured back to the 1850s: when

77

the slaughter of elephants out of Schoemansdal had already reached terminal proportions; when the foundation of Pietersburg lay another 35 years into the future; when the black tribes and kingdoms of the Northern Transvaal still seethed with restlessness in the aftermath of the Zulu-centred Mfecane and the struggle between Mzilikazi's Ndebele and the finally victorious Voortrekkers; when the entire region between the Vaal and Limpopo rivers was inhabited by only 15 000 whites, a tenacious and often ruthless collection of individuals and groups, clinging on to land as they tried, against a background of constant argument among themselves, to establish their republic.

Here at Moorddrif stood a squat sandstone monument – rough-hewn blocks cemented together – looking more like a plinth from which the statue has been toppled than a monument in its own right. But a monument it was, and I translated the inscription from the Afrikaans: "To the memory of 33 Voortrekkers who in 1854 were treacherously murdered by Makapan." Beside the monument, and enclosed with it by a metal fence, stood a dead tree with gnarled and flaking trunk, and intricate white branches etched against the scorched blue of the afternoon sky. Stark tree, stark monument, stark hatreds then.

Members of a hunting expedition returning south had camped here beside the shallow crossing place of a river marked now only by seed-laden water grass and reeds. It seems that a few of the men had gone into nearby African homesteads to barter for ivory and livestock. They were killed there. Then the main party, here at the river, was attacked by warriors of Chief Makapan's Tlou tribe. Perhaps some Tlou taboo had been unwittingly broken; or perhaps for the Tlou, who were part of the now scattered Ndebele people, it was an act of revenge, an act of defiance against their victors. Whatever the reasons, men and women were killed and, according to one source, mutilated for medicinal and ritual purposes. Children had their skulls smashed against the trunk of the now dead acacia tree. The leader of the party, Hermanus Potgieter, had been held down and flayed alive. No one survived. But vengeance followed revenge. The nephew of Hermanus led a commando against the Tlou who had gone into hiding in caves in the Makapan-Strydpoort escarpment. Piet Potgieter laid siege to the caves. After a month, thousands of Tlou had died of thirst and hunger, but Piet Potgieter had also lost his life, felled by a bullet aimed from the darkness of his enemies' last retreat.

I stood by the palings of the monument fence and watched the traffic on the Great North Road; vehicles rushing to and fro on the bridge across the shallow river. Dusty mini-buses headed south, no doubt still returning from Moria's renewal, roof-racks piled high, tarpaulins flapping; the interiors crowded with the faces of the renewed. Beyond the road, east-facing hillsides were steeped in shadow; closer at hand, the thick bush (out of which Tlou warriors had once leapt) surrounded the monument, but slashed back and at bay.

I returned to Potgietersrus in the early evening. The woman at my lodgings had small jewels embedded into the frame of her spectacles. I spoke to her in Afrikaans. She smiled at me through the smoke of her cigarette. "But you are English," she said. "My dear, let's talk English. I came down from Northern Rhodesia nearly 30 years ago; couldn't face the thought of black rule; but look at South Africa now, teetering on the brink." She sat at a ball-and-claw bureau with a flap-down lid to write out my receipt. A large television screen flickered in the background. I asked her to recommend a place to eat. "If you're talking about licensed, there's the Park Hotel; and then the Spur Steak Ranch is quite nice. But whatever you do, don't go to the Orinoco." I asked why. She grimaced. "Shall I say it? It's a real dive. It's all black now, my dear."

Walking in the streets of the once white town in the fading light. Here a beach buggy filled with blond youths in vests, wondering what to do for the evening. More young whites dawdling beneath the neon of the steak ranch in the warm and slightly humid evening. I looked for the post office to make a telephone call, and across the street I discovered a mound of boulders, small jacaranda trees growing at angles out of it. Only just sufficient light to read the bronze plaque set into the paving.

"Commandant-General Pieter Johannes Potgieter was born on 24 December 1822 and died in action at Makapan's Cave on 6 November 1854. He was buried on his farm Middelfontein near Nylstroom; and reburied on this site on 30 May 1964 with full military honours. Potgietersrus was named after him. We honour his memory."

From somewhere in town, a set of electronic bells chimed out the tune of a hymn, a slightly mournful reminder of more assured days, perhaps. I looked at the mound of big brown boulders, and beyond it, over the tin roofs of suburban streets, to a horizon of hills and some shreds of grey cloud against the fading orange of the western sky. I was thinking of 1964, those days when apartheid had seemed as immutable as these stones, and when no black man would have cared to mount the front steps of the Orinoco Hotel for fear of being immediately bundled down them. But times change, even though the tunes of the hymns remain the same.

Black drinkers sat scattered about the lounge and garden of the hotel now, but without much enthusiasm, as if it was almost time to go. Then I remembered the public holiday; they had perhaps been there since lunch, and for most of them it definitely was time. Like the young woman here, one leg on a table in the garden, a big brown thigh exposed, and her sleeping head at rest on the shoulder of her companion who sipped morosely at a milky-coloured liqueur.

The public bar, by contrast, remained a white male preserve, a group of noisy young men playing darts and shouting to Wilfred for more double brandies, a few older men sitting at the three-sided bar. At one point two black men came in and sat down at a table in the corner. I detected no hostility, only the smooth workings of an un-written law. Wilfred ignored them until they came to the bar to place an order; he then directed them to the lounge. A big unsmiling man, this Wilfred, a black barman doing as he was told.

The Orinoco public bar: a utilitarian drinking place; grimy walls adorned only with ageing cigarette advertisements; poorly lit, except for the dart board; a television droning in one corner; the raucous group at darts, big legs jutting out of running shorts, the drunken guffaws; the faces of the men at the bar; Wilfred's cloth endowing the shiny bar-top with dull arcs of moisture; but nothing at all to link the place to a South American river. The men at the bar: one with a hard but intelligent face, gold-rimmed spectacles, a military-style shirt, talking to an older man with some shame or sadness in his eyes; another had an immense black beard, looking like the por-trait of a Voortrekker, and left foam on his moustache each time he drank his beer; several others displayed the thick necks and paunches of those habituated to quantities of meat and dairy produce and beer. The darts players: uncouth, masculine, countrified, strangely innocent and blatantly sexual; lusty young fellows shouting "check those tits, man" at a provocatively dressed woman who had appeared on the television; and afterwards one of them rubbing the front of his silky running shorts and offering to have sexual intercourse with another's wife; and then the glinting eyes, the sudden stiffening of assertiveness and defence.

All this – the swagger, the emptiness, the humiliation – indicative of the final hiding place of white manhood.

I DROVE in the morning into the hills and valleys of the Makapan-Strydpoort escarpment. I had gained permission to visit the caves, which were on private property, and I stopped at the farmhouse – thatched roof and evidence of bougainvillaea – to ask for directions. A pleasant young man with an English accent gave me a hand-drawn map, then indicated a certain point on it. "This is a stone archway over the road. Stop here and hoot. Johannes is expecting you; he will take you further." I thanked him. He smiled engagingly. "I hope you enjoy the experience," he said as I proceeded in the direction he had indicated.

A narrow road, hardly more than a rough track and frequently patched with a white substance looking like lime, led me into dense bush and towards a range of hills, euphorbias growing like stubble on the steep and stony sides. Even though I drove slowly, white dust billowed out behind the car; and I had a sense of going into the deep and burdened silence of earlier times. On my right, before long, I saw the pale heaps of lime, quite dazzling where they had been recently disturbed. I knew that lime was mined here in the 1920s and early 1930s. I knew more. But before me now, straddling the road, stood the rough stone arch.

No need to hoot for Johannes though. He had seen me coming and I watched as he strode down from a collection of thatched huts at the foot of a sharply rising hill. I got out of the car to introduce myself. Firm handshake; steady eyes engaging mine; a lean body, hardened by physical labour; a short black beard enhancing his handsome face; then the polite smile in the sunshine: "I can show you the caves now."

Children had raced down from the huts to open gates for us and to wave. We passed through them and almost immediately into wild and precipitous country. We were driving into a narrow valley, and the track had degenerated, made tortuous by half-buried boulders and eroded channels, and the car in first gear groaned and jolted on a ledge – the track was little more than that – cut into the side of the valley. A few more gates, down to a dry riverbed, and then Johannes told me to stop the car. I parked in the shade of a spreading acacia tree. He pointed to the steep hillside which enclosed the valley on the south-eastern side, the summit crowned by rock outcrops. "Up there the caves," he said. We began to climb.

Thorns clutched at my clothing as I went. The way was steep and perspiration began to flow. Sometimes I used my hands to climb, grasping at rocks or at the trunks of small thorn bushes. Johannes went ahead, sure-footed, and then he would look back and wait politely as I toiled up behind him.

The view from the top was of the vague shape of mountains beyond the half-circle of high cliffs which enclosed the valley at the upper end. Evidence of a waterfall, but without water. I asked Johannes whether there had been water the previous year. "Yes," he replied, "a little bit." And in the river, the one we had crossed down below? "A little bit," he said again.

This part of the escarpment was a haven for plants, its sides and floor dense with vegetation. I had read somewhere that around 800 different plant species flourished here, everything from temperate-zone flora to tropical evergreens and, lower down, some desert plants of the Kalahari. The brisk calling of birds nearby served to enrich the silence of this ancient and versatile place.

We now descended by a vague pathway and came quite suddenly to the caves, a large yawning cavity which sloped down into the earth, the entrance guarded by a small forest of euphorbias. We went into the cavity, the roof high above our heads, yet almost immediately a sense of the strangeness of light, as of a twilight transfixed. Johannes had assumed the role of guide. "Tlou inside. Boers outside, over there," he explained, pointing to the far side of the valley. "The Boers shooting a big gun at the caves." As we went deeper into them, he began showing me things in a manner which suggested he had played guide many times before. Hollowed grinding stones, bones, pieces of sleeping mats, broken pots, all laid out carefully at various points. He stooped down now and took grey sand between his fingers. "Ash from their fires," he said. The roof of the cave still showed black in places. "Also," said Johannes, "the Boers tried to make smoke to bring them out. But they did not go out. They die inside here." When the Boers had finally stormed this last hiding place of the Tlou, carrying their flares into the twilight, they had been overwhelmed by the stench of death.

We clambered down into a corner of the cave, so that the entrance was high above us, and then passed under a lower ceiling of rock and began to ascend to a new entrance. Johannes showed me the beginnings of the deeper caves. "I walk that way to Potgietersrus," he said, "all the way under the ground." I shone a torch into one of the holes, but the feeble beam was swallowed in a profound blackness. From the roof, as we climbed towards daylight, stalactites had grown, but no glistening moisture enhanced their tapered ends in these days of drought. A sudden noise jarred through the cave. I stood still. Johannes offered me a flash of teeth in the gloom. "Dassies," he said. We climbed over hastily built Tlou defences, the trunks and roots of trees incorporated among the rocks of a crude mound, and emerged into sunlight. I asked Johannes if he knew where Potgieter had been killed. He pointed to a ledge of rock above the mouth of the cave. "I think he was standing up there."

The valley lay silent beneath us, thick with growth under a powerful midday sun. I wondered suddenly if it might be possible to hear dust settling, that small sound of the passing of hours and years and centuries, of the covering up of life and reality, one layer after the other. Where was the Tlou agony now, with birds fluttering among the thick fingers of euphorbias? Or what of the Boers in their khaki hats and their lighted flares inside the earth, stumbling against littered corpses where now only dassies rattled the stones? This was the starting point, and beneath it the dust settled and the questions multiplied for thousands of millennia.

Here in the fenced enclosure at the entrance to the Cave of Hearths (Johannes had unlocked a gate to let me through) was a visual manifestation of how much dust. In the late 1940s archaeologists had taken away the soil and stones for at least ten metres down a cliff-face. I stood on the floor of their excavation, the narrow valley at my back as I looked at the markings they had left upon the exposed rock of the cliff. High above me, a thick line represented the surface where they had begun to dig. Bird droppings had partially obscured the markings, but I was able to follow the ages through which they had excavated: Smithfield Iron Age culture, upper Pietersburg culture, middle Stone Age, middle Pietersburg culture, lower Pietersburg culture, lower Fouresmith, upper Chelles Acheu (now called Acheulian, to describe the ancient hand-axe cultures), then earlier stone age and another Chelles Acheu only about a metre above my head. And below that, the exposed entrance to the cave itself. How much dust? Probably about 150 000 years' worth. I looked out over the hot and silent valley, my heart all at once gripped with the staggering age of the human adventure. Nor was this the only excavation. When the lime workers had blasted out their lime, they exhumed the fossil remains of apemen who had inhabited the hills and valleys of the Makapan-Strydpoort escarpment between two and three million years before. The limeworks itself had been a cave, but the roof had finally weathered away and collapsed. The silence throbbed against my ears as I stared into the valley. Johannes stood waiting in the shade of the cliff.

I turned to him, asking if he had ever helped the people from the university with their excavations. He shook his head. But his father had helped them. His father was now very old. "I think he is one hundred and three. He is blind and he cannot hear. He just sits, and then he lies down." So Johannes, who had told me he attended church in Potgietersrus, would soon bury his father in this ancient earth, and then turn his still youngish eyes towards another century in the endless flow of them here.

So it was here, and especially in the caves, that humanity had played out the first slow acts of its astonishing drama. Here in this ancient escarpment, and of course in many other places in Africa and the world. But the thought of it happening here, even where I stood, gripped my mind. Would the landscape have appeared perceptibly newer then, the hills and mountains sharper, rawer, less worn away? Would water have surged over the half-circle of cliffs for tens of thousands of years without ever drying up, even in the winter months? And had Makapan, the Ndebele chief, fled to the caves through some embedded intuition of their safety? Had apes learned to walk upright here, to run in the hunt, to fashion stones and bones for the cutting of flesh? Had the sexual allure of females begun to shift from rear to front, woman at last standing upright with her lips and breasts and hips, fascinations which the dart players in the Orinoco instantly recognised through some embedded intuitions of their own? Had fire been harnessed here? Had self-awareness slowly come to those sloping foreheads and puzzled eyes I had thought of as I drove with warrant-officer Serfontein on the southern bank of the river Limpopo?

The valley lay beneath me now as cradle, as starting point, as area of commonality in all the confusions and divisions of the world through which I travelled. And a vision came indelibly to my inner eye: strange human or half-human creature scrambling from his cave and looking out over this primeval valley, but with haunted eyes and the pain of consciousness upon him in the morning sunshine now, and then filling his lungs and shouting out for the first time, yelling at the earth and at himself, the sound tearing at ancient silence forever, a single syllable perhaps, expression of the predicament and joy of life itself. Om; I am; now that I know I am alive, what am I to do with my life? That was the pain of consciousness. Predicament and joy; puzzlement and opportunity. He is, this strange creature emerging from his cave, our prototype, an expression of the commonality within us all.

6

FILLING THE VACUUM

THE PAIN of consciousness. The phrase is not mine but Eugene Marais', the Afrikaner poet and naturalist whose collected works I had seen when I went with Sidney and Karen to that astonishing house on the dry side of the Soutpansberg. Sitting in the heat, waiting for Petrus Uijs who never came. I remembered Sidney with a certain warmth. "Civilisations rise and fall," he had said, "and I think we're living in another decline." The rapaciousness of Schoemansdal, that sharp perception of resources being plundered, the doubt and the thoughtfulness: these things were what clothed my memory of Sidney now, as I drove towards the Waterberg.

I had become inured to driving, and my mind was freed by the monotony of it, by the rushing air, the harsh light, the gliding relationship of objects in the middle distance to the more static nature of the horizon. I had left the Great North Road once more, driving west towards a range of mountains which must be surmounted to get into the highlands of the Waterberg. Mountains crowned with rocks, and the road descending towards them so that with every moment they appeared higher and more imposing. Sheer cliffs made out of horizontal strata all weathered and cracked, as if the cliffs had been built up of stones, course by painstaking course. My mind drifted off to Mapungubwe and to the stone ruins I had visited in Venda. Perhaps the people who had built those places had first seen such cliffs, seeing how they appeared to be built of individual stones, seeing further how they shielded the high places and how they directed men in a specific direction as they attempted to ascend.

And now, to the right, a huge conical mound free-standing on the plain and surmounted by a sheer rock point. One of Sheba's breasts, perhaps. My mind slid away to Rider Haggard and the mounded and nippled landmarks he had invented for Allan Quatermain's great journey into the heart of 19th Century European mythology concerning the dark continent. Yet in the late 1870s, Haggard had been a British civil servant in the Transvaal. He travelled frequently. Not surprising that, in the heat and flies and profound loneliness of the bush, his imagination had seen in these massively proportioned natural features an echo of the delights of women. Not so surprising, either, that such fancies had fed the flowering of a preposterous romanticism in his stories of African adventure.

The road swung round a shoulder of the mountains and began to ascend, cliffs towering overhead, the road carved through solid rock at their base. Now, man-made walls did appear, presumably built to hold the base of the mountain away from the road, the walls stepped upwards, the rocks used for the building of them bound and contained behind sturdy wire netting and steel stakes. In places the sides of the mountain had been hacked away to allow the road through, turning to gain height, crossing a curved bridge over a deep and wild ravine, hugging the sides of amassed boulders as it climbed. I saw broken rocks on the road sometimes, fallen from the heights; and the marks of pneumatic drilling in the mountain's side, where parts of it had been torn away. And then without much warning, except that at last there were no more cliffs above, I emerged onto an undulating and treeless plateau.

Eugene Marais had lived in the Waterberg between 1907 and 1917. He was 36 years old when he arrived, perhaps running from an unhappy love affair in Johannesburg where he had practised as a lawyer, almost certainly attempting to escape from his addiction to morphine. He prospected for tin and platinum. He continued his study of primates, living in a narrow gorge filled with baboons. Later, he lived in a rented room in a house on a farm named Rietfontein, where the farmer's wife, Tamaria, dispensed his morphine in small doses. He went to the two neighbouring towns – Naboomspruit and Nylstroom – in a Cape cart and fashionable clothes. He became the doctor at a tin mine, even though he had never formally studied medicine. He developed a reputation of being a learned man, widely known for his miracle cures in which hypnotism often played a part.

He went on hunting expeditions as far north as the Limpopo. He fought a losing battle with morphine and Tamaria. He befriended an Indian trader in Nylstroom who was able to supply him with opium. At times he wrote brilliant poetry and prose; at others he came close to physical and mental collapse. When he finally left, but with a longing to return which was never assuaged, he could hardly walk he was so ill. He was also penniless. His young son went ahead with his luggage, and then Marais himself was coaxed onto a train bound for Pretoria and the benevolence of friends. Yet he lived with the torment of his addiction, and his sporadic attempts to break it, for a further 18 years. He was a man who fought constantly against the pain of his own consciousness until, one afternoon in 1936, he put the twin barrels of a shotgun into his mouth.

These darknesses of the Waterberg invading my thoughts; and now, by contrast, the sight of a blonde-headed young woman, her car at an angle across the sandy road.

I had turned off the tar just short of a small town called Vaalwater, and had driven on rough dirt roads, looking for a particular farm I had been advised to visit. While waiting in Pietersburg, I had chatted to a man who had done research into land tenure in the country to the east of Potgietersrus. He found, on average, that farms changed hands every three years. "People wear themselves out trying to make a living in the harsh conditions, vulnerable to drought, equally vulnerable to bank interest rates." But someone else had told me about Charles and Nina, fourth generation Waterberg farming people. So it was that in looking for their farm I came to a fork in the sandy road, and to the right had seen the young woman. I drove towards her to ask directions.

"Take the other fork," she said pleasantly, "down the avenue of pines."

I glanced at her car standing at an angle across the road. "Are you stuck?"

"No," she replied. "I'm looking for the horses."

I reversed and drove in thick sand between the trunks of pine trees, a direction which led me straight into a gathering of buildings topped with thatch.

NINA SAID: "My husband, Charles, originally hired the farm from his father and started with a plough and four oxen. His father was badly injured in the First World War, wounds in the shoulder and leg which never healed. We've done everything here ourselves. Carved the farm out of the bush. The house has grown from rondavels. The tennis court we had built by contractors, but the swimming pool we made ourselves. Mind you, I must tell you that the most avid swimmer is one of our dogs."

She laughed. She was a woman who seemed at peace with herself and her world, this high farm (4 700 feet above sea level, she told me) where the main activities concerned the growing of tobacco and groundnuts and the rearing of Bonsmara stud cattle. The veranda where we sat looked out upon gently sloping land, the foreground of which had been taken for a garden: spacious lawns, established trees, vivid flower beds. I remarked upon the flowers, but Nina was slightly disparaging.

"Oh, the garden's not good this year. We do use a little water from a borehole, but it's rain we need. We've had less than half our normal quota this summer."

But as far as I could gather, the farm was by no means in crisis. She showed me round a little. We looked at the first farmhouse – indeed a collection of rondavels – which was now used by her children when they came to the farm and by guests. She had three children, she said: a son at Cambridge, another in the army, and a daughter who was living at home and teaching in a nearby school.

"For a long time we were concerned about education for the children of farm workers in the area. I finally wrote to the President. Yes, of South Africa," she said with a smile, and I saw some of her determination then, yet tempered with her gracefulness as a woman.

"I told him in detail," she went on, "of the problems children faced who tried for secondary schooling here, and I received a very courteous reply. Then the Minister of Education wrote to tell me that he had set in motion the procedures necessary to establish a secondary school at Vaalwater. So we got our school, built with Government assistance on an English-speaking farmer's land near the village. There are seven white teachers, including my daughter, seven black teachers and about four hundred and fifty pupils."

We walked through the garden on our way back to the main house. The young woman who had been looking for the horses stood on the veranda. "My daughter, Juliet," Nina said. "Hullo again," the young woman said with a slight laugh. It was lunch time, but Nina said that they would wait for Charles, who was somewhere on the farm, before having the food placed on the table.

I asked if there were many English-speaking farmers in this part of the Waterberg. Nina nodded. But there were many Afrikaners as well. Near Vaalwater especially: many Afrikaners who had come south from Zambia farmed with tobacco there.

"We have a very good relationship with them," she said. "Charles has started all sorts of study groups which they attend. Study groups on groundnuts, maize, tobacco. And also on the Bible."

Nina read the look of inquiry in my eyes. "We are loose Anglican, and a bit Pentecostal," she said with a smile. "It is interesting how many Christians there are here in the English community."

They, Charles and Nina, held Bible study with the "cattle boys", but Nina did not know whether this had changed their lives. "They've got a lot to give up," she said thoughtfully, "lots of girlfriends, and so on." Then she talked about their church, designed by South Africa's most prominent architect, Sir Herbert Baker, and built in 1914. Well worth seeing, she said, perhaps Juliet would take me to have a look after lunch. Two old family aunts had been responsible for persuading the famous man to sit down at his drawing board. When he sent his account, however, the aunts wrote back and said: but surely, Sir, you did this for God. Nina's eyes were amused, then she raised them to Charles who had parked his car under the biggest tree in the garden.

At lunch, Juliet looked at me with her cool blue eyes and asked what I was doing in the Waterberg. I replied that my purpose was fairly general, but that I did have a special interest in Eugene Marais and the time he had spent here. Did she know of Marais? "I've heard of him," she replied, "but I've not read anything."

Charles had a weathered face, with eyelids which drooped slightly at the outer corners of eyes as blue as his daughter's. He was genial with me, yet guarded also, as if he wanted to let me know that he was undeterred by my presence. "It's about time somebody wrote something about the Waterberg," he told me, "it's one of the most interesting parts of South Africa." But he did not tell me in which way he thought it was so. We chatted about ecology and conservation, about the drought and the proliferation of game farms in the Waterberg. Then he said he was going to Vaalwater after lunch to play tennis. "What's for pudding?" he asked his wife.

When the meal had been completed, Juliet took me to see the church, St John the Baptist, a small stone and thatch structure standing alone in an area of silent veld. A line of mature gum trees stood to one side; otherwise the setting was the dusty grass and wild syringas of the Waterberg plateau. Inside the lich-gate – also designed by Sir Herbert, Juliet said, and also of stone and thatch – the churchyard had its share of graves. We walked among them for a while, Juliet pointing out the names of family members on the headstones. The two aunts, Juliet's great aunts, were in the churchyard now, and here was uncle so-and-so, and here a tiny grave. "My sister," Juliet said quietly, and then passed on. She reached up and rang the bell. She stood listening for a moment to the sudden richness of sound. "Shall we go inside?" I followed her. She seemed rooted to her place, this young Englishwoman of the Waterberg. She had told me she had spent some time in Europe, but had returned knowing that it was here in South Africa where she belonged. Here in the Waterberg, embroiled in Third World education and in the continuum of life and family. Yet I sensed a level of remoteness in her also, as of a small act somewhere of self-denial. No need to ask: clear enough to see that she too was "loose Anglican and a bit Pentecostal". She would, I knew, speak of herself fearlessly as being a Christian. Was this in itself a renunciation of self perhaps, an abandonment of doubt where doubt and puzzlement persisted?

Inside: the pews, the glass, the muted light and slightly musty smell of sanctuary, Juliet's thoughtful face. The church would not take many more than 50 worshippers, yet it was beautifully proportioned, the famous architect having done his work well. In the tiny vestry, a framed certificate proclaimed that Juliet's great-grandmother had been received into the Order of Cyrene, a high honour in recognition of her service to black women in the district and for playing the organ in the small church for 30 years. Then Nina had played it. Now Juliet did.

"And look here," she said, pointing to the door which led from the vestry to the church. I saw heavy scratch marks, more like a succession of gouges out of the timber of the door posts and on the cross-pieces of the door itself, as if the door had been attacked. "That's exactly it," Juliet said in some amusement. "We forgot to close the vestry window once and a baboon got through and mauled the door, trying to get into the church."

We went out into the sunshine of the church yard once more. I said: "You know that Eugene Marais studied baboons quite extensively when he lived in the Waterberg."

She looked at me with steady blue eyes. "And what did he discover?"

"He learned a lot about human beings. He talked about our pain of consciousness. I suppose you could call it the predicament of consciousness which he believed he saw in the baboons as well. What are we to make of life, now that we know we have it? What are we to make of the feelings of futility and irrelevance and sadness, and of course also of joy and ambition, which this consciousness all too often evokes?"

"Only God can truly fulfil us," she said.

We passed through the lich-gate and got into the car. I started the engine and drove slowly along the road, and then turned in the direction of the farm.

"People are born with a vacuum in them," she said, "which only God can fill. It's a God-shaped vacuum. But people turn away from this truth. They try to fill the vacuum with something else. But what is there? There's nihilism at the one extreme, existentialism at the other. The hopelessness of the moment, no past and no future; or the nothingness of annihilation."

"Do you think that God, in this sense, can take many forms?"

"How can he?" she said. "God is God, as he reveals himself in Jesus and through the Bible."

I said I respected what she said. I said that her image of a vacuum was good, and that it seemed to me to be a parallel for Marais' sense of pain. Then I suggested that perhaps the Afrikaner belief of being part of a covenant nation, or the Zionist hunger for uMoya, were other forms which, for the people concerned, could fill the vacuum and assuage the pain.

She had turned to look at me as I drove down the avenue of pines. "I don't think so," she said, her voice oddly emphatic.

I said with a smile that I was quite wary of exclusivist beliefs, that such beliefs had caused considerable misery through intolerance.

"But the truth is not tolerant," she said. "I know this sounds horribly dogmatic, but the claims which Jesus made about himself were exclusive. 'I am the Way,' He said, 'the Truth and the Life; no man comes to the Father except through me.' "

She was silent a moment, then said: "In accepting Jesus I accept that His exclusive claims are true. Our God is a jealous God. His truth is supreme."

"Have you never doubted that?"

"Yes, I have," she said. "But no longer."

Again, the emphatic tone, that abandonment of doubt. We spoke about these things no more. Yet even then, as I drank tea with the young woman, as I accepted an invitation to return, as I said goodbye to Nina, as I drove across the plateau and then down towards Na-boomspruit, I was haunted by an image, many-sided and ambiguous, which became a potent undercurrent through all my time in the

Waterberg. Those gouges on the vestry door: the image of an un-comprehending beast standing upright at the door of sanctuary.

AND SO in the golden afternoon I went through grass in seed which swayed gently over the undulations of the plateau, or through venerable autumn fields, cattle standing deep among dry stalks of maize, and I saw the shadows of poplars flung out like a grid across the unpaved road, and then the tar began and I descended through bush-filled hills all dusty blue with shadows now.

Half dark when I reached Naboomspruit, Afrikaans for euphorbia stream, a few neon signs flickering in the main street where buildings hardly ever reached a second storey, a street from another age perhaps, as if one might clatter in on horseback, or in a Cape cart as Marais had done, and find the only hotel, the Naboom, and inside it a ladies' bar filled with men in short trousers, drinking hard.

Two young women behind the bar, smoking and sometimes being coy or meaningful with their eyes, and trying always to be feminine, their fingers laden with rings, their lips well-defined in the dim light, and ignoring the swearing and obesity as if, perhaps, they longed for a coconut island sort of dream where their throats and shoulders might have been more in keeping and less crudely admired. But as it was, the sound of piped music provided more noise than moonlight, and mingled easily with the bursts of laughter and rugby on the smoke-belaboured air.

A man said to me: "I hope you enjoy your stay in the Waterberg. I'm a game farmer myself." A large man, bursting out of his khaki, and with clever children at Potchefstroom University: a daughter becoming a chartered accountant; a son with an applied mathematics doctorate, and physics next. But this well-meaning man with an enormous stomach had not always been a game farmer. "Cotton seed," he said. "I had a farm to the west of Louis Trichardt. But then I gave it up when I split with my wife. Now it's game farming for me." I asked him how he made a living from that. "Hunting," he said promptly. "There's someone coming up from one of the big banks next weekend. He's looking for a trophy. Kudu. I've got six kudu which are bigger than the minimum measurement. He can have one. But he'll pay. I'm talking three-and-a-half thousand." He then asked me what my business was in the Waterberg. I mentioned Marais. "Yes, I've heard of him. A very clever Transvaler. But isn't he dead?" I nodded. He then spoke to me about the Northern Transvaal. "The place has backbone," he said. "There's nothing fancy about it, but the people are tough. I've been round the world seventeen times with my cotton seed, and I know what I'm talking about. Tough people, strong, hard-working. They can take it. Drought. Hardship. They'll rise again. They always have. They're pioneers."

Marais as pioneer, I thought after the big farmer had left me. Born in Pretoria when the capital city was hardly more than a pioneering village itself; educated in the Western Cape at a time when Afrikaans was beginning to emerge, and be nurtured, as the real language of the Dutch-reading Boers. He published his first poetry in his teens, some of it highly patriotic; later, as a journalist in Pretoria, he pioneered the writing of Afrikaans. He began using morphine, a freely available and acceptable drug in those days, in his early twenties to relieve the stress and insomnia caused by his hectic lifestyle; he used it even more when his wife of 11 months died in childbirth; and by the time he went to England to study law at age 26 he had been addicted for some time. More a Bohemian than a pioneer, perhaps, more a frontiersman of the mind than of the open country.

Of his life in London, not much is known for sure, except that he did not do particularly well at his legal studies, that he had an affair with a 16-year-old girl, and that he kept a chimpanzee and a marmoset in his rooms. This handsome young man from the Transvaal Republic, probably living a dissolute and aimless life, a Bohemian life almost certainly, but aimless perhaps largely in the sense that he had too many interests, the chief among them being the natural sciences, medicine, psychology and virtually anything to do with the supernatural, above all hypnotism. And all through those years, until the Anglo-Boer War temporarily trapped him in England, he fought a losing battle against his addiction. The dreams of bliss had turned to nightmare; what he had adored, and adored still, became invader now, clawing with brutal intent to enter and defile.

Over the loudspeakers in the ladies' bar, and over the jokes and guffaws, a song with calypso rhythms – Give me hope, Joanna, hope, Joanna, before the morning comes – to which one of the young women behind the bar, her hair tossed back as it would be on a coconut island perhaps, mouthed the English words.

"HAVE YOU seen the school?" Japie asked.

Yes, I said. In a quiet Naboomspruit street I had come across a junior school called the Eugene N Marais, the name prominently displayed at the gate. To one side, mounted on a brick wall, a large coat of arms incorporating a euphorbia tree and a motto in Afrikaans: do your best.

"Inside, they have a chair which was used for many years by Marais."

Japie: a slim young man, crisp-looking, efficient, neat clothes, pleasant grey eyes, and a genuine willingness to be of service. I wanted to learn what I could about Marais' time in the Waterberg; he, as a municipal employee, would do everything he could to assist me. Did I want to see the chair? I said I did not wish to disrupt the school for so slight a reward. Well, if I wished, he would accompany me on a sort of Eugene Marais tour. "There's quite a bit to see," he said.

We drove out into Waterberg hills clothed often in boekenhout trees which provided an elegant cover, sparser than acacia bush; no thickets here, no secrets, and a sense of light pervading the graceful slopes. Japie spoke about Naboomspruit, how comfortable the climate was in winter. In winter, the town had a unique atmosphere: biltong, rugby, the smoke of braais, travelling to Loftus Versveld, the big rugby stadium in Pretoria, "our holy ground," Japie said with a smile. "Yes, I am keen on rugby," he went on, "but also tennis. I play tennis. That gives my sport a balance, I think."

He struck me as a young man for whom balance was important. As he spoke, he seemed anxious for me to understand that the Northern Transvaal clichés, the stereotypes, were only on the surface. Certainly, here was political conservatism and machismo and rugby. But that was not the whole story: there were also people, like himself, who did not smoke or drink, and there were people who liked tennis as well as rugby. "But it is a special atmosphere here, when the Blue Bulls play." And there were people who didn't necessarily believe in the conservative thing, not completely. I liked his thoughtfulness and his candour.

He said: "My feeling is that there is a broad front of people who want to get on with their lives in the Transvaal. And I don't mean in a white homeland. That is not a feasible idea. We are going to have to learn to live together, but I do have reservations."

I asked him what they were.

He hesitated. "I think I would like to determine who I live with, and I would like to keep my own culture."

Marais formed a part of that culture: a champion of Afrikaans and author of some of the most elegant and moving poetry and short stories in that language. I was interested to know how much Japie knew of Marais' life, but did not ask for fear of embarrassing him.

I had developed a sense that, at least from a popular point of view, an Afrikaner writer of such stature should be seen as nothing but upright and patriotic. It was perhaps indicative of a young culture, especially that of a people steeped in religious conviction, that any shameful acts by its protagonists must be excluded. I had read of a bust of Marais which had been suppressed because it showed too clearly the baleful physical effects of his addiction. Not long before I began my travels, I received from the Nylstroom municipality a typed but undated summary of Marais' life, which frequently mentioned his deteriorating health but never a word about morphine. And I thought of the Naboomspruit school's motto and wondered how it was linked to the man whose name the school carried. Here is the great man's chair. Do your best to be like him. But not his excesses and his tragedy which must be discussed in whispers or not at all.

Marais returned to the Transvaal by joining a secret mission in Europe, the aim of which was to travel down the east coast of Africa and then, cutting across Mozambique, to bring urgently needed supplies of ammunition and explosives to the commandos fighting in the last bitter stages of the Anglo-Boer War. By the time he finally arrived, however, the war had ended. For five years he worked as a journalist and newspaper proprietor, and practised law in Pretoria and Johannesburg, all the while battling with malaria which he had contracted on the east coast, and with his addiction. He then fled to the Waterberg to prospect for tin and platinum. He teamed up with another prospector, Alec Austin. They built small cottages at the bottom of a narrow gorge called Baboon Kloof. Japie had driven me there, and I stood looking at a pair of rough stone foundations, all that remained of the cottages now.

"This is where he studied the baboons," Japie told me. "If you come here in the evening you can still hear them sometimes. That's what I've been told."

Beyond the foundations, the kloof narrowed and steepened, both sides thick with trees which nevertheless revealed high ledges of rock. The place, according to Marais himself, where he had been happiest, where he had seen in the baboons the tentative beginnings of the human psyche, and from where, every morning, he had gone up into the hills to do his prospecting.

At the top of the kloof stood the tin mine where Marais had served as doctor. It had been closed for several years and stood derelict and silent, save for a demolisher's block-and-tackle, the clash of chains against steel. A clutter of machinery sloping down towards the head of the kloof, grey mine dumps on the farther side. It was strange to think that what Marais had searched for, with the gambler's excitement of prospecting, had now played itself out. "We'll cover it over and plant grass again," a man said. He was the only mine employee left, serving a caretaker role as the machinery was taken away. "There's plenty of tin still under the ground. But the price . . . It's just not economic any longer." Then he told me, prompted by Japie, that Marais had lived in the kloof with the big apes. Had I heard the story of Marais, stark naked among the apes, when two of the females had begun to take a particular interest in him? "I'm telling you, he got a terrible shock." We laughed pleasantly together.

Japie told me that the farm, Rietfontein, where Marais had boarded for many years, was now a hot springs resort, but that the old farmhouse still stood there. We drove through imposing gates and along a brick-paved drive to the main resort complex. Japie said he would need to get permission to proceed further. While he did so, I looked at holiday-makers sauntering in the sunshine, at children splashing in a naturally heated pool, at teenage girls in daring swimming costumes, and at a notice-board advertising film shows, darts competitions and an opportunity to play American baseball.

Marais had called the Rietfontein farmhouse "The Ark", perhaps because of the collection of animals he kept there, but also because, dove-like, he left it, sometimes for many months on end, but would always return. His relationship with Tamaria degenerated over the years he spent there. Her photograph shows a hard mouth, small dark eyes, hair pulled back from a central path. She had perceived his weakness too well, and she was the keeper of his daily salvation. No doubt she learned what it was to have power over him, to allow his pleading to go unheeded, to use and to manipulate, so that when he finally left he said to his son that it felt to him as if he was escaping from a prison.

What drama, what pain and restlessness must have been played out in these crumbling rooms, deserted now, smelling of rats and decay. The house stood on sloping ground some distance from the resort. The iron of the roof had rusted and sagged, the walls were of patched plaster, dirty, with red stains of sand seeping up them, as if the earth would slowly claw the structure back into itself. The yard was of bare ground, with a row of jacaranda trees, and I thought of the otter Marais had reared here, of the baboons he had kept, of the snakes. The house faced across a shallow valley to hills in the north east. A deep veranda ran along the front where Tamaria's husband often used to sit and smoke his pipe, and the small outside room used by Marais led from it. The chair had been here, perhaps, in this empty space lit only dimly by one small window. I heard from Japie that the resort was planning to turn the old farmhouse into a restaurant, with a Eugene Marais museum in the outside room. The atmosphere seemed all at once oppressive: the closeness of the rooms, the sense of soaring creativity and anguish enacted here. I turned away.

"Let me not die before I reach the hills I love." Marais' words. Those hills across the shallow valley, folding upon each other and clothed in the elegant boekenhout trees. I thought of Marais standing where I stood now, looking at the hills and longing for peace, longing for the needle, longing even for death.

As we drove back to Naboomspruit, Japie said: "He was a good man, Eugene Marais, very kindhearted. He was also a very gifted man. There were many sides to his talent. But he took morphine, and he became addicted. But at first he took it for the pain."

I offered no reply. In the deepest sense, perhaps, what Japie said was true.

WHEN THE Group Areas Act arrived in Nylstroom, the Indian trading community was forced right out of town. The row of shops which they were obliged to occupy after their properties in town had been expropriated stands in the veld, and across the road the veld stretches away. But when I asked the town secretary in which direction to find the Indian shops, he said, and for some reason he looked vaguely amused: "They're still in town. They're opposite our industrial area to the east." He remained standing behind his desk and he did not ask me to sit down. This was the man who had sent me the typed but undated document on Marais, but he seemed determined now to offer as little as possible. So I thanked him for his time and left.

Nylstroom got its name from a group of Voortrekkers who became known as the Jerusalemgangers. With nothing to orientate themselves but the maps in their Bibles, they mistook the nearby north-flowing river for the beginning of the Nile, and decided to press on to the Holy Land in order to get as far as they could from the British, whom they considered the Antichrist. They got no further than the Waterberg. Nor did they escape their Antichrist indefinitely. There is a junior school called Unity in Nylstroom which has a sombre yet strangely grandiose gate: curved and free-standing walls linked with stretches of huge barbed wire. A brass plate offered an explanation: "Thanksgiving gate," I translated. "To the honour of God who out of death gave life. In memory of the sorrow and suffering of the women and children in the concentration camps during the Anglo-Boer War, 1899-1902. A gift from the Standard 5 pupils of 1972." A large mural attempted to depict the inscription. At the bottom the suffering of children, the tents and the misery; in the centre a man and a woman reading by candlelight; and at the top once more children raising a flag. I remembered that the house at Rietfontein had been partially burned down during the war, and that Tamaria had lost her five youngest children in a concentration camp. Could such grief engender a hardness of heart, a dimming of sympathy? Could this also account, at least in part, for the dismal row of shops in the veld?

Ebrahim Ravat: the trader who befriended Marais and supplied him, at exhorbitant prices, with opium. There were Ravats still trading in Nylstroom, but they had not responded to my letters. I had spoken briefly about the matter to Solly Noor in Louis Trichardt, and he had suggested another family. They owned a large furniture shop in the row. I went inside and spoke to a man named Goolam.

When I mentioned Solly's name, Goolam immediately drew from his wallet an ageing newspaper cutting. He made me sit at a shiny dining-room table. He placed the cutting before me. It had been folded and opened so many times that it was in several pieces. Cut from a Johannesburg newspaper in 1953, the story had to do with the Group Areas Act. Goolam hovered over me. Then it came pouring out of him: the ruination, the problems, the humiliation of it all. He certainly looked like a humiliated man, a man who had gone almost beyond self-respect. He called me "Sir". In his late fifties probably, with a thin trimmed beard running round his face from ear to ear, an emaciated body, excitable hands, rapid speech, a small and slightly breathless laugh which possessed no mirth. When the Act had finally been implemented in Nylstroom, he said, the expropriations were sinful, the prices out here in the bush exorbitant. They also had to buy houses for their families. The Nylstroom council comprised white business people; they wanted the Indians out; they disliked the competition. On and on, his tirade punctuated by the small, breathless laugh.

I glanced about the shop: a sea of furniture, cupboards and wardrobes against the walls, a raised office in the centre. An old man sat placidly in an easy chair not far from the door; two men worked in the office; and a striking Indian woman, hand on hip among the furniture, looking at me. When our eyes met she smiled, but in a knowing sort of way, as if she wished to indicate that she knew the topic of Goolam's monologue. I turned my attention once more to him.

He said: "I want to fetch my file. Then I'll show you all the letters, Sir, all the fighting against this robbery and theft. Ravat. You must speak to my father." He called out loudly to the old man in the easy chair. "He knows a bit, but his memory is shocking. Don't go away. I'm going home to fetch the file." Leaning forward in his urgency, he hurried from the shop.

The old man stood before me with a placid smile. He wore a white embroidered skullcap. I rose to greet him and introduce myself, then we sat facing each other across the dining-room table. He folded his withered hands on the shining surface, as if placing them carefully over their own reflection.

"I'm eighty-two," he said in a gentle voice. "I was ten when I came to Nylstroom from Bombay in 1920." Then he looked at me in a slightly puzzled way. "Are you a rooinek?"

"He'll understand you better," the Indian woman said, "if you speak to him slowly in Afrikaans." She had moved nearer to where we sat.

I told him in this way that I was interested in Ebrahim Ravat and his relationship with an Afrikaner poet.

The woman's voice interposed again. "Oh, you mean Marais and his cocaine?" She laughed.

"Opium," I said.

"Oh, yes," she said carelessly, "opium."

She was a beautiful woman, statuesque, upright, looking at me with dark and uncowed eyes. She seemed slightly out of place in the sea of furniture, with the plate glass behind her providing a view of the open veld.

The old man said: "Ebrahim Ravat died in 1936. His son died in 1954."

She had turned partially to look through the glass. I guessed she had married into this Nylstroom family. She was in her late thirties now, disillusioned perhaps, yet proud and holding some anger also.

"Those were the good old days," the old man said in English. "Then Satan got loose and became Prime Minister." He gave me a peaceful smile. "I have a doctor son in Botswana, married to an Irish woman. I have children in Canada, and two daughters in Pietersburg. In 1966 we went to Dublin to see my son become a doctor, then we travelled in Europe."

Another interruption from the woman. A young man in thick spectacles hovered at the entrance, and she advanced upon him with a mocking smile. She turned to me with her bright eyes and said: "Here he is, the fool. He's to tie the knot. He's getting married. What a fool." The young man smiled and turned awkwardly away. The glass of his spectacles glinted momentarily. He looked trapped. Then he walked out and across the road and into the veld on the farther side. The woman laughed, looking at me again with her amusement and contempt. I wanted to talk to her, but it seemed impossible. The old man was talking of his European travels, and after all she was a woman. I wanted to ask: what's it like, living always with this vague stench of humiliation in every corner of your life? But I was a man and I was dealing with the men here.

"We travelled in Europe, all the way to Istanbul. Then I wanted to see the Berlin Wall so we went to Germany. I saw the Wall."

"It's gone now," I said, suddenly remembering how Solly Noor and his German friend had wept together on the long-distance telephone.

The old man looked at me, uncomprehending. His mind had wandered on to other things. Then Goolam came back, bustling in a self-contained squall. He dumped a battered file on the table and sat down beside me. His voice was swift and incessant, his fingers fidgeting through the papers in the file which was like an archives of wrongs done to Goolam and his family and all the 300 Indians in Nylstroom. There were also scores of letters to politicians. Here a reply from a past Prime Minister, thanking Goolam for the generous gift of food; another from the leader of the Conservative Party, thanking Goolam and his family for their good wishes. An archives laced with obsequiousness, Goolam's file.

More obsequiousness in action. A red-faced man coming into the shop and, seeing Goolam seated at the table, immediately putting his hands around his throat and in a half jocular way pretending to strangle him. "I want my receipt tomorrow, you fucking little coolie," he said. Goolam laughing in his small and mirthless way. All at once the old man saying peacefully: "I watched the World Cup on television when we were in Europe. England won four–two after extra time." Goolam laughing. The woman laughing, a sudden harsh burst. I stood up. "Time for me to go," I said.

Goolam sprang to his feet. His mocking adversary had strolled deeper into the shop. "But first I must show you, Sir. You must see for yourself. Where they stole all our property in town."

I felt a growing dislike for this fawning man, for the servility of his will to survive. I nevertheless agreed to go with him. I turned to the door and found the eyes of the woman upon me; bright eyes, seeing too much perhaps, with a sort of contemptuous good humour overlaying the despair.

Goolam drove me into the small suburb of Indian housing. Around one corner, a surprise: a low building, and the sandy yard in front filled with children, the girls in flowing white garments and head-dress. "Our religious school," Goolam explained. It was a sight which soothed me, it was like an assertion of a reality that surmounted all the odds, even habitual humiliation. "Look at the disgraceful condition of the roads here, Sir . . ." But I hardly listened now.

In town, he showed me the ostentatiously modern mosque. "They dare not tamper with religious places," he said. He explained how the Indians had occupied either end of the long main street. I asked where Ravat's shop had been. Over there. But it meant nothing to me, evoking no image or idea of the past. I kept thinking of the woman's bright eyes and her anger. Goolam's voice again: his own family's land had been here and here and here.

"The Indian shops were bulldozed, Sir. But now it has all back-fired," he said. "Look at them now." He gave his short and breathless laugh. "South Africa is finished now. Ruined by their pride."

AS JAPIE had suggested, I went to Baboon Kloof below the tin mine late one afternoon. I went alone. The sun still slanted across the tops of the western-facing hills, but the kloof was in shadow, the sky bright white above it. I sat on a boulder close to the foundations of the two huts, hardly three metres square, each hut. When Marais had lived here, a stream had splashed down from the high places of the kloof and flowed only a few paces from the huts. No stream now, only grey sand and some litter from the mine caught in the under-growth. No baboons either in the bird-rich silence. But then, during the first decade of the century, a large troop had lived in the kloof, using a cave in the cliffs as their sleeping place. For nearly two years Marais moved among them in their natural state. And for years afterwards he continued to conduct experiments on the farm Riet-fontein and elsewhere in the Waterberg region.

He began to distinguish two elements which underlay all patterns of animal behaviour: the first was what he called phyletic memory (roughly equivalent to instinct), and the second he called causal memory, the ability to retain specific knowledge relating to the process of cause and effect (in a word, intellect). While living on Rietfontein, he had rescued an otter cub after its mother had been killed. The cub was reared far from water, in the company of a litter of puppies, but when it was returned to the river as a young adult, it swam immediately and within 30 minutes had killed its first fish. Phyletic memory pure and simple. But at a given point in the evolutionary journey, causal memory began to appear. It did so because it enabled animals to adapt more successfully to the perils of existence. Marais knew that causal memory had almost completely ousted instinct as a determinant of human behaviour, but he used hypnosis in a number of remarkable experiments to indicate that strong vestiges of an ancient phyletic memory still remained. He found the animal in humanity, and saw a single continuum of life from the otter, even from the ants, to *Homo sapiens*, with the baboon standing at the halfway point, possessed of both memories, but with the causal predominating. He called them twilight souls and through them he found profound traces of humanity in the animal.

The consequence of causal memory was mind, the consequence of mind was consciousness, the consequence of consciousness was pain, a vacuum of puzzlement and incompletion. And then the great cry at the mouth of the Makapan's Caves. Marais saw all this in embryonic form in his baboons: this perpetual crisis of conscious existence. He saw their depressions, their melancholy in the evening times, he even noted (but perhaps fancifully) that they, like humans, often sought an altered state, an escape from "some kind of suffering inseparable from the new mind which (the baboon) has acquired in the course of its evolution." Intoxicating berries for the baboons, even alcohol for those in captivity; for the man, morphine, processed from opium which in turn is extracted from a flower.

The man: in Naboomspruit, thanks to assistance from Japie, I discovered a retired professor who had a bust of Marais in his living room. He had received it many years before from the sculptor himself who had then destroyed the mould. The story went like this: the professor had bought an early edition of a Marais anthology of poems at a street sale. It had been inscribed by the author: to Joan, followed by a quote from one of the poems. At a public function where the book was displayed, the sculptor, Joan Couzyn, claimed it as a book he had lost. He offered to cast the bust in exchange for the return of the book. I wondered if I was not looking at the bust which had been suppressed. Sadness and puzzlement irradiated from an ageing face, a ravaged face made all the more stark by Marais' baldness, sagging flesh under the eyes and about the neck, the haunted look in the eyes themselves.

In Baboon Kloof, as I thought about that face, the sky had turned to grey, and in the air the constant sound of wings against foliage as birds sought roosting places and called for the last time; the doves, the hadedahs, a limpid piet-my-vrou; and then the silence descending into a kloof turned slightly chill with the approach of night. In the gathering darkness, I heard a baboon bark from the high places at the top of the gorge. Three barks and then silence. It seemed a desolate place for Marais to have quietly thrust the needle in. I saw the upreaching arms of euphorbias still etched against the weakening purple of the western sky. Marais as outsider, I suddenly thought, the evolutionist in a society of stern Calvinists, the sceptic, the poet, the drug addict, buffeting and bruising himself to gain access to the peace of absolute truth or absolute oblivion.

AT CHARLES and Nina's farm again, they pressed me to have lunch, and I stayed, but the family seemed preoccupied with visitors. Juliet greeted me from an inner room where she helped an accountant friend with the records of stud cattle. I stood on the lawn and spoke to her brother, home from an officers' course for a few days and with a powerful handshake, who told me he had done his history honours thesis on South Africa's involvement in the Angolan war. An elderly woman talked to me in passing: she had spent some time in Umtata, the capital of the independent homeland of Transkei. "It was a taste of an African state," she said with a slight shudder. "The chaos. I'm glad I'm in the exit passage. I wouldn't be able to adapt." I sat on the veranda, looking out over the colourful garden and beyond. Charles came out and apologised that I was being neglected. He sat down, looking thoughtfully at me. I asked how his tennis had gone. "Fine," he said, "fine." There was a short silence.

Then he said: "I hope you won't mind me asking, but are you a man of faith? A believer?"

I looked at his weathered face, the slightly drooping lids over the bright blue eyes. I wondered whether Juliet had discussed with him some of the things I had said to her. I replied that I was more a man of doubt than of any one particular faith.

"Well," he replied, "I always say to people: you owe it to yourself to think of death. You owe it to yourself to consider the possibility of eternity. Do yourself a favour. Read the New Testament. Read it as a novel. It will make you think."

I told him then of some of my experiences. I said that his daughter had used an excellent phrase: a God-shaped vacuum. This was another way of saying what Marais meant when he talked about the pain of consciousness, the knowledge of being which often leads to a sense of futility and incompletion. A vacuum which is a consequence of the painstaking evolutionary process from instinct to intellect, or rather the gradual overlaying of the former with the latter. Marais thought he saw the vacuum in baboons. Almost certainly it would have existed in the apemen of Makapan's, and definitely in the early, axe-wielding *Homo erectus* and *Homo sapiens* who came after them. All with consciousness and a sense of incompletion. If we were prepared to accept a biological evolution, I said, then should we not also accept an evolution of need and thought? Hundreds of thousands of years of need perhaps. In this perspective, could a 2 000-year-old religion which had been fundamentally reformed in the 16th Century claim to hold the one, exclusive truth? Could any religion, for that matter? But the vacuum undoubtedly existed; the need to fill it presiding as a fundamental human trait. And the vacuum was filled, by a host of religions and other belief systems, in millions of people. But the pain of consciousness seemed only capable of being assuaged by the idea of one supreme truth, and thus seemed also to be the cause of much dogma and exclusivity and also much division and downright conflict.

Charles looked at me with his serious blue eyes. He said: "All this might be so. But for you, now, the certainty of death and the truth of the Bible are tangible realities. They're realities which are certainly good enough for me." Then he added: "I see that lunch is ready. I'm sorry we can't continue with our conversation right now. But I hope you think seriously about what I've said."

I did think about his words, and of his refusal to admit the beast of doubt into his sanctuary of certitude and faith, as I drove south-west along the Waterberg plateau that afternoon. I admired his con-viction, as I had admired Juliet's. Loose Anglicans with a charismatic bent. They stood in the foreground of a growing crowd. Besides being a slow meandering to the south, my journey had become a steady process of collecting people. I thought of Japie and the Indian woman in the Nylstroom furniture shop. And Goolam. And Marais. And beyond them, the people I had met and seen in places further to the north, all the way back to the neat Major standing on the bridge. Was there in them all a need to assuage the pain, to find certainty, and above all to look towards the king, that perfect symbol of purpose and direction up there in the sunset above the cliffs? And then my inner eye turned forward in expectation.

A rocky pass brought me down through steep crags. They were of the same texture as the ones I had ascended, that sense of them having been built of stones rather than left there when everything else was worn away. A view of a flat plain stretched out before me. The pass, twisting and steep, eventually delivered me to it. Out of the Waterberg now and driving across the plain, thick with bush, but sometimes with cleared areas of grass in seed and silvered by the sun. Before me, new hills appeared, and as I approached I saw that they were ravaged, eaten away in even bites, like steps, and rock pouring down from the workings, as if in a landslide, and then strange olive-coloured vegetation clinging to those parts which had not been eroded by rain. They were the mountains of iron.

7

MYTHS AND LEGENDS

THE STORY which is told in Rider Haggard's most successful novel – King Solomon's Mines – is one of high adventure in the pursuit of essentially noble quests: to find a wronged brother, to regain a kingdom, and in Quatermain's case to help a man in need. All these quests find common expression in a fantastic journey which begins by heading north into "the dark heart of Africa", as Haggard himself describes it. First, a terrifying desert must be crossed, then the adventurers must "climb the snow of Sheba's left breast till (they) come to the nipple, on the north side of which is the great road Solomon made, from whence three days journey to the King's Place" in Kukuanaland, and after a bloody battle there they proceed to the diamond mine, and then to the cave where they find, as if in reward for the nobility of their various quests and the courage of their perseverance, treasures without end.

A story tailor-made to fit, and to feed, the fanciful mysteries which Africa evoked in the 19th Century European mind.

In 1907, 21 years after the book's first publication, Haggard identified his mythical Kukuanaland as Southern Rhodesia, now Zimbabwe. He talked about the hundreds of stone ruins in this vast area between the Zambezi and Limpopo rivers. He believed that they had been built by Phoenicians who came south to exploit the region's mineral wealth. The Phoenicians, who perhaps had been sent by King Solomon himself, "enslaved the local population by tens of thousands

106

to labour in the mines and other public works . . . forced them to quarry the hard granite and iron-stone to the shape and size of the bricks whereto they (the Phoenicians) were accustomed in their land of origin, and, generation by generation, to build up the mighty immemorial mass of temple-fortresses" of which Great Zimbabwe provided the most impressive example. The Phoenicians must have stayed for thousands of years, because Haggard believed that they had already established themselves in Southern Africa by around 2000 BC. And then they vanished: this notion of a lost race which he exploited more fully in other novels, most notably perhaps in *She*.

I pondered these things as I lounged in my Thabazimbi hotel room on a warm evening. I could smell the scent of big flowers on the trees outside my window. It interested me that Haggard, "in spite of the newest theories to the contrary", should hold these views. Although the discovery of Mapungubwe, and its links with Great Zimbabwe and Venda, still lay a quarter of a century into the future, archaeologists were already beginning to challenge the myths by suggesting that Africa had its own dynamic beyond the perpetual recycling of darkness and savagery.

How to understand the lure of the 19th Century myths about Africa. The ignorance, and the sense of mystery which ignorance engendered, was fair enough: Africa had kept the world at bay for millennia. And the Eurocentricity was inevitable, especially in the sublimely self-confident and imperialist atmosphere of Victorian England. Then of course there was all the excitement of witchcraft, the cutting off of genitals, the wood carving for religious purposes, the dressing in skins and feathers, all those dangerous or noble savages speaking in unknown tongues. But deeper than these elements of the multifarious myth lay a sense of Africa's boundless wildness and generosity. In a cramped and often impoverished Europe, the idea of great space and vast treasures must have been a seductive one. Not a bag of diamonds for Quatermain and friends, but huge chests of them. Africa, continent of limitless resources upon the surface – the forests, the grasslands, the rivers, the wild animals swarming everywhere; continent also of limitless resources under the ground – the diamonds, the gold, the silver, the mountains of iron. This was the essence of the myth.

Earlier that day I had visited the Thabazimbi municipality where a friendly man had answered my questions: about 7 000 white people lived in the town; 10 000 blacks, largely Tswana's from the independent homeland of Bophuthatswana further to the south. The town served a farming community which dealt in cattle and game. And there was mining in abundance: iron, of course, right here in town, in the mountain on whose first slopes Thabazimbi had been laid out. Then the man said: did I know that Thabazimbi stood on the northern rim of the Bushveld Igneous Complex, a large but shallow depression caused by subterranean subsidence and in which inestimable wealth had collected over several thousands of millions of years? Three platinum mines not far away, and a tin mine. Also, the man said, untapped reserves of diamonds, chrome, uranium, gold and lead in the area.

I accepted the brochures he offered and wandered in the tree-lined streets for a while, remembering Japie, who told me he had gone to school in Thabazimbi. "It's very beautiful," he said, "it's like Jerusalem – or how I imagine Jerusalem to be – completely surrounded by hills." I thought though that perhaps Thabazimbi had more trees, and lusher trees, than might be found in the Middle East.

On one of the brochures I had been given was reproduced the Thabazimbi coat of arms. The head of a zebra occupied the crest: indicative of Africa's wildness. The base of the shield contained the heraldic sign representing iron: the reason for the town's existence. The top of the shield was occupied on the left by the head of an Afrikander bull, and on the right by the crossed pick and hammer of the miner: symbols of Africa's plenty. The 19th Century myth reduced to signs. Even the motto – *labore omnia florent* – might be a euphemism for the sentiment that if, like Quatermain and friends, you did not stint your duty, the rewards out here in Africa were always lavish. I thought of the coat of arms quite often as I stayed in the town, and afterwards, as I journeyed across the shallow basin of the Bushveld Igneous Complex.

"THERE ARE only between nine and fifteen years of iron ore left here now, and that includes a new section at the eastern end of the mountain. Production will be starting there quite soon."

These were the words of a young public relations man in horn-rimmed glasses and a hard hat, his hands knotted over the steering wheel of a four-wheel-drive truck as he took me to see the workings of the mine. "But it's had a good run. Since 1932."

What would happen to the town when mining ceased? The young man shrugged. "I'm sure it'll survive, even though we employ about thirty per cent of economically active whites." He paused to make a calculation in his head, shutting one eye tightly as he did so. "And about fifty per cent of economically active blacks, perhaps higher."

We drove past dusty structures and conveyor belts laden with rock, and then onto a broad road which in a series of zigzags ascended the side of a high hill. At the top, he stopped the truck and we walked to the edge of a three-sided crater which must have been a kilometre wide, and considerably more than that in length. The entire bowels of this bulging piece of the earth had been removed. I looked down with a slight dizziness at the stepped sides.

"From here," the public relations man said, "you can see the first section where mining began." He pointed away to the back of the mountain, gouged and looking wounded, against which the trees and roofs of Thabazimbi nestled. "But the workings became subject to landslides and were abandoned about sixteen years ago. Operations moved here to Donkerpoort. But this is now worked out. We could go deeper, but then we'd disturb the water-table. That wouldn't be wise. A lot of the town's water supply comes from underground."

I asked where they were mining now, and he said: "Around at the back of this. I'll show you."

As we drove, he explained the open pit method of mining. Blasting would take place between shifts. Then the big trucks would come in, driving along the steps or terraces in the sides of the crater to remove the ore-bearing rock at the bottom. A lot of non-ore-bearing rock could be visually identified on site, and this was dumped down the outsides of the hill being mined.

I remarked that this did not appear to be particularly friendly to the environment.

"We are making a strong conservation effort," he said. "The mine has its own nursery. We've imported a special grass from Kenya which is doing well." He pointed to an expanse of that olive-coloured vegetation I had noticed when I first arrived in Thabazimbi. "We also plant trees. Over a thousand last year alone; nine hundred of these have succeeded."

We were driving on a broad and sandy highway up the side of another hill. Huge yellow trucks ground down the slope in low gear, raising storms of dust against which water tankers waged a losing battle. Graders kept the surface of the highway smooth. The section of the road to be used by the trucks for that particular shift was marked by a long line of chevrons, and all along the verges old tyres had been suspended from poles, as in a children's playground.

"For the baboons to play on," the public relations man said with a grin. "And it works. Before we put them up, they'd play with the chevrons, moving them around and causing delays in the traffic." He also told me that watering places had been made on both sides of the road "because these big trucks can't always be stopping for the game to cross".

These arrangements struck me as faintly bizarre: the idea that wild animals would want to have anything to do with this gigantic renting of their natural habitat. Yet they had to live somewhere, and in any case the Ben Alberts Nature Reserve was not many kilometres away. According to some publicity material I had seen, it was home to more than 1 000 buck, some white rhino from Zululand, giraffe from Hoedspruit, and oryx and rooihartbees from the Kalahari.

But thoughts of adaptation and co-existence were pressed from my mind as we passed over a crest and descended into a dust-choked inferno. Donkerpoort West. A glimpse of terrace after terrace of smouldering earth above us. The big trucks, tyres several times higher than the vehicle in which we travelled, looming out of the dust, black exhaust smoke spurting with each gear change. At the bottom we watched a big machine with jaws load a truck with 170 tons of rock. Bite by bite in this way, 240 000 tons of ore eaten out of the mountains of iron each month. The truck driver emerged from his cab, climbed down a ladder mounted in front of the radiator, and stood to one side, smoking a cigarette. Heavy dust rained down from the loading, billowing out as it hit the ground.

"Awkward things to drive," my young guide said, looking at the truck. "As you can see, the engine obscures the driver's right-hand view. One of them once ran over a parked bakkie. Squashed it flat. When the driver was questioned he replied: yes, he had felt something, but had thought it was just a big rock."

As we drove back out of Donkerpoort West and back towards his office, he explained to me another mining method which was being used. Sub-level caving; tunnelling horizontally into the hillside near the top; then tunnelling again lower down; then collapsing the material between the two tunnels; on and on until the whole hill was hollow. He impressed upon me the extent of the mining operation by remarking that Thabazimbi mountain was riddled with a total of 421 kilometres of tunnels.

Then he said: "I don't know whether its true. It's certainly become a sort of mining legend. Thabazimbi is supposed to mean mountain of iron. But there's a spelling mistake or some misunderstanding. For years, many blacks understood the name to mean mountain of evil."

I offered no comment.

When we parted, he asked me where my travels would take me after Thabazimbi. I told him I was going to Sun City, that most lavish of pleasure resorts set in the Pilanesberg hills. His eyes brightened.

"Hey, you must see the new development they're building down there. It's called Lost City or something like that. Fantastic. It reminded me of a film I once saw. Fantastic sets. Did you see a film called *She?*"

I shook my head.

"I can't remember who was in it," the public relations man said, frowning in an attempt to do so. "But the sets were fantastic."

"All I know," I said, "is that the film was based on a book by a writer named Rider Haggard."

"That's it!" the young man in his horn-rimmed spectacles replied, obviously pleased that I at least knew something about the matter. "Rider Haggard."

WILLEM SAID: "They came here with their blêddie cattle. It was heaven for them. The sweet veld. Cattle thriving and getting fat. But in hardly eighty years, cattle farmers have seen their backsides here. I'll give another ten years, then cattle will be gone from this region altogether."

He sketched out the situation for me. The plains around Thabazimbi, even to the foot of the Kransberg, those high cliffs I had seen as I came down the steep pass from the Waterberg, had once been open savannah country. Chief Makapan used to come this far to the south-west, moving along the Kransberg with his cattle, grazing and moving, thereby giving the savannah time to recover. Later, the Boers trekked up the river courses in winter, their cattle also grazing and moving on. It was paradise. But then, not long after the turn of the century, came the enclosure of the land. Fences. Then the reduction of the size of the farms, followed by inevitable over-grazing, hammering the pastures into the ground, so that the bush encroached upon the grassland and finally smothered it.

A smallish man, dark and watchful eyes, unshaved stubble covering his firm jaw. His father had been a zoologist and wildlife photographer who was interned during the Second World War because he was German. Willem himself had studied botany and zoology before training as a veterinary surgeon.

"I would have loved to see the place two hundred years ago," he said, looking thoughtfully at me; "it must have been beautiful. Great herds of game. Even fifty years ago it must have been impressive.

Even less. As a student, I went from Pretoria over the Waterberg and then down into these parts on a bicycle. I saw the plain from where I camped high up in the Kransberg – the plain is called the Zebra Flats: you've seen the zebra on the coat of arms? – and the open grassland was scattered with clusters of tambuti trees which grew on fairly evenly-spaced termitiaries. That was eighteen years ago. Now the whole plain is thick bush, except in small places where a farmer has poisoned it and hacked it out. The bush is so thick over large areas that even game can't get through. We're in the exponential phase of this ecological change, this explosion of trees. We're over the edge, I think. In some places the change might now be irreversible."

He said that sickle bush was "top of the hit parade", followed by knob-thorn and yellow-thorn trees. Their rapid proliferation was a direct result of the abuse of paradise. "It was an ecological disaster to bring cattle here and then to enclose the land. You can't impose a cattle-based monoculture on such a diverse ecology. And by putting up all those fences, the ancient migration paths of animals coming from Botswana to winter here have been wrecked, and along with them the ecology.

"But," he went on, "of course the farmer has had to live. Because the farms are too small – only two thousand hectares, most of them, which is ridiculous – the veld has been hopelessly overgrazed and the bush comes pouring in. One consequence is that farmers no longer have a commitment to the land. They are struggling to survive, and because of this no longer care about the ecology. They try for as big a profit as possible and then get out. All my good clients, the serious cattle farmers, have sold up and gone elsewhere – many to the Vryburg area in the Northern Cape – looking for more suitable land."

We sat in his office which was unadorned save for a few diagrams which explained the characteristics of various animal diseases. He offered coffee. I had warmed to this thoughtful and intelligent man. While we drank, I explained to him some of my ideas regarding the great myth of Africa's limitless resources.

"Exactly," he said. "There's plenty here. Take as much as you want. It's a myth that has led to Africa's ruin."

But to be fair, I said, we need to think of Africa's own contribution. I told him of the suggestion that the amassing of cattle and the consequent over-grazing had contributed to the fall of Great Zimbabwe.

"We're treading the same path," he replied. "The European greed in Africa has been terrible. Our need to exploit quickly, our acquisitive instinct and lack of commitment, have wreaked havoc here. But I think that Western civilisation will have its influence – it's had its influence – and then it will pass. If only we can get the elephant and all the other species to survive, then they will multiply again and Africa might return to itself."

He told me he wanted to give up his veterinary work and move forward as a consultant offering a more holistic approach to the predicament of his bush-ridden landscape. He said that the increase in game farming had been a response to the forcing out of the cattle. Some collectives had formed which were trying a more diverse approach, attempting to find economic survival by combining cattle and game with tourism.

"But except where big business has bought out whole blocks of farms the fences aren't coming down. That's what is needed. Space. And sensible stocking levels. The land has a huge inherent power to recover if we can just relieve the pressure."

And the pressure was appalling. He told me of large areas where the roots of trees had been exposed, although still holding the soil together within them, while the rest of the surface had sunk by at least 15 centimetres to a hard surface which the sun had baked like pottery and into which the rain could not penetrate. The question was: how long had this erosion taken?

He answered it himself: "The roots certainly wouldn't have lasted a hundred years; I'd say about ten to fifteen. That much soil lost in so short a time.

"It must have been lovely here even 50 years ago. I've spoken to many old farming people. They say you could see the bottom of the rivers, the fish swimming. Now, it's a brown soup released from some dam, or nothing at all. There used to be natural perennial springs and fountains, but irrigation systems were developed from them. Considerable systems. Now the fountains are dead."

"Don't you attribute this to the drought?" I asked.

"Not altogether. Of course, the drought will have serious consequences, simply adding to the pressure. But the climate isn't changing that much. I attribute it more to the whole chain of abuse and pressure. We have to reverse that pressure. We need to achieve the old balance. Less bush, more game and more grass; more grass, more retention. An inch of rain a hundred years ago was worth a great deal more than an inch of rain today."

I asked how long the reversal of the pressure on the land would take. He replied: "After five hundred years it might look quite similar to how it looked before we came." It seemed an almost hopeless task, I said. He nodded. "But it's got to be attempted."

One of the biggest problems was the high price of the land, and the tendency for ownership to fall into the hands of people who cared little for the ecology of their properties. The struggling cattle ranchers had been only too glad to sell to wealthy city dwellers who used the farms as weekend hunting places and retreats. A sort of gentrification of the ruined grasslands.

"These weekend farmers," Willem said, an active dislike invading his tone. "They thought it would be easy. They thought it would be fun. The neglect, the irresponsibility. You should see their cars coming in at weekends. Pulling trailers for the meat. It's a rotten system."

He had received a call from a farmer who urgently needed his services. We walked out together into the garden which surrounded his rooms and which provided a good view of the mountain of iron. He showed me a dark green band of tambuti trees growing on the summit at the eastern end. "Iron bearing rock under there," he said. "That's what the mining people are about to take off." He extended his hand. "It's been nice talking to you," he said, smiling at me for a moment with his thoughtful eyes.

I watched him drive away in his truck. Helping a degraded Africa to return to itself. A sense of vague restlessness, as of a bystander a catastrophe, and a sense of respect came to me as I thought of that.

THE DAPPLED shade of a Sun City eating place; blue and white table linen adorned with silver, with glass; long counter-tops of sumptuous and varied food. I had driven down from Thabazimbi that morning through country which flattened, although the rim of the Igneous Complex saucer showed in the lingering mountains to the west. The veld was littered with mine dumps, the morning air tangled with electric wires for the railway running alongside the road, and telephone wires, and pylons with their looping loads. And the level symmetry of dumps again, and processing plants, and superstructures and headgears, or rents in the earth for the open pit operations, and chimneys, and the dust raised in the taking out of the hundreds of millions of years of accumulated treasures caught in the saucer. And now I was at lunch at Sun City in the Pilanesberg. Many men in ties and shirtsleeves, as if there might be a business conference in progress. Peacocks walking between the tables of diners. The view, through trees extravagantly laden with fruit and flowers, was of orange umbrellas and white furniture by the pool. Supine bodies. Closer at hand, a few vervet monkeys coming down with their young to walk on the low wall separating terrace from garden. To one side, the sound of water falling into a pond, a width of water as if flowing from the hotel itself and pouring down in a solid sheet. Some Chinese tourists being photographed in front of it. And here was a middle-aged man in baggy shorts trying to get close enough to the monkeys to photograph them.

The Pilanesberg, a ring of volcanic hills pushed out of the floor of the Bushveld Igneous Complex long after this saucer of treasures had been formed, lies close to the centre of one of the pieces of Bophuthatswana. Like all the independent homelands, Bophuthatswana enjoys the freedom to decide on matters such as gambling. In consequence, the Sun City casino is the most famous in South Africa, a country which itself has always disallowed such diversions, as it has traditionally frowned on most of the gamut of what is called adult entertainment: topless floorshows, pornographic films and so on. Sun City has it all, as it has fine sporting and outdoor facilities, and international entertainers performing nightly in the Super Bowl. Hundreds of thousands of visitors a year, most of them South Africans, enjoy these delights and also the unbridled luxury which the resort offers.

From the balcony of my room, I could look out at the Pilanesberg hills, and at the artificial lake with water-skiers swerving through the V-shaped wakes of motorboats, and at the lush green golf course, and at tennis courts and bowling greens and the dazzle of water in the various ponds and pools.

In the black and copper coloured foyer, I watched the glass-walled lifts ascending and descending and the jackpot to be won rising by the second. Water splashed softly from fountains. People moved noiselessly on thick carpets. In the centre of the foyer, a sunken area filled with batteries of slot machines and flashing neon: easy money, sun treasures, dream machine, mystical magic, silver falls, odds aplenty, moonlight mania; and the more sobering sign: cashier – check your change. The pings and constant soft discord of electronic noises, the occasional harsher sound of falling coins; and the flashing and liquidity of lights, the faces of the players caught in their sometimes lurid hues. Attractive young women served glasses of champagne to arriving guests. Porters in striped shirts came and went. The doors of the foyer glared white with the daylight beyond. Then a red-headed woman approached me with a friendly smile. She had come to show me the wonders of Sun City's newest development: the Lost City and the palace it contained.

She took me along passages and up in lifts and into a windowless room somewhere. Here, intricate architects' models had been set up on tables, and the walls of the room itself were filled with drawings and photographs. The redhead's assistant made me a cup of tea.

"Now," the redhead said, "let me try to explain how it all came about. The board wanted another hotel here at Sun City, but something special. What could be its theme? There were all sorts of ideas. The chairman wanted a jungle, a palace in a jungle, a lost palace, ruins. But let me show you the video."

On the screen: pictures of the existing complex, roulette wheels and young women temporarily clad in feathers; people playing games and dining by candlelight. On the soundtrack: Sun City, situated in the crater of an extinct volcano, a million visitors a year, the resort that has everything. But now it's getting the unimaginable: the palace of the Lost City. A long time ago, the commentary explained, a cultured and elegant people moved south until they came to the crater, this valley of the sun, where they settled. They discovered platinum and gold here. They flourished. They built their city and its palace. Then an earthquake disrupted everything. The populace fled. And all that was left was the lost city, searched for but undiscovered until the final decade of the 20th Century. This was the legend. Now it was being made into reality.

An explosion occupied the screen, flying rocks and dust as the excavations for the new development got underway. Cameras tracking through buildings in various stages of construction. Through the main foyer of the palace, parts of a 25 hectare jungle garden will be seen, the commentary explained; to the left a floating restaurant, to the right a huge bronze of the biggest tusker of them all. A mysterious, sacred place, the palace. And in the Lost City itself, a giant wave pool capable of making two-metre waves which break upon a sandy beach; a temple of courage with six-storey-high supertube rides; a fantasy island where patrons can dig up hidden treasures; an earthquake every evening with appropriate sound effects and flowing lava; and a great deal more.

When the video had finished, the redhead said emphatically: "No one will have any doubt when they are here that they are in Africa."

The models gave an even clearer indication of the complexity of the design. The city itself, which lay as it were at the feet of the palace, but not visible from its terraces, was being built as if still in

ruin, broken masonry and cracked walls among the various enter-
tainments and adventures. An elevated walkway linked the existing
entertainment centre with the City itself; while from the City, access
to the palace would be via a long stepped staircase through a part of
the jungle. "And here, look," the redhead said, "the Entertainment
Centre is being made to look as if it is housed in a huge cave, the
hall of treasures. Here's the entrance, with huge animals carved into
the solid rock. This leopard is over seven metres tall and twelve
metres long. And over here, the first subterranean supertube rides in
the world, coming down from the gold and diamond mines. The
whole thing has been incredibly well thought out."

She and her assistant donned hard hats and took me onto the site
itself. The towers and domes of the palace were already in place, the
highest of them rearing 70 metres into the air. The domes were of
elephant tusks and the fronds of palms. The columns inside the foyer
had been made to look like clusters of bamboo tied together with
leather thongs, their bases the feet of elephants. In spite of the dust
and scaffolding of construction, the monumental proportions of
everything showed through. The floating restaurant partially complete, and where water would everywhere fall and glide and cascade,
outlined now only in raw concrete.

My guides bombarded me with facts: 5 600 square metres of marble
flooring, and a further 50 000 to be carpeted; 350 bedrooms, all the
doors of which are being hand-carved; over 1,5 million trees to be
planted in the jungle surrounding the palace; 8 000 tons of natural
rock plus 48 000 square metres of artificial rockwork in the city; 70
500 square metres of artificial lakes and pools linked by 13 major
waterfalls, 20 cascades, two mountain rivers and five wetland areas,
all requiring 10 million litres of water a day when operational. A
massiveness about everything which only the Pilanesberg hills and
the piling of stormy-looking cumulus behind them could surpass.

I asked the redhead whether the legend behind all this monumental
activity, the one I had heard on the video, had been taken from a
specific source.

"Oh, no," she replied. "They've dreamed it up. I think it's very
good. You see, there's so little of African history to draw from. So
little has been written down. And there isn't really anything from
Africa from an architectural point of view."

"But," the redhead's assistant said, revealing that she was new at
her job, "what about when the Egyptians came down and found all
that treasure and built Zimbabwe?"

"I'm sure they've drawn from that, and from all sorts of other sources," the redhead replied. "But what they've ended up with is unique, I think."

"Uniquely African," her assistant added.

I strolled in the Entertainment Centre after the tour had been completed. When she saw me heading that way, the redhead told me that "the tired glitz of Las Vegas is now out, replaced by a much more African look". I could see what she meant: warm and muted colours, artificial rocks and palm trees, long murals of rock art, a gathering of giraffe, the whole place resembling a cavern with no neon and into which the rows of dust-coloured slot machines were made to blend. A cave of treasures without end. And other caves of pleasures. No need to brood with Haggard over appropriately rounded peaks. Sheba's snowy breasts and jutting nipples – and Nora's, Amelia's, Bertha's, Liza's and Sylvia's as well – are made of flesh here, though sometimes delicately clad in feathers.

From my balcony that night I listened to the storm which had gathered over the Pilanesberg hills: thunder, and a gusting wind which flew and swirled in this now darkened valley of the sun. Leaning out over the railing I could see in the frequent lightning the pale towers of the palace of the Lost City. Palm fronds and elephant tusks. The thunder clapped and roared. Was this Africa returning to itself again? But the towers of the myths and legends did not topple, and the thunder brought no rain.

8

TO THE LAST GENERATION

AS I drove down into the Western Transvaal, my mind returned quite forcefully to Pietersburg, to all those statues among the shrubbery, and to Johann, the round-faced academic who had spoken to me about the frontier mentality and how this mentality had been transmuted over the century into the political conservatism of the North. Holding on to what they've got, he had said. But he had intimated to me during the course of our conversation that I might find the West even more intransigent. More encumbered perhaps by their own 19th Century myths, those of which Sidney had spoken, the Israelites looking for their promised land, and the special covenant with God.

But if these were myths, what was the reality? The eastern frontier of the Cape Colony; the isolation of the Boers' lives so great that they effectively missed the 18th Century in terms of the development of thought and social organisation which had occurred in Europe; the consequent dismay at the interference of the British when they began to administer the Colony at the beginning of the 19th Century.

Although the Great Trek in the mid- to late 1830s gave voice to a rejection of British colonialism and also a rejection of British ideas, not least Britain's new intolerance to slavery, the Trek itself was an act of determined colonisation. In less than a decade it brought European expansion across the central South African plateau, and as far

119

north, for a few decades at least, to the rowdy outpost at Schoemansdal. The early years of the Trek and of the two republics it
spawned were marked by struggles against the indigenous black popu-
lations and by their retreat or subjugation.

But the old imperialist enemy was never far behind. As early as
1845, the British effectively ended the short-lived Natalia Republic
in Natal, and those Boers who had settled there were obliged to trek
again to find their independence. The discovery of diamonds in the
late 1860s brought a border dispute which Britain ultimately won,
ensuring that the main diamond fields at Barkly West and then at
Kimberley fell within the Cape Colony. Meanwhile, visions of a
British-dominated Southern African federation had begun to take
shape. In 1879, and at least partially with this federation in mind,
the independent Zulu kingdom on the eastern seaboard was smashed.
The British had already turned their attention to the Transvaal. They
annexed the ailing republic in 1877, Rider Haggard being the man
to hoist the Union Jack in Pretoria's Church Square. But the Boers
soon fought back, and the Transvaal commandos under Piet Joubert
(I remembered him on his horse in the Pietersburg gardens) finally
humiliated the British at Majuba in 1881, thus securing Transvaal
independence once again. But not for long. Within five years, gold
had been discovered on the Witwatersrand. Men and nations, scram-
bled after Africa's bounty; and the growing economic importance of
the gold fields became one of the main causes of the bitterly contested
Anglo-Boer War.

After some resounding initial successes in the field, the men of the
Transvaal and Orange Free State republics were forced back by over-
whelming odds, and after just over seven months of fighting the
Union Jack was flying in Pretoria once again, and the Transvaal
president, Paul Kruger, was on his way to Europe where he would
die a sad and disillusioned exile. The War was far from over, however.
For another two years the Boer struggle took the form of highly
mobile guerrilla commandos which harried the British wherever they
could, often with remarkable success. The British response was a
form of scorched earth collective punishment, the burning of farms,
the destruction of crops, the impounding in the notorious concentration camps of tens of thousands of Boer women and children.
Fresh bitterness overlaying old. Concentration camps were erected
all over the two Boer republics, as far north as Pietersburg. Apart
from peripheral skirmishing in the North, however, the main battles

were fought and the most ruthless collective punishment meted out much further south, with the West shouldering its fair share.

Even after the peace had been signed in May 1902, much bitterness remained and surfaced 12 years later in the so-called Rebellion of 1914 when the hard-liners in the Western Transvaal – notably the courageous and austere General Koos de la Rey – and in the Orange Free State again took up arms. The rebellion was suppressed, but the bitterness and a wounded republicanism remained. These emotions emerged once more in the late 1930s with the formation of the anti-British, Nazi-influenced Ossewabrandwag. When General Jan Smuts, the then Prime Minister, guided South Africa into the war on the side of Britain, the Ossewabrandwag went in for sabotage and the harassing of military volunteers. But even before the war was over, the movement fizzled out. For the most part, the hard-line Afrikaner stance became absorbed in the rising Afrikaner nationalism, and was silenced for more than 20 years by the political success of 1948, when the Nationalist Party came to power, and the establishment of a republic outside the British Commonwealth in 1961. The battle had finally been won. But as Johann had told me: from around the middle of the century a whole generation grew up adjusting to a new enemy, the black danger. Afrikanerdom was under threat once more, and the extremist hard-line attitudes resurfaced in the Western Transvaal, in 1973, in the form of the Afrikaner-Weerstandbeweging (AWB), which means, literally, Afrikaner Resistance Movement.

"The Ossewabrandwag was part of the lunatic fringe," Johann had said, "but they managed to recruit nearly four hundred thousand members. The AWB? Yes, I think it's part of the same tradition. It appeals to a certain type of youth, rebels without causes, who fasten on to an extremist form of patriotism. They've probably heard of Robey Leibbrandt, a South African boxer in the 1930s, who went to Germany and was then sent back, ostensibly by the Nazis, to assassinate Smuts. But nothing came of it. Yes, I think the AWB is to an extent Nazi influenced. People point to their insignia which is reminiscent of the swastika, but which of course also has biblical connotations. They salute with the right arm raised, but with the fist clenched. I don't know how strong they are. But I don't believe they are representative of the far north ethos. In the West maybe, but not here."

More bitter here in the West, perhaps; more sullen, more conscious of their previous defeat, more threatened by the possibility of another, more intransigent; and a sense of being more surrounded by the enemy, especially in Rustenburg, than anything I had experienced in the integrated towns of the North.

Yet not in reality surrounded, although the road from the north, from Sun City, ran through Bophuthatswana to reach the town. At first, a peri-urban litter of houses poured between hills which looked worn out, the soil long ago eroded to leave only rough piles of rock and thorns. Closer to Rustenburg, a shanty town began and spread away on either side of the road, bare earth between the structures of old corrugated iron and wood, and litter everywhere, caught in barbed-wire fencing, lying in drifts by the roadside. Then a sign indicated the position of the Bophuthatswana border with the Republic of South Africa, but the shanty town paid no attention, ending only at the outskirts of the town itself. The town lay under a slight pall of smoke, and beyond it the Magaliesberg mountains seemed close and solid.

Rustenburg. Described by Baden-Powell, the British general who captured the town in the Anglo-Boer War, as "the Mecca of the most old-fashioned and bitter of the Boers". Mini-bus taxis filling the streets now, the spires of churches visible above them. Pavements thick with black pedestrians in some places, much whiter at the centre.

I wandered into a commercial art gallery: landscapes, flowers, birds. The proprietor was Bill, himself an artist, who told me they had been lucky enough to get a contract to do something for the new development at Sun City. People strolled in and out of the gallery. Bill said he was organising an exhibition of some of his own students' work. He also spoke to a young man who brought in a leaded-glass table lamp. "We must have an exhibition of your stuff soon," he said. The young man looked pleased. Bill always lowered his voice when he spoke about money, as when someone came in and commissioned him to do a painting of Rustenburg, something historic.

Not far from the gallery, in a small pedestrianized square, the bronze sculpture of a young woman in a long dress, quite boldly open at the throat, holding a lighted candle in one hand while running the other through her hair. An inscription provided a key to its understanding: "This sculpture commemorates the establishing of civilisation in Rustenburg environs with the arrival here of the trekkers in the eighteen-forties. The girl symbolises the trekkers, and the candle symbolises the light of civilisation."

More statuary outside the municipal buildings. President Kruger, whose Boekenhoutfontein farm lay not far from Rustenburg, sat brooding on his plinth. The statue had been made by a French sculptor in 1901, not many years before Kruger had died in exile. The sculptor, Jean Georges Achard, said that the tragic greatness of the Transvaal leader had been so indelibly chiselled on his mind that he was compelled to make a statue. The piece was discovered and purchased in Paris after the First World War. Being too small for Pretoria's Church Square, General Smuts donated the sculpture to Rustenburg. At the unveiling, Smuts said: "I hope that the life of this man will set an example to us right to the last generation."

In the building behind Kruger's statue, I discovered the small Rustenburg museum. On the ground floor, some artifacts from the Sotho-Tswana settlements of the Western Transvaal were displayed. Upstairs, a stained and frayed Transvaal Republic flag, the Vierkleur, stretched out and framed, and a neat inscription saying how a woman had saved the flag from capture by wearing it as a petticoat under her crinoline dress; and a glass case containing small objects made by Boer prisoners of war on St Helena and Bermuda, in India and Ceylon.

Walking later in the warm evening streets of Rustenburg, I came across a young father standing at his front gate and dandling a baby in his arms while on his hip, like a contradiction or an expression of high resolve, was strapped a revolver.

In the hotel bar, English technicians from the huge platinum mines not far away in Bophuthatswana, keeping to themselves and talking about standby and weekend work, and Liverpool's last match. A few groups of Afrikaners in desultory conversation. And then an authoritative trio slamming through the swing doors, looking around, moving to the bar. Large men, the largest, blond-bearded and pale-eyed, in an unzipped jacket with the name of a make of tyre written across the back.

"Hey, kaffir," he said in Afrikaans to the barman, "step closer. Now make your mouth so." He puckered his own. "Ja, you poes. Now give me three beers."

The barman, a slender, youngish man, turned away with inscrutable eyes. He returned with the bottles and glasses, and stood waiting for the money.

The man in the jacket said: "I said give me; you've given. I didn't say sell me. So fuck you, kaffir."

The trio laughed uproariously. But this encounter had simply wetted the appetite of the bearded man in the jacket. He kept openly humiliating the barman, who by now had moved away, kept calling out insults and mockery at the man who, when I entered, had been reading a Johannesburg newspaper. Did he endure this every night? Hey kaffir, hey poes (a vulgar Afrikaans word to denote the female genitals), a single black man bearing the brunt of such venom. I doubted, as I looked into the pale eyes of his tormenter, whether this was a racial thing at all. More like the bullying of brother against brother. More like this simple longing for physical superiority. I watched the trio turn once or twice to glance at the Englishmen. A longing to smash something and to degrade, now in a world that was collapsing for them. For all of them. The grins and smirks of the entire bar as the trio performed. The responses of a beaten people, I thought, the bitterness of defeat, the bitterness of doubting God's guidance, covenants lying in shreds, all the valour of past battles reduced to this. Fighting for their independence again now, and again it would be loss and, for these the chosen people, humiliation. So fuck you, kaffir, in the meantime. Yet with a hidden sadness in the pale and arrogant eyes, and the hair of masculinity bristling with physical assertion.

"More beers."

A muscle flexed in the side of the barman's face; he ignored the coins tossed deliberately into spilt liquid on the counter.

"Ag, shame, my poor kaffir, don't sulk there with a thick mouth."

But they were, after all, no more than three individual men enjoying another night out. The largest of them kept putting his finger into his companions' drinks, pretending to stir, then offering the wet finger to the owner, then sucking it himself when the offer was declined. Once, in retaliation, one of the trio took the large man's half-empty glass and made as if to urinate in it. The whole bar rocked with laughter.

Had they sensed it all along, I wondered, Smuts and others, this foreknowledge of demise which told them that there would one day be a final generation?

GETTING OUT to the old Kruger farm, I passed through a busy section of Bophuthatswana: fruit sellers at the roadside, cement-block housing, people walking with supermarket bags – and a dilapidated trolley once – on verges which had become wide and dusty. Phokeng: a cluster of shops; big advertising hoardings, one of which showed a shapely black couple splashing together in clear blue water; mini-bus taxis disgorging their passengers; gatherings of children and idle youth; then out once more into open country, telephone poles at untidy angles, the bodies of several dead dogs dragged just off the tarmac. And then the turn-off to Boekenhoutfontein and the rough dirt road.

A row of four restored houses presented themselves as I drove into the yard and parked under a gum tree. They were built at the foot of a low hill, and faced down a sloping yard to a dam upon which a few ducks swam. Otherwise no signs of life. I got out of the car and stood in the shade of the tree. The closing of the door had sounded brittle in the silence, and the sun beat down, shimmering across the long view. I thought of Kruger, the 11-year-old Voortrekker; Kruger, the young fighter against indigenous tribes; Kruger, the diplomat, advising the wild residents of Schoemansdal to withdraw; Kruger, the stern Christian and father of 16 children; Kruger who had said that Pietersburg was the bastion of the north; Kruger, the statesman, dour and uncompromising; Kruger in exile while his country crouched low in defeat.

"Good morning."

I swung, half startled, and looked into the face of a youngish woman with fair hair. I returned her greeting, but she did not smile. She asked if I had come for a tour. I said I had. She said: "Very well. Will you come this way, please?"

I had the sense of being marched along, as one of a hundred people on a guided tour; but it seemed faintly absurd, with the two of us alone in that silent place. The woman had led me a short distance from the row of houses and then made me turn to face them.

"Do you want English or Afrikaans?" she asked.

"Either," I said with a smile which she ignored.

"You are English-speaking, not? Very well then. The house on the extreme left was built by one of Kruger's sons in the 1890s. Typical Victorian. Note the end gables and the lattice work on the veranda. The house is occupied by the curator and is not open to the public."

She allowed me a moment to absorb this information, then she went on: "Next door is the first Kruger house. Simple thatch and an apricot-pip floor which I will show you later. Then there is the main Kruger house, erected in 1873, in which the family lived until he moved to Pretoria when he was elected State President in 1883."

And where, 12 years later, I remembered, Solly Noor's grandfather had become a close neighbour. She described the main house – a rectangular white facade which concealed the roof – as one of the few double-storey dwellings in the Transvaal at the time, and built in the vernacular style of the Karoo. And on the far right the old farmhouse, probably built by the original owner, a certain Mr Bronk-horst, before Kruger purchased the property in the late 1850s.

"Typical pioneer house," she said in her efficient tour-guide voice. "Rough thatch. Mud walls. Because the people in those days were still taming the country and had little time to spare for luxuries. Come this way, please," she added, setting off at a brisk pace in the direction of the main house.

I asked, as we walked, whether she lived in the curator's house. She merely nodded. I said it must be pleasant, living out in the country, yet not too far from Rustenburg. She answered with a single syllable. She seemed impenetrable, solemn, businesslike, unlocking the door of the main house and escorting me into a crowded interior where the tour went on relentlessly.

Please note, she said, the sign on the pedals of this organ which read: "mouse-proof patented". The floors were made from mud and dung and the blood of cattle. And look at this sideboard and table, made in Germany, timber from the Black Forest, intricately carved, the carving prolific with lions, especially made for Kruger who was often called the Lion of Rustenburg. And did I know what this was: a rectangle of wood filled with holes and pegs? A calendar, she said, which had to be set every day. And here was Kruger's Bible, in Gothic type and High Dutch, difficult to read, but of course he knew prac-tically the whole book by heart. And please note the elephant ver-tebrae as door stoppers. In the children's room, more vertebrae, of oxen this time, used to simulate a wagon and a span of oxen, and a small upright one at the front being the leader. Undoubtedly, Kruger the boy had led his father's oxen as they trekked north in 1836. And look at these dolls, their painted faces protected by dried pigs' blad-ders, objects which were also used by the boys as a football. Step this way, please. A Hollandse trapkas under the stairs where Mrs Kruger kept the milk and butter nice and cool. No, the upstairs part of the house was not open to the public. It had been used almost entirely as storage. Dried fruit in the coffins – always a stock of coffins – which also deterred the children from stealing the fruit. Also maize and pumpkins stored up there. Outside the back door, the old stone veranda, a 120-year-old vine still bearing, and also some powerful-smelling medicinal herbs which the young woman suggested I inhale.

Then she said: "You can look at the Bronkhorst house by yourself. If you want to you can take that path over there to some stones where every day Kruger prayed his morning prayers. Then you can meet me back in the first Kruger house and I will show you the apricot-pip floor."

I took the path which led up the low koppie behind the row of houses. Thick vegetation on either side, small signs attached to the trunks denoting the names of various trees along the way; and then, halfway up, a cluster of stones under a lavender fever-berry tree, leaves drooping in the heat and drought. The stones and the tree had been surrounded by a fence. I read an inscription cut into a marble slab: the stones on this site are precious possessions for the Afrikaner people, and the earth hallowed ground, because here the great peoples' hero, Paul Kruger, kneeled and humbled himself in supplication before his maker. I stood in the silence, trying to take from the place a reality which seemed remote. The inscription had been placed there in 1957. The immutability of marble and of the minds of men. The surety of the voices praising Kruger and bringing even his daily worship into the foundations of an exclusive and ruthless nationalism which was even then being built up. I thought suddenly of the Indian woman in the Nylstroom furniture shop, that profound aura of humiliation; and of Solly Noor's grandfather saying: if Oom Paul knew what the laws would do to us, he'd come out of his grave fighting. I stared for a moment at the long view, the flat brown landscape from which an occasional koppie protruded, then I went back.

The young woman rose when I appeared at the open door of the first Kruger house. She said: "Now this is the apricot-pip floor..." But I hardly listened any longer. I felt a restlessness for understanding. The roof of the house was supported by a rough timber pole which occupied the centre of the floor. I noticed some pegs – no doubt for hats and coats and harness – protruding from this central column. The pegs had been made from the slender legs and upturned hooves of buck. I remarked that the legs looked quite bizarre, sticking out like that. And the woman laughed.

I turned to look at her. "I agree," she said. "I love animals, and I don't like this. But these people had to make do with what they could take from the land."

I nodded. "They were pioneers."

"Yes," the woman said.

Encouraged by her laugh – a gesture which suggested that in spite of herself her guard had dropped – I talked to her of the hardness of heart I had sensed in the Western Transvaal, the intransigence, a sort of bitterness and sullen anger. Was my sense correct, and had it to do with military defeat?

She listened with solemn eyes. She said: "Come and look at this."
I stepped closer to where she stood and she indicated a framed turn-
of-the-century poster, in Dutch, condemning the British for the concentration camps: over 100 000 Boer women and children interned,
thousands dead and dying. "My great-grandmother was in a camp.
My grandmother never spoke a word of English in her life. She
refused. In Europe, Germans are still being tried for their concentration camps. But there's nothing for us. It's all forgotten. We are
just the makers of apartheid."

She looked up at me with some emotion showing in her eyes at
last, and I became for the first time conscious of her slightness. The
slight shoulders, slightly tensed, as she stood before me, in a sense
squarely, in her longish skirt and sandals.

"How long is this going to be here for us to see?" she said, indicating the house in the mud floor of which thousands of apricot
pips had been embedded. "How long? Rhodesians come here and
laugh. This won't be here much longer, they say. Do you know what
they are going to do with this? And overseas visitors, cultural chau-
vinists, saying: how old is everything, only a hundred years, what
history is this? But it's ours," she added with a sudden vehemence,
her finger pointing to her own chest.

I nodded. We stood looking at each other in silence. I said: "Do
the Afrikaners want to fight?"

She half-laughed. "We are not all AWB." She held my gaze with
a sort of defiance, yet in her eyes for a second there seemed to stir
a plea for understanding, but muffled by a private torrent of pride.
"The Afrikaners are a funny people. I think they are trying to make
a community. Trying to find somewhere to belong."

And then, abruptly, she returned to herself. She became again
curator and guide. Did I have any further questions regarding Boekenhoutfontein and Kruger? I said I had none. I thanked her for the
tour. She nodded gravely and, locking the door of the first Kruger
house behind us, walked back towards her own.

NOT FAR south of the Magaliesberg the maize began. The flat land
undulated only gently, and the fields spread in a dry and golden
panorama to the horizon on every side. The only trees were those
which served as wind-breaks, a lonely line of them sometimes de-
marcating the end of one sweeping field and the beginning of another.
The maize for the most part had been ruined by the drought, hardly
more than knee height, the pollen-bearing tassels charred by the sun,

the crops unharvested. Yet not far from Ventersdorp I did see a harvesting machine going slowly along slightly higher rows of maize, and a low heap of white bags on a trailer which no doubt contained something of the diminished harvest.

I was driving down to Ventersdorp to look at the headquarters of the AWB and, thanks to the flatness of the land, I saw the spires of the churches before I entered the town itself. A countrified place, more a village than a town, and seeming strangely empty, the half-somnolent silence broken by the sound of individual vehicles, individual voices. I stopped at a roadside café and bought a sandwich and a country newspaper.

When I had telephoned the headquarters several days before, a deep voice had informed me that it would not be possible for me to talk to the leader, who in any case would be extremely busy for the next few weeks. Now in the newspaper I read that 15 leaders of the AWB were to appear in court quite soon, charged with public violence, conspiracy, and for illegal gatherings. On the same page, an article by a political scientist from one of the Afrikaans universities pointed out that the population of the great Witwatersrand conurbation (which began less than 100 kilometres to the east of Ventersdorp) would have risen from around six million in 1980 to 30 million in 2020, only 2,5 million of whom would be white. My question: was the balance representative of the black danger against which the Afrikaners would fight another war of independence?

The headquarters of the Afrikaner Resistance Movement in Ventersdorp turned out to be a modest single-storey building with a blunt facade, bricks painted dark brown, some white plaster above, and over the entrance the stylised representation of an eagle made from metal the thickness of reinforcing rods, wings outstretched, talons showing, the head turned implacably to the right. Hanging just inside the door, but more like a tapestry than a flag, the famous emblem: three black sevens, joined at the centre by their stems, which occupied a white circle on a red background. I had asked the Greek in the roadside café if he knew why they used three sevens. He said with a slightly blasphemous smile: "They say the sevens must cross out the three sixes of the Antichrist."

On the edge of some public gardens in Ventersdorp, I came across a monument which, with obvious lack of intent, reinforced the direction in which my thoughts were leading me. The monument resembled a constructivist sculpture, the tools used being a cutting torch and welding equipment. A wagon wheel, some of its spokes merging into the background, had been superimposed onto a thick sheet of steel cut out in the shape of South Africa, with the old territory of South West Africa included. Above this assemblage stood a tapering spike of steel which passed clean through a book-shaped construction representing the Bible. It had to do with the reaffirmation of something (according to the inscription), the reaffirmation of the divine guardianship over the Great Trek perhaps, or over the promised land, mandated territories included, to which the covenant people had been brought by the strong wheels of their wagons and by the strength of their faith. But to me, my mind darkened by the thought of sacrilege, it was as if the Bible had been impaled.

I drove quietly out of Ventersdorp and into the empty countryside of the Western Transvaal, the flat horizons empty save for the occasional maize silos looking like rows of giant grey batteries standing on end. I turned in the direction of Lichtenburg.

Dark thoughts. The Bible impaled upon the steel of human need. The ultimate malleability of those truths and covenants which underlie the faith of men. The comfort of supra-human sanction for all-too-human acts of fear or need. The vacuum must be filled. But the danger is of self-delusion for a people who believe that their god is bound by a special and permanent agreement to protect them. And above all, given the fervour of such a people, there is the terrible fallacy of seeing all opposition as anti-christian: certainly the British at the Cape, at least for the Jerusalemgangers. And now? Who must bear the three sixes on their foreheads so that the next war of independence, like the others before, can be a holy one?

I HAD come to Lichtenburg to attend a political meeting. Thanks to the perseverance of a friend, however, I was also able to speak to an AWB colonel, a man with a gaunt face who smoked a lot of cigarettes.

I arrived in the late afternoon and found posters for the meeting attached to not a few lampposts in the wide streets of the town: die stryd duur voort, the posters proclaimed, the struggle goes on. A Conservative Party meeting. A party still claiming it could command a million votes, but disappointed and angered by recent events, by the reforms sweeping the country, by the unbanning of the ANC at the beginning of the decade, by the faltering steps being taken towards a negotiated future by the governing National Party from which the Conservatives, dismayed even then by what they saw as the growing liberalism of government policy, had split in 1982.

In the centre of an area of grass and shrubs in front of the Town Hall (where the meeting was to take place and not far from the venue for my interview with the Colonel) I found a statue of General Koos de la Rey: the sharp features and pointed beard of one of the best and most unyielding generals of the Anglo-Boer War. A Western Transvaler from Lichtenburg, he was one of the men who had proposed and practised the guerrilla style of warfare embarked upon by the Boers after Pretoria had fallen, and one of the prime movers behind the 1914 Rebellion. A man who had in these ways kindled and kept alight the fires of Afrikaner nationalism. Yet at first he had been opposed to Kruger's plans for war, urging that negotiations should continue, or at least that the Republics should not lose the moral high ground by attacking the Cape and Natal. When Kruger accused him of cowardice, De la Rey said: "You will see me in the field fighting for our independence long after you and your party who make war with your mouths have fled the country." Not long afterwards, Kruger gave orders for the Boer commandos to attack the two British colonies.

At the appointed time, I crossed the street and, passing through a pair of heavy steel gates which protected the entrance to a security company, found the Colonel already waiting for me. He rose to greet me, harsh-voiced but not unfriendly, a big middle-aged man dressed in his AWB uniform. We sat in an unadorned office and talked together in Afrikaans.

He asked me what it was I wanted to know. I replied: "As much as possible." He eyed me with slight amusement. He said: "Let me tell you something about our principles." He paused to light a cigarette. "To begin with, we believe in the Holy Trinity. A three-in-one God. No one is a member of our movement who does not believe in this God. Secondly, we believe we have the right to govern ourselves. We do not want to live under blacks or Indians."

I asked where they wanted to govern themselves.

"In our own land. The old republics are legally ours: that is incontestable in the World Court. I'm talking about the Transvaal, the Orange Free State, the republic in northern Natal, as well as the old Northern Cape republics of Goshen and Stellaland."

"What about the so-called homelands?"

"They remain," he said, blowing out smoke. "We don't have a problem with Mangope," he went on, referring to the President of Bophuthatswana. "We don't want his land. He wants to rule the Tswanas, and that's fine. In fact, I have a high regard for him: he's a Christian and he's resisting this re-incorporation rubbish from the ANC.

"Who are the ANC anyway? They're not even a nation. They're a bit of this and a bit of that. How can they claim the right to govern us? We are a nation and we have our land for which our forefathers fought and died. My grandparents died for it," he said, his eyes hard.

Was it not time, I suggested, that people should be finding ways to live together in some sort of reasonable agreement?

"Look, my friend," he replied, "we are not in favour of mixing. Look at nature: you don't get sparrows and starlings and swifts sharing the same nest. Look at the Bible: it never says anything about the mixing of the races; on the contrary, it warns against miscegenation all the time."

I asked him about the claims, often made in newspapers, that the AWB was neo-Nazi.

He laughed. "Ag, it is because of this," he said, pointing to the three sevens on his uniform. "They think it looks like a swastika. But it's the sign of completion; it adds to twenty-one; and it cancels out the three sixes, the sign of the devil. We will fight the Antichrist. We will fight until we overcome."

"Who or what is the Antichrist?" I asked.

"The forces of evil," he said, standing up to fetch a booklet. "The false gods."

He placed the booklet in my hands. I read that the AWB formed a bulwark against liberalism, Marxism and communism. I read also that the AWB considered itself to be the antipole of the ANC.

"I've been in jail twice," the Colonel said; "I'm not worried. I'm fighting for my God, for my people and for my country. What my grandparents died for I will not give up."

He sat down again, busy with another cigarette. He looked at me with hard and steadfast eyes.

I said: "A lot of people think of your movement as just another bunch of ruffians."

"Yes," he said; "a lot is laid at our door which has nothing to do with us. Our members are disciplined; they don't go round hitting kaffirs. You've never heard of anything like that."

"What form does your fight against the Antichrist take?"

"Our stance is no violence, except in self-defence."

"Would that change under a black government?"

He looked at me with hooded lids. "That would be up to the leadership." Then he laughed in his harsh way. "I know what I'd do though. I'd give them hell. But come, my friend, are you going to this meeting? I will walk with you. I must see that my men are in place."

He rose and strapped a firearm to his waist.

I asked how many members the movement had. He shook his head. "I can't give the figure, but let me tell you it is very large."

"Are all members armed?" I asked as we walked towards the Town Hall.

"Oh, yes. You know what we say: an unarmed white is a dead white. Get yourself a gun, my friend."

He walked up the low steps and disappeared into the foyer of the Town Hall. I lingered in the early darkness for a moment, mingling with groups of people who stood waiting for the meeting to begin. The bronze of De la Rey's statue glinted in the spotlights trained upon it. The evening was pleasantly cool.

In the hall, the audience stood for a moment in silence for an elderly Transvaal couple who had been murdered in their home, and whose bodies had been found at a routine road-block in the boot of a car driven by black men. The bowed heads, the beards against chests, then the muffled creak and clatter of the chairs, and the faces looking up towards the platform, as if waiting for guidance.

"One or two disappointments don't make the future," a speaker said; "what makes the future is a nation's determination to struggle for its freedom. A nation that stops struggling is one that lies down in the coffin and waits for someone to nail on the lid. The truth is that unitary states all over the world are breaking down. Federation is not the answer. The way forward is self-determination by the various nations. In South Africa, therefore, partition is the only solution."

Some expressions of approval came from the audience then, but in essence they were waiting to be led. They listened in silence to an erstwhile leader being castigated for having betrayed his people by espousing the false god of negotiation. They listened as one of their ministers of religion said that the broad way, the easy way, was negotiation and power sharing, but that the narrow way of nationhood, although harder, was the right way. "We must continue to struggle until we win. Freedom and self-determination go hand in hand. And without freedom as a nation there can be no peace. We will fight for that freedom!"

The applause rang out. But would these people fight a holy war with the whole of Africa driving south upon them now? Or had they already sensed that they were living in final days, even perhaps as the last generation who would watch the flame go out and in the darkness would perhaps mutate? And what of De la Rey out there in the cool of the evening? I wondered if he would urge negotiation now, and if once again he would be accused of cowardice, seduced away from the paths of patriotic right by the beast of the triple sixes.

9

THE CAPITAL

"WE HEARD shooting in the morning," Joe said; "but that wasn't all that unusual. The Bophuthatswana Defence Force is always doing some sort of practice or other in the veld near town. And then, driving the kids to school, I heard it on the radio. There had been a *coup d'etat*. It seemed absurd. I drove across to Mmabatho to see what was happening. Some Bop army rebels had the President and a few cabinet ministers imprisoned in the stadium. Then the South Africans arrived. I remember it was raining, and the South African assault troops were leaping out of their helicopters into the mud and crawling forward, surrounding the stadium, cutting holes in the perimeter fence, while a crowd of us stood and watched. Then they smashed through the steel gates with an armoured car, and the assault troops stormed in from all sides. There was a lot of shooting in the stadium. I heard later that five Bop soldiers had been killed. After a while, the President was driven out, surrounded by South African brass. And that was the end of our coup."

Four years ago now, these desperate deeds. The Independence Stadium, capable of seating 60 000, still hovered ostentatiously over the flat landscape, floating rectangles of grandstand seats as if hanging from invisible threads, the whole construction in these separate bits, looking like an elaborate mobile which had partially collapsed onto the ground. And the ministerial compound where President Lucas

Mangope lived, not much changed, except that now it was surrounded by two high security fences.

"He used to be very free in his movements," Joe said, "going down to the shop in his 1960s American cars – he's very fond of them – to buy his own Sunday papers. But no longer."

More than 160 men were imprisoned for their part in the attempted coup. Due to various pressures, not least the recent freeing of political prisoners in South Africa itself, all but four had been released by the time I visited Bophuthatswana's capital and the adjoining town of Mafikeng. But an inevitable result of the coup was that the regime became more security-conscious and also considerably more repressive. Joe introduced me to a man involved in the Mafikeng Anti-Repression Forum, a human rights organisation formed early in 1990 following the detention and torture of numbers of school children in Bophuthatswana.

The Maref man told me that of the four Maref chairmen who had held office so far, three had been deported, a black and two whites, and the fourth had left the country because her husband had been deported. He said that in the case of whites considered troublesome, mostly South Africans working in Bophuthatswana, the regime would simply not renew their visas, thus forcing them out.

The central issue exercising the minds of people, whether in favour of the President's regime or against it, was the ANC's demands for re-incorporation of the homelands into a unitary South Africa. Bophuthatswana became independent in 1977. Thanks to Sun International, the owners of Sun City and several similar resorts, and thanks to the platinum mines outside Rustenburg, the country had enjoyed a measure of prosperity unknown in other homelands, and which it was now reluctant to give up. Ethnic federation of autonomous states, Bophuthatswana being one of them, was espoused. Anyone who actively disagreed was severely dealt with.

Although the coup had not been about re-incorporation – the reasons given for the attempt being to oust a government guilty of corrupt administration and rigged elections – its occurrence had alerted the regime to the possibility of overthrow. The major political opposition party was banned, and other parties could not operate without submitting to the stringent conditions of registration. The Internal Security Act, allowing among other things for long periods of detention without trial, still operated in Bophuthatswana, even though the South African version had been repealed.

The Maref man said that the evidence they had collected pointed to a huge increase in the use of torture and violence against political prisoners, and that violence was widely used to suppress political opposition and to intimidate the general population. Naturally, under these circumstances, the regime saw the unbanned ANC as a major threat to continued independence and therefore as a dangerous enemy. On the most recent Bophuthatswana independence day, a man in his fifties had been severely beaten by uniformed police and then exposed to an attack by a police dog for wearing an ANC T-shirt.

But on the surface, thriving and prosperous urban places, these two towns: Mafikeng, made famous when it was besieged in the Anglo-Boer War; and Mmabatho, glittering capital of Bophuthatswana.

The grandiose design and proportions of the Independence Stadium repeated everywhere in Mmabatho. The stylish parliament building set in new-looking gardens; the Ga-Rona, name of the large horse-shoe-shaped complex of government offices, slate and copper roofing beneath which arched face-brick and pillars enclosed several floors of office space; two major hotels with casinos, the Molopo and Mmabatho Suns; and a vast glass-clad conference centre with 4 000 seats, even though the rooms at the hotels numbered only around 300.

I gave a lift to two soldiers on my first day in the capital. Camouflage suits and berets, talking to each other in their own language, then asking if they could switch on the radio. I tried to engage them in conversation, but they had little to say to me. When we passed the conference centre, I remarked on the modern design. "You must go inside," one of the soldiers said; "it's terrific. The luxury." He whistled to give an inkling. "The kitchen is one hundred metres." Outside the entrance to the centre: a gathering of long black cars, shining motor cycles, flags on poles, men in uniforms with flashing brass, others in suits. "Don't you know?" the soldier said, as if my ignorance struck him as something close to a personal affront; "today is the parliament opening. The President's speech."

Not far from the conference centre, I discovered a shopping complex called Megacity, the central plaza surmounted by a sizeable Perspex dome into which soared slender-trunked trees. The complex spread out through a maze of arcades and passageways in all directions. In one of the arcades an incongruity: two red and glass telephone booths from England, and a life-size model of an English policeman making use of the instrument in one of them. The central plaza was filled with people and chatter. Several restaurants beckoned,

including a Trattoria Italiana; and the tables of The Meating Place
were filled with stylish young blacks and a handful of whites. An
unmistakable sense of opulence. The women especially, as they criss-
crossed the plaza, were clothed in the height of fashion, carrying their
lunch-time purchases in colourful plastic bags. Nearly always, jewellery adorned their throats and ears, and sometimes they wore make-
up on their dusky skins.

Mafikeng was older, but the streets bustled. Black people queued
for buses and the automatic tellers built into the outsides of banks.
People shouted. People jostled in supermarkets or sat reading newspapers in tearooms. I joined them. I read about a Bophuthatswana
civil servant on trial for attempting to steal R5 million of public
money. People shouted flamboyantly to each other across the crowded
streets. In the central parking area, a man with wrap-around dark
glasses played a small electronic keyboard: repetitive jive rhythms to
which he sang in a throaty voice. Inside the circle of spectators, an
older man, his face creased and quite worn out with the wisdom of
the street, danced athletically to the music. A few coins tinkled on
the concrete paving. Some applause. A woman with a baby on her
back danced to one side. Some laughter. A sense of vibrancy here,
of the untidiness and energy of Africa: this fragment of a fragmented
country, wedged between the Kalahari and the fearful realities of the
Western Transvaal.

The sunsets over the capital provided a definite radiance. Close
enough to the desert perhaps, or because of the flatness of the land,
the whole sky would be illuminated by the brilliance of the passing of
the day, and even after the sun had disappeared, an afterglow remained, a luminescence which infused the very air with a gentleness
of light. Strange to think, at such moments, of the muffled thuds and
distorted screams of torture.

JOE WORKED for an educational institution in Mmabatho, and
had lived with his family in Mafikeng for some years. He had wide
interests and a healthy scepticism would enliven his dark eyes with
amusement sometimes. He drove an old station-wagon, the back not
infrequently loaded with his children and their friends, and a dog,
so grey and immobile now, that Joe had to lift it in and out. Like
an ageing member of the family, that dog, and Joe's treatment of it
revealed something of the quality of the man. His wife was away
during my visit to the capital, and I became indebted to him for the
time he spent with me.

He drew a rough map to familiarize me with the geography of the place. Here was Mafikeng, straddling the road which would later take me down to Vryburg and the Northern Cape; to the south-west of Mafikeng, the Stat or black village which had taken its fair share of Boer shells and attacks during the siege; a few kilometres to the north-west of Mafikeng lay Mmabatho (the word meaning mother of the people), and between the two towns the suburb of Montshiwa, originally a product of the Group Areas Act, and some industry spread out. Probably about 80 000 people living here, Joe estimated.

Within this broad outline, he sketched in Libertas, where many of the seconded Afrikaner civil servants, and also not a few conservative English-speakers, ex-Rhodesians, lived. Like Sowhito in Thohoyandou and Krematart in Giyani, I thought. But there were differences.

"People are tending to live where they please," Joe said. "There are high integration levels. Here's Unit Six, for example, a favourite suburb for the trendy MCs." I asked what these were. "Mixed couples," he said with a smile.

The degree of integration could in part be attributed to the freehold principle of land ownership in the capital, and indeed throughout Bophuthatswana. "There is tribal land still," Joe explained; "but outside of it anyone can own land, and not only Bop citizens. I own my property here in Mafikeng. This makes it different from any other homeland capital. People are living where they want to live, or where they can afford, and this inevitably leads to residential integration.

"And a result of this integration has been the development of good non-racial schools which sometimes have developed their own syllabuses. I think it would be difficult to find anywhere in sub-Saharan Africa better English-medium schools, predominantly black, where the pupils mix both at school and socially in the suburbs. For my own kids, I can think of no better place in South Africa for them to grow up. They are almost completely unconscious of race."

Ironies also. At one school, more than half the children came from the violent townships of the Witwatersrand where opportunities for education were often erratic. "It's one of the benefits of education in an authoritarian state," Joe said. "The Bop authorities tolerate no nonsense in the schools. There's no politics, no stoppages, no boycotts. Just education. And thousands of Witwatersrand parents are taking advantage of this."

Other ironies as well. While we drove in his station-wagon to look at one of them, I asked if Bophuthatswana, assuming it could retain its independence, stood any chance of becoming economically viable. Joe shrugged. "Is it really independent? I mean all the infrastructure – the roads, the electricity, the water, the telephones – is South African. But given this, it does generate more than fifty per cent of its own revenue. Mainly through taxing the Sun hotels and the mining of platinum, chrome, some diamonds. But then it wastes a lot. Look at this school."

The International School of Bophuthatswana: rolling lawns, extensive playing fields, special housing for staff, swimming pools, glass-walled squash courts; tuition to Cambridge A levels; in short, a show-piece. Attended by the children of cabinet ministers, wealthy chiefs and Indian traders, and also by a handful of pupils with bursaries. "But this one school dominates the education budget every year, starving the rest of the system."

Perhaps it was a longing for prestige, a yearning for recognition, which underlay this kind of excess and imbalance. Like the Bophuthatswana National Orchestra, the musicians recruited from overseas. Like the State Ballet Company. Like the television stations, one local, the other beamed by satellite as far afield as Israel. Like the building of the most sophisticated sound recording studio on earth, and a 17-chalet village (complete with fully-grown date palms) to accommodate the artists and their entourages, hoping for the legitimacy of the Jacksons or Madonna.

Or like the Mmabatho airport opened in 1984, capable of handling jumbo jets, but at the moment used largely by Bop Air for its regular service in twin-engined aircraft to and from Johannesburg. "Although sometimes South African Airways and Lufthansa use it as a training airport for their jumbo pilots. When it first opened, you had to show your passport to get through. Even though you could drive from Johannesburg, or anywhere in South Africa, right into the middle of Mmabatho without encountering a single border post on any of the roads. But it gave the airport a bit of an international feel."

Playing at being a real country, I thought, their only allies now the conservative right, the AWB man in Lichtenburg saying: "We don't have a problem with Mangope; we don't want his land; he wants to rule the Tswanas, and that's fine". The grandiose over-spending in the capital, like the authoritarianism and repression, was fine.

"To be fair, though, they have done some excellent things with their money as well," Joe said.

He took me to see the Mmabana Cultural Centre, a modern concrete building with children playing outdoor chess in the gardens.
Inside, a thriving sense of purpose and activity. In the gymnasium,
a young black using a springboard to lend impetus to his somersaults
and rolls. "There's an anomaly. He's a Bop citizen, but he's a member
of the national team of a foreign country – South Africa." He showed
me the 300-seat theatre, half-built sets on the stage, banks of spotlights
being set. Art classes in progress; pottery; sculpting in clay. Upstairs,
dance studios equipped with barres and mirrors, scores of young
children in leotards sitting in passageways. And a library of toys,
hectic scenes of play all over the floor, very few toys left on the
shelves. And young people with their musical instruments talking in
a foyer which gave access to several soundproof studios. I saw through
small windows set into the doors a young boy playing a piano, another
a flute; and a red light showed above the door of the orchestra room.

We drove into the Stat on sandy and uneven roads. The houses
were built in circles facing on to a central area, usually with a curved
stone wall erected in the proximity of a tree. Here, in the shade, the
elders of that particular circle, known as a gotla or ward in the old
tribal system, would gather. Some of the houses were distinctly Western in design, but old and for the most part dilapidated. Until the
1920s, Joe explained, a lot of Tswanas were wealthy cattle owners
who could afford European builders. "Much the same as now," he
said, smiling slightly; "the wealthy Tswanas using European architectural and engineering expertise to create their capital."

And after a moment: "I don't know where all the money comes
from. The civil service salaries are extremely high. In housing, you
can't buy a great deal for under a quarter of a million. And the luxury
cars. Everyone's got one. At least one. I spoke to a dealer not so long
ago. He's moving up to eighty BMWs a month, that's new buyers
and trade-ins."

But as we drove, the dog asleep in the back of the station wagon,
I began to see another reality: the informal settlements clinging to
the edges of the two towns. The huts and shacks, and sometimes
concrete block structures, spread out in an untidy mess on the flat
country. Joe told me the settlements ran in a 40 by 5 kilometre strip
around the western and southern edges of the capital, and that they
probably housed a further 80 000 people; and in my mind the rural/
capital dichotomy began to take shape.

That evening, I listened on the television set in my hotel room to
what the President had said when he opened Parliament. The people

of Bophuthatswana, he urged, would need to display courage, wisdom and thrift to offset the effects of the economic recession and the drought. He also attacked the ANC, blaming the organisation for the violence sweeping much of South Africa, and saying that his government would not allow the disruption, the fear and the political killings which had become the hallmark of so-called free political activity in South Africa "to wash across our borders".

IN THE Mafikeng museum I accidentally interrupted a man in a back room who was working on some maps spread out on a trestle table. I had thought that perhaps the room contained more exhibits, and I apologised for intruding. But the man called me inside. I asked him what he was doing with the maps. "Come and look," he said; "the shape of the new federal Bophuthatswana."

With the back of a pencil he outlined the current pieces of the homeland, the one in which the capital was situated, stretching north and then east to surround Rustenburg on three sides; two more pieces to the north of Pretoria; two in the Northern Cape; and one tiny piece, an absurdity, hundreds of kilometres away in the Orange Free State.

"It's not absurd," the man said; "not when you think of things in terms of ethnic federalism. That's what's happening everywhere else in the world. It makes perfect sense, too. Now," he went on, glancing at me with his pale but enthusiastic eyes; "look at this. Bophuthatswana could become the most important country in Southern Africa."

Another map was overlaid upon the first. It seemed to show the location of archaeological sites, and when it had been aligned I saw that they stretched across the Western Transvaal. "That's what we're claiming," the museum man said; "all the way to the Vaal." He pointed to one particular site, further north, but outside Bophuthatswana's current borders. "Here were two Tswana cities," he said, "bigger than Cape Town when John Campbell visited them in 1820. Stone built; very advanced. Then Mzilikhazi destroyed them, as he did a great many of these settlements. But the ruins are still there. I'm preparing maps and a report."

The idea, for a start, was that the hills in which the two city sites were situated should be bought by the Bophuthatswana Parks Board and then incorporated into the homeland proper. "This would be another great tourist attraction for the country, and it would be of great cultural and historic value. I even have thoughts, but I admit they are wild ones, of moving the capital there."

An elegantly dressed black woman had joined us at the trestle table. The museum man introduced her as his researcher. She smiled pleasantly at me.

"She's doing the research in support of our land claims to the Vaal," the man said.

"Do you really want the Western Transvaal?" I asked her.

She smiled again. "I used to live there."

"Kicked out, she was. In 1977. Forced removals. Sweeping the Western Transvaal clear of unwanted blacks."

"I remember the day," the woman said.

I asked where she had lived.

"Putfontein," she replied. "Between Ventersdorp and Lichtenburg. They sent us to Ramatlabama near the Botswana border. All we found when we got there were stones and a few tin lavatories."

"The whites of the Western Transvaal will now just have to adapt," the man said; "I believe that ethnic federalism is definitely on the way."

It was a strange moment. The elegant woman standing before me. In my mind's eye, a vision of the AWB colonel standing up after our interview and strapping on his firearm. All the claims and counter-claims, incontestable even in the World Court perhaps; the country itself as if bruised by all the claspings of possession. I saw the pendant earrings of the woman glint as she turned her head to speak to the museum man. Putfontein: 270 families removed between late 1977 and 1979, I read later, just a few of the 160 000 black people cleared from the Western Transvaal between 1960 and the early 1980s. Over a million in the Transvaal as a whole, a large percentage dumped into Venda, into Gazankulu, into Lebowa, as into Bophuthatswana, devoured by the granite jaws of ethnicity-obsessed apartheid. And now, re-emerging, to oppose that folly with a folly of their own? The woman was smiling at me again. "It was so nice to meet you," she said; "now I must fly off."

REFERRING TO the participants of the attempted coup in 1988 the Maref man had told me: "Perhaps a lot of them were opportunists. Others were disgruntled with conditions in the army: too many white officers, and so on. But there were others who genuinely wanted change."

Perhaps there were even some who had begun to see the dangers inherent in the pretentious sense of nationhood being nurtured by the rulers. Certainly there was discontent, even anger. If not, why the repression?

"Some of the rural areas have had a hard time," the Maref man said. "Chiefs not loyal to the President have been deposed, causing enormous resentment among the people, a resentment which is ruthlessly suppressed. To the north of here, villagers killed nine Bop policemen in their attempt to resist incorporation into the homeland. This was a few years ago. Then the heavies moved in and the entire village fled. When they returned, their chief was replaced by someone loyal to Mmabatho. This new chief was so unpopular that he had to live inside a police encampment. Even so, someone shot and wounded him. The case is in court at the moment."

An academic with whom I spoke strengthened my growing sense of the dichotomy between hinterland and capital. "There can be no doubt," he said, "that the president has worked hard at uplifting his people in and around Mmabatho, thereby creating a very strong power-base; but the spending here, and in a few other centres, has angered the majority of people who live in the countryside. Yes, of course there's poverty. You just need to look at the health statistics to see that."

I asked him to comment on the two charges made most frequently against the Bophuthatswana regime: corruption and human rights abuses.

He said: "When South Africa placed a moratorium on capital punishment, the authorities here executed someone immediately. I think simply to show how independent they were. Is there an independent judiciary? I don't know if one can say there is when the Chief Justice sits on the Cabinet as an adviser. But am I answering your question? Human rights abuses. Yes. But if comparisons must be made: nowhere near as bad as most African countries. Corruption. Again yes. But again not on the scale of the rest of the continent.

"The question I often ask myself, however, is this: if there is, as we believe, such widespread discontent, especially in the rural areas, why is there no action? Is the state's power to repress that great? Are the people meek? Perhaps the real answer is that the discontent is often balanced by some measure of material benefit. Also the very real difficulties faced by the ANC and others to organise resistance must be taken into account."

I invited two ANC officials to breakfast with me at my hotel one morning. Joe had provided the contact; I had spoken to one of the men on the telephone; he had told me they were extremely busy;

but, yes, they would do their best to see me in the dining-room at seven. Not surprisingly, I breakfasted alone. Later, I was able to see one of them in his office. He rose to shake my hand, saying with an unabashed smile: "I'm sorry, man. Something came up. We've got all these court cases. We just couldn't make it."

I sat looking across the desk at a youngish man with a round and open face. I told him I had read in the newspaper that the ANC had appealed in the Supreme Court against the Bophuthatswana Government's decision to refuse the ANC permission to hold meetings in the country. He nodded. I asked him to sketch the situation in the homeland as he saw it.

"Let me begin in this way," he said, looking steadily at me. "The regime, and especially the President, has been created and nourished by the white National Party in South Africa. And of course they love him. He's proof that ethnicity works. Even the AWB love him. What kind of credential is that?" He laughed at the thought. "But I believe that if there was open political activity, his power would fizzle out. His power is based on two things.

"First, on his ability to repress political opposition. There's no freedom of political expression here. Second, on his ability to buy support. After the coup, salaries for the security forces increased substantially. Constables and low-ranked people now drive BMWs. Their support and loyalty has been bought.

"This leads me to the serious and endemic misuse of public funds. We've had scandal after scandal, none of them ever properly and publicly investigated. But no one complains, not in the capital at any rate. They're cushioned here by their own materialism, surrounded by all the lavish buildings, soothed by the pulp on state radio and television. But most Bophuthatswanans live outside the capital, and most of them work outside the country. Migrant labour. The old, the illiterate, the sick – these are the people who attend the government meetings and sometimes applaud."

I asked him about the idea of ethnic federalism. He laughed. I said that some people were saying that, given a certain amount of consolidation, Bophuthatswana could become a viable country.

"Look, man, the so-called wealth of Bop is not in the hands of the people. The Sun hotels and the minerals: where do the profits from these enterprises go? There are more casinos in Bop than in any other homeland, but these Suns do not shine for the people. South Africa supplements the budget year after year. South Africa provides the infrastructure. All these things make a nonsense of independence. Anyway, we have always felt we are South Africans. In terms of the land allocated to Bophuthatswana, this was not based on any historical reality, but was arbitrarily done by the South African state."

I told him about the museum man and his maps. He guffawed, his eyes full of merriment. "An unholy marriage, if ever there was one. Mangope and the AWB."

Then he shook his head. "No. If we are serious about reconciliation and democracy in South Africa, we can't keep thinking about this kind of nonsense. We have to open debates about the real issues, not keep drawing lines on maps and closing doors. Do you know that the local press was prevented from reporting the formation of the ANC in Bophuthatswana? The story was already printed, but the authorities demanded that the paper not be distributed. South African newspapers are also discouraged from doing investigative work here. Bop TV is an instrument of the government. There's no local news, except of an official nature. Here's a joke for you: a young pupil was asked by his teacher who Mangope was; the pupil thought he was the main news reader because he was always on the box at news time." Again the merriment in his eyes.

Did the ANC enjoy wide support in Bophuthatswana?

"Our support is substantial," he replied; "even in high government places. But of course these people do not want to be seen as sympathisers. There are also increasing numbers of police and prison staff who are anxious to treat our people well, sensing that we are the future.

"But a great many have been so enveloped by the benefits of the system that they cannot see beyond. It's called the 'luxury syndrome'. It is very seductive. I know," he said, smiling a trifle impishly at me; "I would be dishonest if I said I had not felt the seductiveness. But I am not prepared to abandon my idea of reality for the sake of enhanced material comfort."

Someone hovered at the door of his office, and the ANC man apologised to me that an urgent matter required his attention.

"Two quick questions," I said.

"Sure. Go ahead."

"The authorities obviously know about you. Why don't they arrest you or threaten your job?"

"I suppose because if it happened to any of our officials it would be a public event. We would make sure of that. It would be bad publicity for the regime at an international level: as repressive as the old South Africa. Their longing for international recognition does offer some protection, I suppose. Your second question?"

With a smile, I asked him if he drove a BMW, and the ANC man roared with amusement.

AT THE University of Bophuthatswana, popularly called Unibo, I heard some students stamp and sing. I was sitting in the shade of a courtyard half under a big new lecture-theatre complex when the students, all male to judge by the voices, started the first tentative beginnings of what would become a cohesive chant. They were several floors above me in the windowless complex, like a concrete fort without even any loopholes.

"The whole building is completely dependent on artificial light and air conditioning," someone on the campus had told me; "when it first opened, the electricity kept failing. It was absurd: all the lecture theatres being evacuated every twenty minutes or so, then back we'd all march for another try."

The smart buildings of Unibo standing proud in the autumn sunlight. A new Great Hall, one of the major donors of the cost of its construction being Sun International. A Unibo boast: unlike other homeland universities, no teaching days lost through student action in the last three years. A few small problems: like the issue of re-admissions, conditions in the residences, the quality of on-campus food. Oh, yes, students had recently smashed thousands of rands worth of cafeteria equipment to show their disgruntlement. And there had been an open demonstration against the university administration at the last graduation ceremony. I wondered whether the singing, which had begun to echo through the building above me, had to do with that. Was it another demonstration of anger or displeasure?

Two voices I had heard during my stay in the capital returned to me then. The first, that of a white supporter of the Mangope regime: "One worrying factor is low tertiary education standards and the low skills level of supposedly qualified people. Typists with diplomas claiming forty words a minute battling to do five or ten. Even university degrees can be worth virtually nothing in the real labour market, Communications degrees, for example, held by people who can hardly read and write." The second, a Unibo lecturer: "Students? Not in the real sense of the word. There's very little enthusiasm for knowledge that is considered unnecessary. Perhaps there are one or two exceptions. But generally, all the students want is a ticket to get the sort of job that will enable them to put a down payment on a fancy car."

The singing filled the courtyard now, the voices in powerful unison; and the stamping of the feet at various points in the repeated chorus seemed to shiver through the concrete and the tiling underneath my feet. I saw them descend a flight of stairs, a few steps at a time, in a tight phalanx of swaying bodies. I asked a passerby why they were singing. He looked at me coolly through gold-rimmed spectacles. "I don't know. I think they just feel like it." The students now stood at the bottom of the stairs in the sunlit half of the courtyard. I saw them stamping their feet and at certain points in the lyrics raising their arms and fluttering their hands, an almost mocking gesture; and I felt the vented power of their male voices, and the power of their feet slamming down upon the tiling of their modern campus, as the volume of the singing built to a crescendo and then stopped. They began to drift away in small chattering groups. I sensed neither anger nor idealism. Where would they lead their capital, their country, these young Bophuthatswanans?

10

MERCILESS EYE

ON THE way out of Mafikeng, driving on the road to Stella and Vryburg in the Northern Cape, I stopped for a few moments to look at hundreds of white headstones set out in rows behind a high fence. The gate at the entrance was locked; I stared in through barbed wire at the graves. When the most famous siege of the Anglo-Boer War had finally ended, a British garrison remained while siege hero Baden-Powell marched into the Western Transvaal where he captured Rustenburg without a fight. Then the guerrilla war began, followed by the British response of collective punishment. Concentration camps for Boer women and children; and the graves of those unable to survive standing in a silence broken only by thorn trees scratching slightly in the dry wind.

I drove on into a flat and featureless country, the road running straight for tens of kilometres at a time, the wind stirring up eddies of red dust sometimes from the half denuded veld on either side. A flock of laughing doves raced for a moment ahead of the car, then swerved away on their strong wings, leaving me alone with my thoughts.

The Boers in travail. Turning, after the war, to the desolation of their farms, taking the plough to the land once more and their animals to grass, then watching as their husbandry shrivelled under the blistering skies of drought. The march to the cities had already begun, but the drought of 1913 accelerated it, as the depression and another great drought 20 years later turned it into a stampede. Yet there were those, a minority of families, who clung to the land as their means of livelihood. Protected by the political power gained in 1948, they had endured the droughts of the mid-1960s and early 1980s. But now, when political power seemed already to be slipping from their grasp, they faced the scourge again.

Drought. Appropriate, driving in that half denuded landscape, to turn my attention fully upon this deadly phenomenon. It had hovered at my elbow all through my journey, even from those first moments standing with the Major on the bridge. Now I looked into its pale and merciless eye, and in so doing I remembered Eugene Marais once more, his lifelong preoccupation with drought turning in the end to nightmare.

Doubly appropriate to ponder these things now perhaps, since I was going into the heartland of South Africa's ranching country, and I would also go beyond it to the Vaalharts Irrigation Scheme, "one of the largest of its kind in the world", according to the publicity literature: more than 35 000 hectares of arable farmland and two towns, all dependent upon a single river weir.

I recalled a dam I had seen further to the north, a high concrete wall built across a river as it ran through a narrow valley, the sides of which were composed of reddish-coloured rocks and cliffs. Close to the entrance gate, evidence of what must have been a picnic area: a few acacia trees; an ablution block and low structures intended for the lighting of braaivleis fires built of the red stone; overturned rubbish bins on what must have been a stretch of grass. And here a small sign stuck in the ground said: "Cabbage tree, one of 75 planted in 1987 to commemorate the 75th anniversary of the Department of Water Affairs". No sign of the tree though, only the slight hollow in which it had once stood. An air of desertion which increased as I came closer to the dam itself. The wall had been raised in 1967, possibly as a precaution against future dry periods. This must also have been the date of the construction of what appeared to be a boating clubhouse, a small stone building set into the rocky hillside, but now without a door and with windows smashed out. Directly in front of the clubhouse, a stone wharf against which boats must once have been moored, and to one side a slipway.

But no boats now. What water the dam contained lay in a narrow strip on the far side of the valley, at least 200 metres from and 50 metres below the end of the slipway. An effectively empty dam. And here at the boating club, a sense of human effort gone to thorns and waste. The dry stones of the empty dam glared dull red in the fierce-ness of the sun. I sat on a boulder which, a quarter of a century ago, might have served as a bollard. I searched the rough floor of the dam for holes or fissures. The air throbbed with a thick silence. It was Marais' belief that the world's water was draining away to subter-ranean depths from which it could never be recovered.

OOM WILLEM came out to greet me as I drove into his farmyard. He gave an immediate impression of advancing age, not in the sense of being bearded and venerable so much as caught in that slow turning point which comes to active men when strength is gradually replaced by weariness. He walked with a white stick and wore thick-lensed spectacles, but his sight was not unduly impaired. He had the ap-pearance of having once been ginger-haired, pale eyes and brows, his short-cropped hair gone white now, yet tinged with the faint colour of rust. "Kom binne," he said affably, his handshake firm; "come in. We can drink some coffee."

But we did not go in immediately. His house, a modern bungalow which he had built himself, was surrounded by substantial areas of paving, all cleanly swept, and by a neat garden with flowers edging the lawns. Oom Willem's wife, a broad-hipped and friendly woman, had emerged from the house to join us, and I remarked to her how green the grass looked in contrast to the stark grey farmland stretching away beyond the fence. "Yes," she said, "but see how the termites are eating it. They are looking for water to store up for the winter months." In a sheltered corner not far from the kitchen door, Oom Willem showed me a guava tree which he had nurtured so that it had gradually become inured to frost, and, he said with obvious pleasure, had provided them for the first time that summer with a modest harvest of fruit. Then we went in for the coffee.

In the sitting-room, dark furniture – ball-and-claw and scalloped edges – gleamed with polish; doilies adorned every flat surface; and a large television cabinet occupied one corner. We sat in deep chairs. Oom Willem told me he owned two farms: this one on which he lived, mainly arable land, although he kept a few cows and sheep for the kitchen; and then another, some distance away, devoted ex-clusively to cattle. His father had farmed here before him. He referred to the old republics of Goshen and Stellaland, now incorporated into the Northern Cape, as "our places". His farms lay in what had once been Goshen. Yes, he thought like a republican. He did not really want to share with other races. But they were surrounded on three sides by Bophuthatswana now, and stock theft had become a serious problem.

"They come from the homeland on horseback at night," he said, looking at me through his thick spectacles; "they drive the cattle over the border before daybreak. The drought has made it worse. They eat the cattle, or they sell for cash. But I don't know," he continued, his voice bland, his eyes momentarily on the spoon as he stirred his coffee; "to me it was madness to stop the death penalty because you have to make people afraid before they stop doing wrong things. Everybody knows that theft is wrong. Maybe for cattle theft they should bring back the death sentence. Or they should do the Middle East thing and cut their right hands off."

He told me then, but without any sense of irony, of the farmer who lost 13 head of cattle and quite by chance had found 11 of them on the back of his neighbour's lorry. "And the neighbour was a white man!" Oom Willem said, clearly intending that I should be shocked.

Later that afternoon, I drove with him in his bakkie to a place where he needed to give instructions to a few of his labourers. We went on rough roads between his fields: maize even more stunted than I had seen in the Western Transvaal; sunflowers; many fields lying fallow. Oom Willem told me that the tendency was to turn from these crops and to plant grass for the support of cattle. In times of drought, this provided a lower risk than the seed crops, but also lower profits. But the farmer who banked too heavily on seed crops, with input costs so high, could ruin himself in a single season. And yet the farms were generally too small to provide a living from cattle alone.

While he spoke to his men, I stood by a windmill and listened to the laboured clanking of the pump. A thin trickle of water splashed down into the corrugated-iron reservoir. Not enough to irrigate a single field of all those fields stretching away on the flat earth. They were dependent on the heavens. And the heavens, glaring a fiery red in the west as the sun set, had failed them.

AT BREAKFAST the following morning I met Oom Willem's son, a handsome but reserved youngster who had recently returned from agricultural college and the army to help with the work on the farm. During the meal, another young man, a neighbouring farmer named Hannes, appeared and brought a gust of chatter and laughter to the table. Oom Willem teased him gently about his recent marriage, but Hannes was unabashed. He said he had already eaten – "she makes a good breakfast" – but that he would drink another cup of coffee with the family.

They spoke about the weather. Hannes said: "I might have been dreaming, but I'm sure I heard a long-range weather forecast which said that next summer would be worse than this one, and after that it will never rain again."

"Oh, nonsense," Oom Willem's wife said with a laugh, and then urged him to indulge in at least one slice of toast.

"I mustn't eat too much," Hannes said, buttering the toast; "I've got rugby this afternoon. I think we're going to thrash them. Are you coming to watch?" he asked Oom Willem's son.

"I might make a turn there."

They spoke about the redness of the sunsets. "All the ash from that Italian volcano," Oom Willem's wife said; "that's what I heard on the news."

"The world has gone mad," Hannes said cheerfully through a mouthful of toast.

They spoke about farming matters and about debts to the bank. "I've found out a thing," Hannes told them. "Do you know that if you can't pay last year's debts they charge you less interest on new debts? This means I'll never pay last year's debts again."

Everyone laughed. Hannes said he was feeling slightly nervous, slightly wound up, about the rugby match. His eyes were bright and alert. He was powerfully built, with immense thighs and a neck as thick as his head, but slightly overweight around the middle. "The rugby is not so important these days though. My wife now comes first," he said with an expression of proprietorship, almost a gentleness, lingering momentarily in his young male eyes.

Oom Willem said with a smile: "You're a good husband, Hannes." Then he stood up. "We must go," he said to me. "I want to be back by lunch-time."

We went out onto the country roads and drove fast in the direction of Oom Willem's cattle farm. The country spread out in a flat continuum, much of it ploughed, a few windbreaks of towering gum trees, some gatherings of windmills, but for the rest it was bush, becoming perceptibly denser as we travelled.

I asked Oom Willem whether he had been born on the farm. Earlier that morning, I had seen to one side of outbuildings a small graveyard, his surname repeated on many of the stones, with birth dates going back into the first half of the 19th Century.

Now Oom Willem nodded. "Born there, yes. And I'll die there. But you must know that things were very different when I was young. It was very wild. The only telephone was at the post office in Stella. Man, it was less than ten years ago that we got electricity. Of course before then we generated our own. Yes, as a young man I went to the cities to earn my fortune. I did shift work in Springs. But I came back. We all come back to the land. Hannes, the youngster at breakfast; he left; he joined the prison services; then his father died and now he's come back to the family farm. He won't leave again."

The bakkie drifted suddenly in a stretch of thick sand. Glancing through the rear window I saw dense dust gushing out. "It's not yet Kalahari sand," Oom Willem said, "but if we turned west it soon would be."

We passed a farmhouse protected by a high fence topped with coils of razor wire. Oom Willem told me that in the insurgency days of the 1980s, their district had been classified a border area. The government had paid R500 a month to induce farmers to stay. "But now they've stopped the payments. They say there's no more danger." He snorted. "They should keep paying now because of the cattle theft." I asked why his house was not fortified. "Man, it's so easy to get through with a pair of pliers. But the woman in that house we've just passed says: 'well, at least the fence keeps the sheep out of my garden'."

We drove through bush and thick sand. The bush seemed impenetrable in places, and I was reminded of that other Willem I had met, the small dark man with watchful eyes in Thabazimbi, who had spoken so clearly of the phenomenon of bush encroachment, a result of overgrazing. "Cattle farmers have seen there backsides here", he had said; "many have gone elsewhere – to the Vryburg area in the Northern Cape – looking for more suitable land." But Oom Willem offered another explanation for the thickness of the bush: "In times of drought the trees take the moisture first, starving the grass. Then the grass dies and the trees, Kalahari yellowwood and camelthorn mostly, take over."

The road had ascended a slight rise, hardly more than a ruffle in the immense landscape, and from this vantage point a tract of suddenly treeless land spread out. "This is now my kingdom," Oom Willem said, his old eyes keen as they looked ahead. His cattle farm, a piece of pale brown grassland hacked out of the bush; its full extent visible from the slight rise; the boundaries obvious, marked as they were by the walls of bush beyond.

We drove on, and by the roadside as we approached a huddle of low farm buildings, the gnarled trunks and branches of the trees he had taken out were piled up in long banks. Firewood for generations from this back-breaking task. Glancing at Oom Willem's profile as he drove, I had a sudden sense of something almost childlike and heroic, this old man fighting such a rear-guard action, no doubt with bakkie-loads of labour from the homeland, but in his own stubborn essence alone beneath a searing sky. The wind stroked the tall grass of his cattle farm now. Windmills raced. The old farmhouse was in a state of advanced disrepair, yet it was where he lived when he worked here for any length of time. The living-room had become seed storage: grass seed reaped in the autumns piled to above the picture rail against one wall. On another wall a few crooked pictures still lingered, and also an empty frame with broken glass. "And there hangs a portrait of me," Oom Willem said jocularly, once again unconscious of any irony.

We went out to look at the cattle. They stood and lay about the various watering points, each point with its own windmill, blades whirling in the sunlight. The dark eyes of the cattle watched us. A hundred cows and a couple of bulls in the various camps, he explained; and keeping it at that level by selling off the excess. Oom Willem moved among them, prodding them with his white stick to make them stand up, looking at them with his practised eye, moving among them, slapping a rump here and there with the palm of his hand. The simple relationship of farmer with his livelihood. And the grass was spread thinly in places, I noticed, still standing in the rows in which it had been planted; and the bush stood far off in a solid grey wall.

I asked Oom Willem how he had known where to drill for water. Had he used a diviner?

"Man, there are two things I have never seen," he replied. "One is a ghost; the other is a successful water diviner. I've seen all the instruments a geologist uses, all the maps. And they're not much better than the forked stick of the diviner. No one can really tell me where the water is. If I use a geologist, a diviner or just someone with a bright idea, the success rate is the same. About thirty per cent. You just have to keep looking."

He spoke for some time to his labourer who lived on the farm, a wizened man in a ragged coat. We walked out onto the planted grassland, and he showed me where tiny thorn trees had taken root once more. They would have to be dug out individually . The country needed rain, he said suddenly, then the grass would establish itself and spread and choke out the young thorns growing between the planted rows.

Rain. He stood leaning slightly on his white stick, looking away across this cattle farm, his kingdom in the wind. His pale eyes seemed perplexed. He said: "The world has changed." I waited for him to continue. "People have changed," he went on, and I saw him reach back into himself for an anecdote, rather than to think of rain.

"When I was at school it was a shameful thing, getting lice in the hair. The head was shaved. But no longer. I have grandchildren in Lichtenburg. They told me that now the children sell lice to each other for fifty cents. They put them in the hair to get a few days off school. This is how the world has changed."

Yet the perplexity in his eyes remained. We began to return to the crumbling farmhouse. He walked in silence for a few moments. Then he said, and I felt that it was a release for him to say it: "I am trying to imagine what it would be like if it did not rain at all. Farmers always say they've had no rain. But all of them have a little. I've seen many droughts, but never once has there been no rain. If it did not rain at all, everything would die. The underground water would dry up. Maybe there'd be some thorn bushes. Everything else would die. And men would fight and kill for the last remaining drops."

The wind stroked the thin grass, so that it bowed and darkened in waves as we walked.

PEOPLE IN Stella told me that the wind, which by the afternoon raced menacingly across the flat country, would bring a cold front all the way from the Western Cape. I had read, but could not readily see, that Stella had been laid out in the shape of a star. Rubbish bowled along its wide and empty streets. The only sign of activity: crowds of black people queueing outside the town's bottle store. And later the welling up of drunk shouts and lamentations when I stayed in the hotel, the only guest, and by seven that evening even the staff had gone. I walked in the passages and sat in my room, conscious of being alone, conscious of the tight-locked silence of the building closed in by the roaring of the wind, by the incessant banging of a gate or metal window somewhere outside in the dark. I thought of the drought, and in so doing once again remembered Marais.

As a 15-year-old schoolboy in the Western Cape, he had written a poem entitled, "There shall be no more sea". Even then, this preoccupation with the draining away of the world's water, the ultimate catastrophe, and how humanity would flee for refuge to he who had "stilled the waters of stormy Galilee". By the time of the 1913 drought, Marais had no belief in God. Nature was his goddess, a beautiful but callous being who had made fear and suffering the dominant features of life, whether animal or human, both of which in any event were elements of a single continuum. He studied with some suffering of his own the effects of extreme drought in the Waterberg. He expounded his theory: that vast quantities of water were penetrating the earth's surface "to subterranean depths from which no natural cause releases it again and where it is apparently beyond the reach of man's utmost ingenuity". Beyond this, he recognised the swing in nature's rhythm, when drought would be replaced by wetter years, and wetter years once more by drought, but even here he retained the pessimistic conviction that "the oscillations of the pendulum are gradually lessening round the dead-point".

By 1933, when the next great drought reached its climax and when Marais' life was drawing to an anguished close, his views had become even more doubtful. He misquoted a French astronomer as saying what Marais himself wanted to say: that the world was drying out because a large quantity of underground water was being broken down by the earth's central fires and that the vapour was disappearing into endless space. Scientifically doubtful, certainly; yet his obsessions seemed to contain an inner truth, an inkling of that sense of impending calamity which characterises the human response to drought.

Also in 1933, Marais wrote of this calamity in a piece of quite terrifying science fiction. Volcanic activity; rivers and the sea itself pouring into fissures in the earth; human cruelty and misery and collapse; and then silence. Perhaps no more than a gate or a metal window banging in dry wind. One survivor with a secret water source high up on a mountain. Going at last into the deserted streets of Pretoria, treading between thirst-contorted corpses and looted shops, making his way along the dark passageways of an empty hotel, being shot at suddenly from across a street. The shock of not being alone. The banging on my window, knuckles urgent against glass.

And a voice in the wind: "Tieners! Tieners, are you there?"

I shouted back, my own shock transmuted into irritation, that Tieners most certainly was not.

The voice went on: "Tieners! Tieners!"

I switched off my reading lamp and pulled open the curtains. By some faint illumination, I saw the head of a man not much higher

than the level of the windowsill. I saw wild hair ruffled by the wind.
Wild eyes.

"Tieners," he said.

"No."

"I'm looking for Tieners." Suddenly I saw an urgency in the eyes.
A dishevelled tautness of emergency and threat in the way he looked
up at me, swaying slightly from side to side. "Where is he?"

I said I had no idea.

"Where the fuck is the idiot?" The voice flared out in desperation.
"I've got to find him."

Was anything wrong? Had something happened?

He stared up at me blankly for a second, then turned away, staggering slightly. He mumbled something, but I caught only the word
cattle. Then he said, using the Afrikaans idiom, and more to himself
than to me: "Tonight the puppets are going to dance."

In the early morning I left the small star-shaped town and drove
towards Vryburg. The straight road divided the flat landscape equally
to the right and to the left, and the wind raged unabated across it.
Windmills thrashed and shuddered. Dust marred the morning air.
The red fields, devoid of crops, looked as if they burned, dust billowing out from their exposed rawness, and also from the open
country where the grass had died away. Marais' survivor had seen
catastrophe coming. He had read the headlines: Thames dry from
source to mouth; thousands of ships on the sand; Mississippi sinks
100 feet in a single day; lakes in America and Switzerland disappear.
But his friends in the Transvaal village where he was living were
unconvinced. Ag, you know what the Press is like, they said, it takes
a small thing and blows it out of all proportion. But then, one day,
the boreholes were suddenly dry.

Vryburg, the Texas of South Africa, according to a sign by the
roadside which welcomed visitors to the town. Set out on the flat
country with mature trees lining the streets and standing in the gardens of the houses. The plentiful spires of churches. The sound of
bells on Sunday morning; and the crowds of parked cars; and the
men in flapping suits, the women holding onto their hats as they
bent towards the various vestibules.

Texas. I asked a coloured man about the label and he said: "Oh,
yes, it's because of the cattle, the meat. This is the butchery of South
Africa." It had also been the capital of a republic once. A bronze
bust of the first and only president was displayed outside the municipal offices. The Republic of Stellaland: 1882 to 1884. And then

it was overtaken, but peacefully, by the British. Above the main entrance to the municipal building, a coat of arms with an aggressive motto: "armed and justified". A reminder that the original residents had been mercenaries for nearby African chiefs, freebooters and cowboys.

Texas. I came a day too late to witness the end of Vryburg's great Desert Race, but I caught the aftermath. Unruly young men and women in the hotel, their blood roused from the rallying over the weekend, their motor bikes on trailers in the car park, their eyes bloodshot from the sun and dust, and from the contents of empty cans rolling in the passages. And in the streets, the raw faces and leather jackets of youngsters and their molls, swaggering at filling stations, preparing for their race back to the teeming towns and cities of the Witwatersrand.

Texas. In the hotel, the staggering drunkenness half-way through the afternoon, young coloured women gyrating and enticing in the foyer; and the destitute coloured man living in a shed near the hotel parking, emerging unsteadily when he heard my car, Arend, longing for home in Port Elizabeth, hating the people of Vryburg who were all against him, his misshapen face and sunken eyes and grey stubble, coughing, and the welling up of anger and shouting one afternoon after which Arend was no longer in his shed; and the drifts of hopeful men, beers in their hands, hanging about a row of outside rooms where the cleaning women lived with a multi-hued herd of children; and the single street of commerce, neon and plastic in the wind, the filthy café with half-frozen fish lying on the floor between the foot-steps of shoppers; and the thickset aggression from a police van in the night, and the music bursting inside the bar, and the cold wind and the taste of dust in the cold darkness; and the shrieks and shouts in the passages late at night, most of the guests black and many profoundly drunk, while I lay in bed and thought of Marais' survivor and the shock of being shot at.

Pretoria. Behind cover for an hour, waiting, watching, enough of a hunter to know the rules of being hunted, and then through his binoculars he had seen his attacker behind the curtains of a second floor window. She had tried to kill him because she was gripped at the heart by an almost insane fear.

THE SOUTH African flag flew briskly above the sandy yard and four-wheel-drive vehicles of the police stock theft unit in Vryburg. The policemen inside the building, all armed and in plain clothes, were friendly, but said I should wait for the Captain. They provided me with a powerful cup of coffee with which to while away the time. The policemen sat at a big table trying to do some work on their budget. "To estimate these things is impossible," one of them said; "how do we know what's going to happen?" On the wall, large colour photographs showed policemen leaping from an armoured car behind a big puff of maroon smoke, policemen dangling from helicopters, policemen going fast over blue water in a motor boat.

In the Captain's office a map of the whole of the Northern Cape, studded with red and blue pins, occupied a large portion of one wall. "Red for cattle; blue for sheep," the Captain explained; "but small thefts — less than five cattle or ten sheep — are not marked." The pins were very much clustered around Vryburg and Stella, and I wondered suddenly whether Tieners had been found. Other pins formed a fairly dense string along the various borders of Bophutha- tswana, and also some along the boundary with Botswana. "Yes, we can go in," the Captain said; "we get good co-operation from the Bop and Botswana police. But we have no powers of arrest in those countries."

He sat down, inviting me to do the same. A smooth-faced man, straight-forward in his manner, accustomed to authority yet with no trace of bombast. "You must remember though," he went on, in- dicating the pins, "that these are the points of our investigations. In seventy per cent of the cases there is no evidence that it's theft. Shortages, yes; or claimed shortages.

"We struggle because of lack of evidence. To provide us with evidence it is necessary for the farmers to do four very basic things. These things would also help to prevent stock theft. First, the farmer should keep his fences in good repair. A few have electric fences, but of course this costs a lot of money. Second, the farmer should mark his cattle. Eighty per cent of cattle in this region are not properly marked. Branding also costs money. The cutting of the ears is not evidence that will stand up in court, unless supported by other ev- idence. Third, the farmer must make regular and accurate counts. And fourth, he must keep proper records. Some figures on the back of a cigarette packet aren't good enough. I came across one farmer whose stock records consisted of notches cut into the leaf of a sisal plant." He smiled easily. "Yes, quite unusual. But it makes our job almost impossible."

Nevertheless, the unit had the previous year been successful in bringing suspected thieves to court in 116 different cases. They had also recovered 1 000 animals worth nearly half a million rand.

I asked about the impact of drought, whether it had led to a sharp increase in stock theft.

The Captain spread out his hands. "Not a huge increase. But you've probably seen the situation. Crops on the ploughed lands have failed, or at best the harvests are small. Farmers have always relied on seasonal labour from Bophuthatswana for the harvesting. In the drought this work has got less. The blacks still have to live though. Yes, theft is an alternative.

"Probably there's a bigger increase in theft by white farmers," he went on. "But I can't give figures. A lot of these cases aren't reported to us. The thing is sorted out between the neighbours themselves. These cases, too, are related to the drought. Many farmers are feeling the economic squeeze. They have big loans which have to be paid, and everywhere profits are down."

Even after I had left the Captain, my thoughts lingered with the white farmers, men like Oom Willem and young Hannes, talking incessantly about debt and rain, the great pivots on which their lives turned. White stealing from white in their efforts to survive. The thought of the death sentence and the cutting off of hands; the thought of no more water, and Oom Willem saying: men would fight and kill for the last remaining drops. In Marais' story, hundreds of people were killed with bayonets as they attempted to gain access to the water lying in Pretoria's delivery pipes after the flow had stopped.

I spoke to a Vryburg agricultural economist on the telephone. "I will give you a brief overview of the white farmers' position," he said in a friendly and businesslike Afrikaans voice; "will that help you?"

I said that it would.

He said: "It has been traditional to farm with cattle in this area. The country is ideally suited to it. But for the average farmer the profit margin is fairly small. Modest. Then in eighty-one eighty-two, they turned in a big way to ploughing and seed crops. They were good wet years and they were harvesting three tons a hectare and making good profits. By eighty-four, the weather was dry. To keep going with seed crops the farmers went into debt. The input costs – for seed and fertiliser and so on – are high, but the profits can be huge. It was a gambler's chance: maybe the rains will come; just one good profit will repay the debts. Although rainfall improved in the middle and late eighties, it has dwindled again now. Are you following all this?

"Good. In the Vryburg area the average annual income from seed crops was around R95 million. This season, some rain came early and then stopped. Then the heat damaged the flowering. And the result is an income of less than R30 million. On average, this works out to a loss of around R200 000 per farmer. A very serious situation. They are now being paid R180 per hectare to plant grass. The state is thus urging farmers to return to beef. In spite of this, there are sequestrations now, empty farmhouses, and the value of land is falling. It has dropped by fifty per cent in the last few years.

"Those who have stayed purely with beef farming are better off. The input costs are much lower; in consequence there is not so much need to borrow. But meat prices are low at the moment, and this places added pressure on the farmer. And the drought could have very serious consequences. If it does not rain heavily next spring, there is veld for the cattle to eat only until the end of the year. Those with too many cattle on the veld are already on dangerous ground. They are having to import feed at high cost.

"The cattle are drinking underground water or what still remains in the dams. But there are problems here too. The underground water is full of lime. The dam water is salty, becoming increasingly so through evaporation. Fourteen cattle have recently died due to the high salt content in the dams."

Not far from Vryburg I came across a cattle research station, and there I met Alfie who said he would be happy to show me around. We went in his bakkie, bouncing along rough tracks and ultimately over the open veld. There was something cavalier and likeable about Alfie himself, and about the enthusiasm of his ideas. A young man, perhaps in his late twenties or early thirties, he wore a camouflage jacket over his khaki clothes, and his long hair was hardly contained by a jauntily angled cap; a good-looking and lively face, in a wild sort of way, and adorned with the large fan of a trimmed moustache. "I'm not a scientist," he said, although he had told me he held an agricultural degree; "I'm a technician. Now let me show you my experiments."

A black man in overalls stood on the back of the bakkie, jumping down each time it was necessary to open a gate. There were many gates as we drove from one camp to the next, looking at the cattle and the condition of the veld which each contained. His experiments had to do with the carrying capacity of the land. The norm, set by the state, was eight hectares for one large beast.

"For decades it's been eight, but I don't know where they got that figure. All I can tell you is that those farmers who have followed it are in trouble now. It's too heavy. What I'm trying to do is establish what it should be. I'm experimenting from five hectares to ten per beast. Continuous and non-continuous grazing. What are the vegetation types that do best? What is their nutritional value? And also the licks, calcium and salt. I'm experimenting with various combinations to bring down the cost to the farmers.

"I know it's harsh," he said after a moment; "but bugger it: the farmer who has damaged his land should be got off. Withdraw his subsidies. Let the farmers who can do the job, and there are plenty, get on with it. The nutritional value of this northern Cape veld is high. But some farmers get greedy. They load the cattle in and then pray for rain. They don't realise that what they do in one season will have an effect on the next five or ten."

We drove window-deep sometimes in grass and scrub, with Alfie talking all the time, telling me the merits and demerits of the various plants, and also explaining the condition of the cattle in each camp. Then he turned onto a sandy road, which seemed much used, to take me to another portion of the farm. All at once, the black man banged on the roof of the cab.

Alfie stopped the bakkie, then watched in the rear-view mirror as the man loped back and picked up something from the roadway. The man grinned as he clambered back onto the bakkie, holding up a pair of socket spanners. Alfie laughed. "The desert race," he said; "we're on a part of their course."

He drove more slowly, stopping each time the man banged. He told me he had watched the race the previous weekend, how organised it all was with the red stickers on the trees, showing left or right turns, showing hazards.

"But the manne are mad," he said; "they care nothing for their vehicles. They crash down the gateposts. I was standing on that drinking trough over there to get a better view as they came through the farm. Here the manne were coming straight for me. I dived into the bush. They crashed through the trees and went on. Mad. And here was a man coming first in his class or division. Then his gearbox went. He couldn't move. No problem: he stripped the thing and fixed it right here by the road, in the dirt, and he got it going and came third. I couldn't believe it. Yes, right here," he said, watching the man in overalls retrieving more tools half-submerged in the churned up surface. "All they take away with them is an empty toolbox," he added with a laugh.

His eyes became animated as he spoke about the desert race, and once he pushed open an unlatched gate with the front bumper of the bakkie. He told the story of the motor cyclist who had broken his leg and his arm in two places. Alfie had asked him how he had managed to do that. In his first crash he had broken his arm, but he went on. In his second crash he had fractured his leg. He continued and crashed again, this time breaking his arm once more. Then he was too sore to continue. Alfie had asked him if he was mad. "No, man," the motor cyclist had replied; "I was winning."

"He was completely mad," Alfie said. "Imagine his parents at his grave saying here lies our son. He nearly came first, but broke all his bones in the process."

We spoke about the drought. Alfie told me that the rainfall in the area had dropped 300 millimetres below the average of 500. Then he told me of his father's sheep farm in southern Namibia where he had grown up. The harsh country with virtually no rain at all. One bad mistake over the carrying capacity of the veld could result in ruin. "But all over Southern Africa it's the same. Mistakes over carrying capacity. Then there's the debt. It's a spiral. People are expecting too much from the land to keep pace with the demands of the banks. Then the droughts come and there's panic."

We had stopped again in the middle of the road while the man on the back collected more spanners. Alfie called to him: "Now you'll want to resign, hey, and start your own garage." The man laughed.

Alfie turned to me. "I think the drought makes people mad. Even these city people. Look at all the tools! They come here into the dust, and they get dizzy from a bit of dehydration, and then they go completely mad."

IT WAS during 1933, the year that Marais wrote his story of the calamity of a waterless world, that thousands of impoverished white South Africans, many drought-ruined farmers among them, set to work to build the Vaalharts Irrigation Scheme. They dug the canals with picks and shovels. From a weir across the Vaal, the water was diverted through the scheme and then into the lower-lying but normally dry Harts River to the north-west. Nearly 850 kilometres of concrete canals and community furrows. Over 1 200 small farms of 25,7 hectares each. By 1938, the first families had moved in, but under strict conditions: one farm per family and no black labour. A sub-economic scheme to assist people stricken by drought and depression. But no longer. The rules and conditions have passed into history. Now, to remain economic, many farmers work three or four of the original farms.

The crops lay spread out on the flat lands. Cotton, seeing it against the sun as a sweep of dark brown filled with white flecks, and the women (from the southern parts of Bophuthatswana) seeming to be waist-deep as they reaped. And the pecan nut and citrus trees, the vineyards and the vegetables. A frequent glimpse of tractors. All this made possible by water, the constant gurgling in the canals. This enclave of wetness in a brown and dusty land. The water made manifest, a dazzle of spray against the setting sun. The lavishness of it, the sense of life. The rich growth of grass and weeds beside the furrows. And a white vapour clinging like a blanket to the lands in the evening, and standing as a grey-white haze between the trees in endless rows along the sides of all the roads. The consciousness was of moisture, soothing and calm, as of the return to comprehension after fever.

By a circuitous route through backyards and ravaged shops, Marais' survivor had surprised the woman who had tried to kill him. A girl of perhaps 20 years old, bedecked with looted rings and watches. At the sudden sight of him, she had screamed and screamed, and then she had wept with relief. "I must have been mad," she sobbed.

In the morning I drove to the weir. The water lay as an expanse of blue against the concrete structure, enlivened by thousands of ducks and other water birds. A few caravans stood under the trees on the bank; deserted caravans with flat tyres and tattered cloth at their windows. On the far side of the water, dense clumps of reeds, and beyond the reeds the darker bush, and beyond the bush nothing but the hugeness of sky. A slight breeze darkened the surface of the water sometimes. Like a secret source it was, lying here concealed in the flat country, while the rest of the world died of thirst. The girl's source had been a forgotten concrete container, part of a system to cope with rainwater running from the various roofs of the building where Marais' survivor had found her. On the downstream side of the weir, I saw a big canal carry a strong-flowing current away towards the farms.

The girl had stories to tell. About the bayonets at the delivery pipes. About increasing panic. About a man who in a hoarse voice, and finally with thirst-cracked lips, shouted out the message of the Second Coming. About the crowds who gathered about him. About those who climbed onto the roofs of their houses to be closer to the appearance of Christ in the cloudless sky. About another man, dressed in a sheet and with a petrol can which had seen duty as a flowerpot on his head, calling the people away, saying that Christ could not return because there was no room for him to land, but that he, the man with his makeshift crown, would lead them to the New Jerusalem; and great crowds had followed. About the ruthless gunning down, in the name of water conservation, of Pretoria's entire black population, 20 000 armed whites blazing away after innumerable black families had been assembled on open ground by municipal proclamation. About the ultimate collapse of order and control, the rampaging of thirst-crazed crowds, the looting, the convulsions, the drunkenness, the bellowing of despair, the whimpers of sublime pain, and then at last that fearsome and unhinging silence.

Strange to think of these dark things amidst all the wetness and water of the irrigation scheme. Marais' morphine-tormented imagination? Nightmare of the European mind in drought-ravaged Africa? But beneath these considerations lay the deeper imperative of survival, and I thought I saw a pattern emerge which underpinned this elemental thing. The scarring pull and sadness of drought; the heat and dehydration; the faint dizziness; the hallucinations of hope and divine salvation from the cruel goddess of nature; the ultimate tearing madness to come through, as in a desert race, everyone else a competitor and a threat; the searing loneliness of thirst and precious resources sucked away; the sense of stampede inherent in the idea of drought; and in the end that supremely amoral sense which comes with isolation, when friendship and loyalty, and even gregariousness, are crushed beneath the merciless boot of individual survival.

The looted gun shops in Pretoria, and the two survivors, the man and the girl, turning ashen at the sudden sound of singing. Three drunken Africans marching down the street. To kill them becomes the immediate and unquestioned imperative. The shots ring out. In the end, the last of the Africans kneels wounded before the young woman. His blood has splashed onto a new white outfit she has taken from a looted fashion shop. He pleads for his life. He calls himself her dog and servant. He calls her his nonnie, his young mistress. She lifts her revolver for a second time and shoots him through the head.

I stood by the fence of one of the farms in the irrigation scheme. An old white man leaned on his spade, looking blankly at me. Running water sparkled at his feet. I asked how things were going on the scheme. He spoke in a slow voice, as vacant as his eyes. Things were going well, he said. But without rain the water could not last. Only one more year, he had heard. I asked what then? He looked at me incredulously. He spread out his hands. I turned away, remembering that someone, perhaps it was Johann in Pietersburg, had told me that the history of South Africa could most properly be understood in terms of the constant struggle over scarce water resources. I got into my car and drove out into dusty autumn landscapes which lay silent and enormous beyond the watered enclave.

11

RIVER OF SHAME

A LANDSCAPE of grey and secretive bush, unrolling itself to low horizons on every side. A huge emptiness of country which invaded and lulled the mind. Yet I drove with a consciousness of the river as a small knot of expectation in my thoughts. In the bush somewhere, the serpentine water, but always concealed and silent in its flow. Same river as had fed the irrigation scheme for more than half a century, yet in a different context now. An older context: the river as bearer of wealth and transformation. The Vaal, Afrikaans for drab and grey; yet bringing on its currents a dazzling harvest and a drove of ragged miners to its banks. I thought also of a young Jewish child, a tomboy of a girl named Sarah; but she would not have lived on the river, and perhaps would have developed into a different woman, had it not been for the diamonds.

The great rush began in 1869: thousands of men from all over the country, and from many parts of the world, converged upon the river and began to dig for the alluvial diamonds strewn out in the gravel of the bed itself and across the river's ancient flood plains. Rumbustious new towns sprang up. Financiers, estate agents and sophisticated diamond buyers from London and Paris strode between the wood-and-iron structures of Klipdrift (later renamed Barkly West), as they soon would in Kimberley 35 kilometres to the south-east, where the so-called dry diggings proved even more lucrative than those at the river. The rush was the start of South Africa's transformation from a colonial backwater. By 1871, hardly a hundred kilometres of railway had been built in the debt-plagued Cape Colony; less than 15 years later, when the first train steamed into Kimberley, a network of 2 200 kilometres had already been laid.

But from the beginning these advancements exacted a high social cost. Indigenous communities had been seriously disrupted by the discovery of diamonds, especially the Griquas. These were people of racially mixed descent (predominantly Malay and Khoikhoi mixed with some white blood) who, dissatisfied with white rule at the Cape, had moved north of the Orange River around the end of the 18th Century. The discovery of diamonds seriously damaged their economic independence, and alienated their traditional land around the Vaal and beyond. The resulting dissatisfaction led to a Griqua and black uprising in 1878 which was brutally suppressed. The Griquas especially never recovered; they clung to the fringes of the mining towns, subservient and depressed. The discovery of diamonds also, and for the first time, raised an insatiable need for large quantities of labour. During the early 1870s, black labourers were entering and leaving the diamond fields at a rate of 50 000 each year, thus beginning a process in southern Africa which has not completed its fateful cycle even today. But above all, perhaps, the discovery of diamonds brought about an enmeshing of races on a scale unknown in the slave days at the Cape or even on the rough frontiers of the expanding colony and the republics to the north. Generally favourable male-female ratios among the white settlers had tended to limit miscegenation; the reality on the diggings, however, was markedly different.

The Jewish child, Sarah Gertrude Millin, saw this with a sharp clarity; she wrote of it in her first novel, *The Dark River*.

A time of tumult and upheaval having its roots, then, in this river embedded in the bush; unseen, except once or twice, a sight of darker trees which plotted certain points or turns in its meandering course. And the torn earth sometimes, the lumpiness of old diggings, softened somewhat by what vegetation had found root in the heaps of stones and gravel, but a desolation still. At Canteen Koppie, just outside the town of Barkly West, a whole hill had been dug down. An unimposing monument of stones with a bronze plaque bearing an inscription: "Originally known as Klipdrift Canteen Kopje – the site of the first alluvial diamond workings in South Africa in 1869. The exposed deposits contain many stone tools and weapons as well as fossil

remains of animals which prehistoric man hunted in this neigh-
bourhood." All around, the heaps of stones, the holes, the thorny
scrub lay silent in the heat and glare of piercing autumn sunlight. A
blasted and inhospitable place, and offering evidence of some litter
as if people picnicked there sometimes with beer cans and paper
plates.

The main street of Barkly West ran through in the rough shape
of an S, testimony perhaps to the haphazard disorder of the town's
beginnings. No disorder now: the neat buildings of commerce standing separate and spread out along the pavements; dwellings secluded
in their gardens filled with fruit trees; an old stone church, St Mary's,
built in 1871. But still no sight of the river, even though I knew it
to be close.

On the western side of town two signposts pointed to De Beershoogte and Mataleng. I drove towards Mataleng on a gravel road
leading over a rocky rise. The country had become uneven and strewn
with boulders as it approached the river. Once over the rise, the road
curved into a huddle of sub-economic houses – raw cement blocks
and asbestos roofs – set down among thorn and pepper trees. A hand-
made sign welcomed me to Mataleng. At the entrance, the Superstar
restaurant and nightclub was housed in a squat brick building with
liquor advertisements adorning the walls. In an open space to one
side, a wrecked car lay upside-down in the stones, like an abstract
sculpture against which a small boy urinated while his mother, a
woman with immense hips, waited for him to catch up. I drove back
to the tarred road.

"That is the bantus' place: Mataleng," said a polite and friendly
man I picked up not far from the De Beershoogte sign. He wore a
knitted balaclava rolled above the ears. He worked on the Kimberley
railway station, he told me, and every afternoon he hitched a lift to
work and every morning he returned home by the same method.
"There are no buses, master," he said, when I remarked on the uncertainty of this method of transport. I asked if he lived in De Beershoogte. "We have to live there; it's the coloured township." I reminded him that the Group Areas Act had been repealed. He laughed,
a sudden loudness of amusement in the car. "Not yet in Barkly West,
master." He had the yellowish skin and slightly Eastern features characteristic of the Griquas. His use of the word "coloured" was typically
South African, a generic term for people of mixed descent, mixed
blood, bearing the taint and shame of miscegenation in their past.

The taint and shame of interracial intimacy: inevitable that one should think of these things here, and in such terms, so close to Sarah's dark and shameful river.

As I drove through Barkly West and out onto the Kimberley road, I asked my Griqua hitchhiker whether he knew of a vantage point which afforded a view of the river. I said I had driven down from the irrigation scheme and had been waiting to see it all day. "Have you come to see the diggings?" he asked. I said I would like to see them. "Then you must go the other way, master. Back past De Beershoogte to Gong Gong and Waldeck's. But you can see the river nicely over there." He directed me along a side-road which cut straight through a rocky ridge ahead. "Drop me here," he said at the turn-off. I went alone through the cutting blasted in the rock and found a reach of river suddenly exposed to my gaze.

Deep water darkened by the shadows of the afternoon. High banks of black boulders, with the spreading trees of the bush beyond. The current looked strong in the narrowed bed. A stone and steel bridge, built in 1884, still spanned the river, but the doorway and windows of the old toll house had been bricked up. A little way upstream stood a derelict pump station with arched windows and grey walls crammed with graffiti – a great deal of love, especially for Wimpie, and even more for Antoinette, my darling; also some racial hatred and how the AWB would manifest it – and a set of steep concrete stairs descending through the floor to a dark and uninviting lower level. But beyond such details lay the consciousness of Sarah's river flowing silent and relentless between the blackened rocks.

She was born in Lithuania in 1888, but her parents had immigrated to South Africa before she was six months old. She spent her first six years in Beaconsfield, a small town not far from the Kimberley diamond fields. Then her father gained trading and ferry rights on a section of the Vaal, and the family moved to Waldeck's Plant. She would have played among black rocks like these with her brothers there. They were the only white children, and she the only white girl, at Waldeck's, one of the many places on the river then crowded with diggers. Sarah also began to read, and to write poetry, in the solid security of her parents' wood-and-iron house. The family played chess or cards, or made its own music, while beyond the middle-class curtains the squalid lives of the diggers were always present.

In Sarah Gertrude Millin's first novel, she draws a detailed picture of life on the diggings: the heat and aridity; the hopelessness of hoping for something that never materialises; the real poverty of most of the diggers; and the unerring ability of the diggings to degrade the individual man. The degradation comes in many forms, but the chief of them is interracial physical intimacy. Millin's tone is always shrill with disapproval. These white men who had sunk as low as their diseased and filthy lovers. And there is no redemption after that, especially if a child is the result. Like her character John Oliver who, after one such relationship on the diggings, marries a white woman. When she discovers his secret, however, she leaves him in horror and disgust, but primarily because Oliver's half-caste child is wandering about on the diggings.

It is essentially her own disgust which Millin describes, her obsession with what she ultimately perceived to be the moral and intellectual inferiority of people not white, and above all with the evil of miscegenation. Those flawed and tainted coloureds, God's stepchildren (as the title of her most celebrated book describes them), doomed to the shortcomings, the bad of both sides, inherent in their blood.

I turned from the graffiti-crammed pump station, and from that uninviting lower level. The stone piers and steel girders of the old bridge stood vague in the half-light of evening now: she would have used it frequently to cross what, for me, had been no darkened flow of shame at all but simply the river of my boyhood.

THE MINING commissioner's museum in Barkly West turned out to be a single cluttered room in a building now used by the detective branch of the South African Police. A black constable unlocked the door for me and I wandered between shelves and cases crowded with an assortment of objects, the majority of them unexplained.

Some needing little explanation, though, like the heads of old picks, a tin helmet, some hip flasks. Or the collection of smooth round stones, tumbled in the river for some millions of years, one or two of them the size of footballs. But only a few in the conglomeration of rock samples had been identified. And the Stone Age tools found on the diggings, hundreds of them, all without the small black numbers of the archaeologist. These tools brought the thought that for tens of thousands of years people had lived on the banks of the river, as they had lived at the Limpopo and the Soutpansberg and Makapan's Caves. Then the Iron Age people had drifted down from the north. And then the rattling dusty diamond rush had come, largely from the south.

Old photographs hung on the walls. One set offered a panoramic view of "the river diggings, 1871": the harsh country in sepia tones, hundreds of tents and shacks spread out in the stony bush, a glimpse of the river in the background. Other photographs showed a group of diggers stranded on an island with the river in flood; diggers working in deep trenches; men digging for treasure, up to their knees in river water and mud; diggers in posed groups outside their tents and makeshift homes, rugged-looking men from another century, evidence of collarless shirts and the twirled moustache. And here was the old bridge being officially opened: a banner – *labor omnia vincit* – stretched across its narrow width, a crowd of men in hats, a few women under parasols.

In one corner I came across a model of the most essential piece of alluvial mining equipment: a circular tub with rotating paddles. The basic mining method was simple: dig out the alluvium; add water until the stones and pebbles were suspended in a slurry; stir the slurry with the rotating paddles so that, by specific gravity, the heavier material drifted to the outside where it was released through a narrow gate in the side of the tub; wash the heavy material in a sieve and then turn the sieve over onto a sorting table.

I had a sudden memory. The bang of the sieve onto the table; brown forearms flexed; and there in the centre of the shining wet stones a white diamond; my father asking why in the centre; and the man saying because of the weight, always in the centre, look I'll show you, and he picked up the diamond as big as a marble and threw it back into the slurry. Dunbar: strange how his name came floating through to me again, and how he had laughed when my father in some alarm had told him he was foolhardy. A childhood memory of some tents and Dunbar's brown forearms banging down the sieve again, and then my father's amazement and relief.

But diamonds had occupied only a small part of my experiences as a youth, more the stuff of legends than reality. A friendly detective chatted to me for a while. I asked him if IDB, illicit diamond buying, was still a problem. He said it always would be. The buying and selling of uncut diamonds damaged world prices. The mining houses, and the few remaining individual diggers, had to be protected. It was the law. I told him that when I was at school in Kimberley great IDB myths would spring up around certain individuals – the new cars, the lavishly dressed girlfriends – they were the gangsters of my youth. The detective laughed. "It's still exactly the same," he said; "it's still going on."

I strolled in the main street of Barkly West, thinking once more of the Stone Age artifacts and of Sarah Gertrude Millin. Her mind seemed to have been blocked by a denial of the slow march of humanity's adventure. Was there a point at which Europe had leapt so far forward from the bulk of humanity that no common ground remained, and the only individual linkage possible between the races was that of master to servant, or that unthinkable coupling of the groin? Some coloured girls in bright dresses walked on the pavement in my direction. I caught the gaze of one of them upon me. She had ribbons in her stiff and crinkled hair. She held her eyes to mine. She seemed all at once to prance slightly, arching her back and swinging out a slender hip. I smiled. And in reply, unabashed and young, she gave me the girlish beauty of her own.

IN A neat brick house, away from the mild bustle of the S-shaped road, I met a man who said: "I am the oldest digger still living on the river."

Johannes Roos Mills, born in 1903, an old man now, his head slightly hollowed at the temples, small veins breaking on his nose and cheeks, white hair neatly combed. "He is very deaf," his wife told me with a cheerful smile; "you will have to talk loudly to him." We sat in a room which smelled faintly of floor polish. Outside, the day was hot and silent.

"I was digging with my father during the First World War," the old man said. "Then when I was seventeen I got my own certificate."

We spoke in Afrikaans. He used the word delwery to describe the process of digging, and for me it lent a rich descriptiveness to his words. This is exactly what these men had done: delving through the alluvium for their fortunes in the precious stones.

"A lot of the diggers made money, and a lot of them lost it just as fast. Many of them drank and gambled too much. I used mine to make a shop in Longlands, and later I bought a garage. But I also lost money trying to help other people to dig."

His voice had gone gentle with age, quavering slightly, but his mind seemed lucid enough. He sat with his hands in his lap, his face turned towards me. His wife smiled cheerfully at us while we talked.

"Yes," Johannes Mills said; "I found many diamonds. I went to the Lichtenburg rush. There I was finding about 20 carats each day. Then when I came back to the river, some of us threw a breakwater there by Longlands. We found three big diamonds, all over one hundred carats. The biggest was one hundred and fifty-six carats, a yellow. I'm sure I have found more than a big soup plate of diamonds in my life."

"Ag, much more," his wife said.

"I took over my father's diggings. My father went farming, but he lost his farm in thirty-three. The drought and the depression. No, I was never alone on the diggings. I always had labourers to do the hard work. The blacks weren't as wild as they are now. Now they push you away from the counter in the shops. In those days, they were very polite. If they weren't, I'd give them a clout so that they only woke up the following morning."

I asked his wife whether she had stayed with him on the diggings. "Never," she said; "I stayed at home."

Johannes Mills told me he had owned a house in Longlands. When he was on the diggings, he lived in a small wood-and-iron shed. But he would always go home twice a week to his family. Then in 1944, the house was washed away.

"But the delvers knew the flood was coming. Before our house went, they moved all our furniture out. I found our belongings lying on the ground higher up. Then I had to buy another house quickly," he said. For some reason the memory of this amused him. His tired eyes showed some gaiety for a moment. "I bought one. That one there."

He showed me a framed painting on one of the walls: one side of a brick-built dwelling with an iron roof and deep veranda. "My daughter-in-law painted that. I liked it and made a frame." I said the painting gave a clear idea of what the house must have been like.

Then I told him of my memory of Dunbar, and asked whether he, Johannes Mills, had ever thrown a diamond back.

"Hundreds back into the mud," he replied. "Once I threw an eight carat back, to show some people. When I turned over the sieve, there were two eight carat diamonds right in the middle. They thought it was magic, but it was just a fluke," he said with an artless smile.

"But it's mostly luck," he went on; "one day up and one day down. An old delver once said to me: it's a funny life – one day you're eating porridge, the next you're eating an orange with a silver knife and fork."

His wife went out to make some tea. I said to Johannes Mills that I was interested in the lure of the diggings, the excitement of turning over the sieve, just one more sieve, then another and another, like an addiction perhaps.

"I got used to it," he said; "I was delving for more than 60 years, until I was seventy-nine years old. But, yes, it's always that chance."

Over tea, we spoke about the Mills' children. Their son had ended up as the managing director of a factory somewhere on the Witwatersrand, and they were clearly proud. Johannes Mills said: "People sometimes ask me what I have done with all the money I made through the diamonds. I say to them: haven't you got children? That's where my money went, educating my children. I also bought my son a car."

"You know," said Mrs Mills, "the children were only allowed on the diggings when they were teenagers."

I asked why. The old man smiled obliviously at me. I asked my question in a louder voice.

"Because," he said, "I wanted my children to make up their own minds about me when they were old enough. People have always said bad things about the delvers. Everyone thought we were poor whites.

"Once a journalist made a story in a newspaper about the shocking conditions on the diggings. I wrote to him and told him I would pay for him to come and look. If he found what he had written was true, then I promised to pay him one thousand pounds. But the journalist never replied. I think he must have got his story from the Hottentots."

"And what about that other man?" his wife prompted him.

"Yes, he came to me and said: you're a digger, how do you live, have you got a house? I got cross," Johannes Mills said; "I got so cross I told him: no I don't have a house, I live under a bush."

His wife laughed. Then she extended her left hand, the fingers adorned with several rings. She pointed to one of them. "This is one he found," she said.

"They offered me a huge price for that," Johannes Mills said; "but I told them, no manne, I've already given it to my wife; if I sell it now she'll murder me."

Mrs Mills laughed once more in her vivacious way. She looked to be at least 20 years her husband's junior.

Then the old man wanted to show me a diamond he had found, and had then had cut, and was keeping as an investment. When he shuffled out to fetch it, his wife said: "I think he's keeping it for another wife he must have somewhere." She laughed. "Ag, I love to tease him, even after all this time."

I asked her what it had been like, being married to a digger.

She said it had been a funny life, ups and downs, but they had always managed. They had lived quite well. "But you must remember we are children of the depression. Hardship is in our blood. The young people now are too soft," she went on; "when things go wrong, they shoot each other, or get divorced, or take their own lives." But she and her husband were getting old. They both had illnesses. His heart was weak. Their dog had died of old age. And the fruit, their lovely fruit in the garden, was regularly stolen by the coloureds. She told me about their orange tree which they had planted, and the first time it bore there had been only one orange, and they had watched it grow and ripen. They planned to eat it together on the veranda. Then it was stolen. "I cried that day over the orange. I cried because I was angry and there was nothing we could do. I wanted to chop out all our fruit trees." She spoke expressively, even dramatically, yet with a fine pleasantness and decorum. She told me about the terrible cost of old-age units in Kimberley, and how they could hardly manage here in Barkly West any longer. "You know, sometimes my husband can't even put the hose on the tap. He has no strength left and his heart is bad."

But her husband, who had returned to the room, heard little of this. He sat with his teacup held in both hands, smiling politely at us, but with suddenly tired eyes. I said it was time for me to go. But he detained me. He wanted to show me his digger's certificate. I saw that it had expired a few days previously. Would he renew it? "Oh, yes," he said; "once a delver, always a delver." Then with slightly trembling hands and with the simple pleasure of a child, he unwrapped a piece of tissue paper and showed me his beautiful stone.

GONG GONG, Waldeck's Plant, Beaumont's Folly, Sidney-on-Vaal, Longlands and Bosman's Fortune: these had been some of the places of great activity along the river, although now not many of them remained on the map. I nevertheless went out to see them, following my Griqua hitchhiker's directions. Beyond the signposts to Mataleng and De Beershoogte, the bush spread to the horizon once more, a monotony of grey. The river was on my left, but I could not see it. Only after some kilometres, and after I had turned off onto a stony side-road, did I come across it, quite suddenly, lying sky blue and glittering in its shallow eroded valley. The level of the water was low, its surface studded with black rocks, some of them in straight lines which I guessed were the remains of breakwaters. I remembered the photograph of diggers up to their knees in mud and water. The road twisted down to the riverside, and then divided. I drove upstream on a surface which alternated between deep sand and pavements of uneven rock. I was going to Gong Gong to meet an alluvial diamond miner named Paul Fourie.

People were living here on the baked and rock-strewn bank of the river. Houses of terracotta mud and corrugated iron had been set down on the narrow strip of ground before the side of the valley sloped too steeply; donkeys stood among thorn trees; small graveyards were surrounded by dilapidated fences; the houses seemed crooked and sunk into the earth; faces peered out at me sometimes, brown and yellow; and once a group of women with doeks stepped off the roadway to allow me to pass. Desolate people.

Desolate and devastated country, as the road climbed now into a landscape of deep holes and mounds of boulders and stones, all of them washed smooth when the river was younger and more wild. For a moment I was reminded of the iron mine at Thabazimbi, that ruination of the earth, that sense of wounding for its treasure, but here on a smaller scale, although I saw exhaust fumes and then a loaded truck loomed over a steep rise not far ahead. I pulled my car aside. They were digging in the alluvium still, but now with mechanical shovels and other earth-moving equipment. Discarded machinery, metal and spilled oil littered the scene; and the vegetation had shrunk back, stunted and cowering and often lifeless in this forbidding landscape of search and ruin.

I found the place where the alluvium was processed. Black and coloured workmen busied themselves at various points. A generator throbbed somewhere out of sight, the whole plant being electrically operated. Conveyor belts carried ragged streams of material; ladders gave access to the larger machines. But easy enough to see that the principle was the same as it had been a century before.

Paul Fourie: a youngish fair-skinned man with a smooth round face, wearing dark glasses to protect his eyes from the relentless glare of rock and sand. He climbed down a ladder to greet me. His handshake was firm. I asked whether he found it exciting to earn his living in this way. "People glamourise it," he said with a slight smile; "but it really is just a living."

We watched the trucks drive up a ramp and tip their loads into a hopper where steel bars discarded the boulders, allowing only the sand and stones through onto a belt which finally tipped the material into a big drum revolving on a set of four motor tyres. This is where the water was added, Paul explained. Then out the muddy mixture would come, down a series of gutters and into several tubs with their constantly rotating blades. Sand flowed over weirs at the centre of the tubs and was taken away by conveyors underneath for washing and then for sale as building sand. The heavier material which gravitated to the outside of the tubs accumulated in a metal container which was emptied three or four times a day, the contents washed through graded sieves which were then turned over onto the sorting table.

"Only I do the sorting," Paul told me.

"But wouldn't your workers be tempted to empty the hopper when you're not here?"

"There are security systems, but they're too expensive for me. My people know: they are not allowed to touch the container. Only me."

While the trucks tipped the alluvium into the hopper, the heavy boulders crashing and bouncing away, and while the plant rattled and hummed, Paul and I stood to one side, talking about diamonds, and about what it must have been like in the old days. Picks and shovels and hand-operated tubs then. At the height of the rush, Paul told me, he had heard that 30 000 diggers had swarmed on the farm Gong Gong alone. "Perhaps that figure is too high, but at any rate there were thousands. It must have been an incredible sight." And down-stream at Sidney-on-Vaal, a sizeable town had grown up. Diamond buyers' offices, trading stores, at least 30 hotels. The wild Saturday nights. Drunk men yelling, and a few of them from time to time drowning in the river.

No town there these days, I discovered, but sufficient remaining to indicate what it might have been like. A large rectangle of open ground: the market square, loud with wagons and trade and whiskered men in their collarless shirts. Now it was covered with grass looking lush under the silvered spray of sprinklers. The whole town had been sold as part of a farm in the early 1960s, but it had died several decades before. Around the perimeter of the market square old buildings still stood, and from a far corner a street led off into the veld, a few wood-and-iron dwellings still lining one side. And here was a church, built as late as 1930, an unadorned interior with wooden pews, the exterior painted brown, the woodwork white, and a superstructure at the apex of the roof which contained a clock. A Puritan chapel, manifestation of atonement for earlier days perhaps, but standing in a silence broken only by the quick spitting of the sprinklers now. The young Sarah had often seen men brawling outside the bars here, or shouting at their black and coloured women.

Other buildings around the square were older: a row of wood-and-iron shops which had recently been painted. A rambling house at the top of the square, once a hotel and now being converted to that use once more, a friendly couple told me. They allowed me inside: gleaming timber floors, rugs, old furniture and on the walls sepia photographs of the diggings similar to those I had seen in the museum at Barkly West. The couple took me across the square to the brick-built library. Turn of the century architecture, tall sash windows, and in the main hall a vaulted ceiling of dark varnished timber. The shelves stood in ordered rows, and they were filled with thousands of books still in their categories, but now covered with thick dust and cobwebs. It was as if someone one evening had closed the door, perhaps half a century ago, and that it had never been opened again, until now. They had closed the door on the whole town and left it there. The carousing of the diggers silent now, only the echoes re-maining, only the mustiness of dust and cobwebs smothering the rows of books and blurring the glass of the elegant windows. I looked in a desultory way for books by Sarah Gertrude Millin – she had written more than 30 – but could not find any.

In one of the wood-and-iron shops a coloured woman sold me a chocolate and a cool drink for my lunch. She seemed astonished when I told her that this quiet place had once had 30 hotels. She looked at me through the bars protecting the counter, and I wondered briefly whether they had been erected to keep unruly diggers at bay, or more recently. She was a pleasant women, telling me her husband had worked as a mechanic with the cotton farmers, but the price of cotton had dropped and now he had lost his job. "But we'll come right," she said, passing me my change. When she smiled she revealed a gap in her front teeth.

I had asked Paul to direct me to Waldeck's Plant. It, too, was down-stream and on the other side of the river. I went there. I had arranged to return to Gong Gong in time to see Paul sorting through the material from the sieves, but now I drove along the river bank, the way at one point becoming almost impassable, low cliffs forcing the track close to the water's edge. Giant kingfishers watched the river, sometimes hovering in the air with a blurred thrashing of their wings. A makeshift causeway, no more than boulders thrown into the water with the track laid precariously on top, took me across to where Sarah had lived. The bank was steep and led directly into a wilderness of diggings; the road switchbacked into holes and over sharp mounds, stones scraping the underside of the car. I came to a battered bulldozer working in one of the holes. Nearby, in the desolation, a coloured man with green eyes and a congenial face stood outside an iron shed with a large shifting-spanner in his hand. He greeted me politely.

"Diamonds? They must find them," he said in response to my question; "otherwise they wouldn't go on. But only two or three carat stones now, I think. Although last year one of the white men found an eighty carat. But that's once in a lifetime. Me? No. I just work here. I find no diamonds."

Was there, I asked, a lot of IDB here on the river?

The skin around his green eyes creased in a pleasant laugh. "What's that? I don't know what that is," he said evasively.

I drove slowly back to the river. Children with stiff hair stood at the doorways of low dwellings, and a young woman walked barefooted among the stones. At the river I turned off the engine for a moment. I heard a few birds, otherwise nothing save the throatiness of the bulldozer in low gear, the clashing of steel against rock. Sarah's playground, I thought, watching coloured children fetching water from the river's edge. Laughing coloured children with pale brown skins, bearing the stigma, in Sarah's mind throughout her life, of how they, or their parents or their parents' parents, had come into the world. Not simply by a sexual act, but by an act of ethnic defilement. Had she fled in horror from such tormenting things? And had she, in her secret heart, found a fascination which perpetually fed her horror? This cycle, inherently sexual, of obsession and disgust: how close it lay to the festering heart of the racialist. So close indeed, and so inexpressible, that it could only be transmuted into intolerance and ideas of superiority. And upon this foundation was built the ideology of blood, the idea of an ethnic hierarchy, the imperative of purity and finally the terrible fallacy of a super race striding forward, armed even with ultimate solutions, to dominate the family of man. Almost without knowing it, she charted with chilling clarity the dark and uninviting lower levels of the bigotry and racialism of her country and my own. More inevitable than ironic, therefore, that this talented Jewess was read quite avidly in the Germany of the 1930s, especially by those who espoused the idea of Aryan purity and its consequent anti-semitism. Inevitable, too, that towards the end of her long life she became an advocate of white supremacy in Southern Africa, avid supporter of Smith's Rhodesian regime and South Africa's disastrous attempts at separate development.

The sun beat down upon the river of shame. I restarted the engine and drove back to Gong Gong.

PAUL TOOK the sieve with both hands and in a single deft movement overturned it and banged it down. Then he lifted the sieve gently, as if turning out a cake, and there on the sorting table lay a circular mound of wet and glistening stones. Using a piece of metal especially shaped for the purpose and shining with constant use, he spread out the stones, examined them quickly, then swept them away. They rattled into a growing pile at his feet.

The sorting table was roofed and closed in on three sides. In this way a private place. I became interested in the discreteness of his labourers. They would bring him the sieves in sets of three, and then retire during the process of sorting. They did not watch this private thing: the expectation, the adrenalin perhaps, the growing anxiety or the sudden triumph. There were flecks of mud on Paul's dark glasses as he worked. But I wished then that I could have seen his eyes.

"This is like gambling," I suggested; "once one tray is done, the urge is for the next. And then the next."

"Yes," he said; "but the stakes are a lot higher. My whole life is here. I found nothing yesterday. The day before I found three small ones, worth about the cost of one day's operation here."

Paul had been mining in this way for the past 12 years. His father had been born in Lichtenburg, during the diamond rush there, but he had studied at night while working on the diggings by day, finally becoming a company secretary. He had been employed by a Johannesburg firm which had mining interests in Barkly West, and was finally transferred there. Paul was five years old at the time. He told me these things as he worked. I noticed that from the bigger stones contained in the first sieve of each set he would swiftly select half a dozen or so and place them in a tin. I asked him what they were for. He said he planned to build a small water feature out of these better-looking stones. He would build it in his garden in Barkly West next to his patio and braai area.

Another sieve banged down. The metal sorter flicked, but no diamonds were uncovered. Paul's mouth was impassive, patient. I caught something of the obsession of chance which had so surely tied men to the river, often for life, regardless of their circumstances. And then Paul lifted the final sieve away from its contents.

"Success!" I said, a pang of excitement flashing in me as I remembered Dunbar and my father and the strong brown forearms. A translucent white pebble lay close to the centre of the mound of stones.

Paul shook his head. He was smiling behind his dark glasses. "Quartz," he explained; "but there's always tomorrow."

12

THE FIFTH WORLD

I WENT to Kimberley with the specific intention of seeing something of George. He had taught me English and history for some years when I was at school there. I remembered a crisp man in horn-rimmed spectacles, articulate and forthright, who told me once that my education could never be considered even to have begun until I had played cricket and read *Alice in Wonderland*. I found a considerably older man, grey-haired and balding now and seeming shorter than I remembered; but the spectacles and forthrightness had changed little. When he had been my teacher he had sometimes worn a clerical collar. I learned, when I made contact with him before the start of my journey, that although retired from teaching he was still the An-glican Rector of Barkly West. He also managed a school at Longlands (where in 1944 Johannes Mills' house had been washed away) which he hoped I would be interested to see. I had replied that I was.

The streets of Kimberley appeared narrower and more mundane than when I had frequented them as a boy. Inevitable, perhaps, how the first view became the richest, how the severe limits of the horizons of childhood would imbue what lay within them with a grandeur and mystique which time so easily eroded. Evocative, nevertheless, to return and to see the first view cut down by the imposition of another scale. Like the facade of the church where my father had preached, tall and severe with brickwork and buttress then, much smaller now, and given over to the signage of the music and hi-fi shop which the church currently contained. And next door, the church hall had become a dance studio. These once solemn places commercialized now; yet I remembered one evening, inside the church, how the lightning had hissed and slithered on the back wall, and how I had sat uneasy with premonition.

The mining house offices had not been altered, white wrought iron still enclosing the first floor veranda. But the windows of the best bookshop in town were now stuffed with roles of fabric below a big sign proclaiming "Bargains Unlimited"; and the library, although still full of books, no longer lent them out. The lending library had moved to the new civic centre which, in my day, had been an emptiness of littered veld filled with those weeds which would bush out and then break off at the stem and tumble in the wind across the open spaces.

The muddle of the streets remained as a reminder of how the town had grown, spreading out around the great holes which the diggers had made as they followed the diamonds down into the blue-grey rock of the volcanic pipes. These were the dry diggings, richest in the world, which had soon eclipsed those at the river. An essential mining town still, when I had grown up there, riding my bicycle through these twisting streets, or down the long Du Toitspan Road to Beaconsfield where I had lived. And in my road, the sidewalks were still unpaved; the intricate iron-work of my front fence unchanged; and the house not much altered, the deep veranda and the coloured glass on either side of the front door still there.

Growing up in isolation, although at the time I could hardly have been aware of it; yet aware of something, perhaps no more than the occasional sense of being besieged, hemmed in by the fire of my parents' religion and by the sterile grey mine dumps upon which nothing but thorns would grow. Beyond them, flat veld extended forever. The possibility of a world beyond my world, and the possibility of a past which might make the present comprehensible, came only slowly to me, through books certainly, but even earlier through the confidence and breadth of knowledge which I had perceived to be invested in the mind of George.

The streets on my route to school had changed little, and the school itself even less. Kimberley Boys' High School, known to everyone as KHS. The Cape Dutch gables of the various facades, the cypress tree in front of the main entrance, the windows of the headmaster's office to the right of the main doors, the two quadrangles surrounded by classrooms and separated by the main hall, all were immediately recognisable, as were the black and white striped blazers worn by the boys.

I remembered standing in line one morning, waiting to go into the hall for the daily assembly. The music teacher played as usual on the piano as the boys marched in. George had walked briskly by, and then stopped. He had turned to me. "What is the piece being played?" he asked. "Jesu, Joy of Man's Desiring," I replied. "And the composer?" "Bach, sir." He had nodded, it seemed to me with a gleam of approval in his lively eyes, and then walked on. I could never have admitted then that my ability to reply was a fluke, much like the two diamonds in Johannes Mills' sieve, that my parents had a scratchy gramophone record, and that on any other day the pianist would have left me submerged in my own ignorance.

When I admitted it to George now, he chuckled. "I don't remember that," he said; "but at least I chose the right day." He had thick grey eyebrows arching above the dark frames of his spectacles, and there was a kindliness in his eyes which his forthright manner might have hidden before.

He showed me around the school, introducing me to a few teachers and to the principal, a young man who seemed slightly on edge but in an urbane sort of way. We lingered in the main foyer outside the headmaster's office. I remarked that I remembered the foyer well, but that I had usually been there under unpleasant circumstances. A teacher laughed. The foyer was filled with glass cases containing cups and other memorabilia. In the hall itself, lists of names in gold lettering on varnished wood: the rolls of academic honour from the past, the head prefects, the Rhodes scholars, the outstanding sportsmen. We spoke for a moment, George and I, about a few of my contemporaries; there were some illustrious names in various fields, he said. He referred several times to the magic of the school which was now over a hundred years old.

I learned, as we went in search of some of my old classrooms, that he had been a pupil there himself. Then he had gone away to university. I remembered that he had sometimes taught us wearing his academic gown, a rather ragged garment we had thought, especially when it billowed out behind him as he strode about the quadrangles. His movements were slower now, his forthrightness tempered with a certain patience. Yet he did not hesitate to speak his mind. As when we came to my first classroom in one corner of the junior quad, now used as a computer room. "Excuse the stench of tobacco," George said, making no attempt to hide his disapproval.

He took me to see the library, a separate building with the same Cape Dutch gables as the school itself. A class of boys, some in the familiar black and white striped blazers, sat at tables, reading. George introduced me. I told them I had been a pupil at the school when the library had been built. "Gee," they said politely, glancing at me from time to time as if it amazed them that I was still alive.

But I caught something from their faces. Was it simply the impatience of youth? Surely their ignorance or innocence could not have been as great as mine had been. At the laying of the library's foundation stone, George himself had said that the list of boys' names, mine included, which had been placed behind the foundation stone would possibly be of interest to those who finally demolished the building. To talk of demolition before the building was complete had shocked me. The thought that time would inevitably crack the deepest foundations brought me for the first time to a realisation of self in relation to a larger process: the perpetual overlaying of one reality with another, the impermanent yet interlocking nature of each segment in the human adventure. Vaguely, through the screen of my ignorance, I found that I wanted to grasp this idea of the impermanence of life with no glove of preconception to guard against the thorns. Impossible to tell the extent of this particular influence or that, but I remembered these things clearly as I lingered in the old school library that day in the presence of George.

WE DROVE to Longlands in the heat of the afternoon. We went in George's car, and he stopped briefly in Barkly West to pick up a man named Russell, a retired electrician now helping to take care of St Mary's Church, and generally, so far as I could make out, serving as George's right-hand man in his activities on the river.

Longlands: a spread-out gathering of mud and galvanised iron houses among the stones and thorns of the veld. George turned in among them and drove slowly on badly eroded roads. Coloured people stopped to look at us sometimes as we passed. He gave me a background to the school we were going to visit: he had inherited five schools when he had taken over the Barkly West parish, all of them in a poor state. Perhaps the worst, though, had been here in Longlands and at Waldeck's Plant across the river. "I combined Waldeck's and this one," he said; "the first buildings went up in 1970. To begin with, it was known as the Forlorn Hope school. Forlorn Hope," he repeated with a slight snort; "that was the old diamond rush name for this area."

I saw immediately, however, that the school had now been named after George himself. The sign was plainly visible. The school presented itself as a cluster of single storey buildings behind a sturdy wire-netting fence. In the fence, an elaborate gateway, roofed like a lich-gate.

"It stands as a symbol," George said; "so that people may know they are passing from the ordinary world, here outside, into a realm which belongs to God."

We walked in the bare school yard. At intervals, umbrella-shaped thorn trees cast their webs of shade onto the thick red sand. "*Acacia tortilis*," George told me; "beautiful trees. I can get quite lyrical about them. And I am determined to preserve them, and in so doing to teach the value of preserving beautiful things."

He showed me the first classrooms, built in 1970: mud-brick walls plastered with cement. But they had been made too low, and without ceilings the heat in summer had been intolerable. With a grant from the British Consul, he had increased the height of the roof to introduce cross-ventilation, and he had installed ceilings and proper flooring. "These first efforts were built on a north/south axis. That was a mistake. The only way to build schools in Africa is on the east/ west axis, to keep the sun out of the classrooms. As you can see, the rest of the school has been built in this way."

Before he took me to see the newer parts, he showed me how one of the original buildings had been converted into a church: rows of pews facing a table adorned with a simple cross. I questioned him about the use of his name for the school, and he replied in his forthright way: "I didn't really want that. It smacked of self-glorification. But the committee pressed me and I finally agreed. At least it's better than Forlorn Hope. That is an extremely poor name for a school." I saw Russell, who had been largely silent since he had joined us, break into a broad grin. Then we both followed as George turned quite briskly in the direction of the main part of the school. I thought of his academic gown flowing out behind him, but perhaps his pace was no longer brisk enough for that. "He's quite a man," Russell said in a shy and stammering sort of way. I nodded.

Juggling with a large bunch of keys, George now began to open doors. The classrooms were attractive, well-built, well-equipped with blackboards and softboards filled with bright pictures and teaching aids. "As good as anything in the white schools," he said. Each classroom had its own storage space, and George showed me how some of the teachers had made small offices for themselves in part of the space. As manager, he had a hand in selecting the teachers: apart from their qualifications, he wanted to make sure that they were not in debt and that they did not smoke. "A filthy habit," he remarked. Fifteen teachers and 425 pupils meant reasonable ratios. He was encouraged by the academic standards being achieved. "In time, we'll have another KHS here," he said.

There were problems, however, and George talked of some of these as we walked in the open space between the classrooms and the school's most recent acquisition, a R70 000 administration block. All the outside taps had padlocks on them, he pointed out, to prevent the theft of water. "We have our own pump station at the river. We pump up to those storage tanks over there. But we can't have the local population wandering about the school, helping themselves to whatever they feel like." The sturdy perimeter fence, however, was primarily to keep the goats at bay. Indeed, a small animal-proof pedestrian gate close to the main entrance allowed access to the grounds at any time. It was used by the caretaker who lived at the school, and by her family. "But the goats were a terrible nuisance, eating everything we tried to plant." I began to get an inkling of George's determination for excellence, his belief in the worth of the school set down here in the dust and desolation near the river, and in a community as desolate.

"We brought in Operation Hunger," George told me; "they established that a third of our children were malnourished. We now have a feeding scheme. But most important of all, we need to teach the children to look at the world in a new way. We need to teach them preservation," he said, indicating the acacia trees; "and a sense of duty, and a work ethic. But where do these things come from? If your parents are feckless, drunk from Friday night to Monday morning; if you kill everything that moves, and chop down everything for food or fuel or building, then there is very little chance. If we can develop a sense of pride, a sense of worth, we could start a revolution here. But it will take time. That's why I agreed to the name change. How can you have pride in a school called Forlorn Hope? Terrible. And also," he added in his direct way; "I want to leave them something that will last after I've gone."

George planned to make a garden between the classrooms and the administration block. A few acacias were already in place. Shrubs and flowers would be added, a rockery perhaps, and (dare one think it?) a small patch of lawn. The garden would be named after one of the school's benefactors. As the raw red soccer field already was, according to a bronze inscription on a plinth of cemented stones. The administration block also, adorned with a plaque indicating the name of the company – run by a KHS old boy, of course – which had put up the money. Inside the building: the neat toilets which George called comfort stops, the well-equipped kitchen and staff room, the offices, including the principal's, photographs hanging on the wall, but not yet any glass cases of cups and trophies.

And I suddenly saw what George was doing: he was consciously building a tradition through icons: plaques, named gardens, photographs, the buildings themselves, the foundation stones, the symbolic entrance gate. "Yes, I think that's probably right," he said matter-of-factly when I put my thoughts to him.

The caretaker appeared, a yellow-skinned woman wearing a doek, her hands deferentially clasped together in front of her. She asked whether the reverend required a cup of tea. "Excellent," George said, rubbing his hands; "Russell, where is our other refreshment?" Russell grinned shyly. He disappeared for a moment, then returned with a bottle of sherry and three glasses. We sat together at the table in the staff room. George looked expansive, his thick eyebrows arching and then lowering as he tasted the sherry.

"Forty years ago I was given the River Diggings congregation," he told me; "then I became rector of Barkly West which includes the River Diggings. So all my working life I've been linked to the river, and to the schools here."

Before we returned to Barkly West, George drove on a bumpy track down to the river. The sight of hovels among the trees served to set the reality of the school in sharp relief: an edifice which shone somewhat in all the dereliction of the old river diggings. Forlorn Hope, with the river gliding between rocks. The school's pump was mounted on a moored raft to cope with the changing level of the water. George pointed to the remains of breakwaters, deploring the ravishment of so beautiful a place. "Be still and know that I am God," he said in his rich cleric's voice. And for a moment, standing on the ageless bank, we were.

We drove back into the low and spread-out habitation of Longlands, the terracotta houses squatting among thorn trees, the weeds and thorns, the mounds of rubbish and wrecked cars, the ragged children, two youngsters carrying a crate of beer, the sound of voices welling up as the shadows of the afternoon began to lengthen, the acrid smell of poverty sometimes drifting through the windows of the car. We drove in silence.

Then George said abruptly: "I call this the Fifth World. Where they live in filth and squalor. To live in squalor is to be squalid. It is to give up hope and self-respect. It is something less than human. The Third World is poor, but it is made potent with aspiration. The Fifth World is where people no longer care. In their hearts – I am sure – they don't want our religion or our culture."

I asked him why he thought that.

"Because they are crushed. The grind of poverty. They have no identity. They are God's stepchildren. Nobody has been willing to look them in the eye as equal human beings. They are rejected by white society. They are even rejected by themselves."

I pointed to a group of children who had rushed out of thorn trees to look at the car. "There's joy there," I suggested, "and potential."

"Yes," George replied: "but generation after generation it gets crushed out of them."

"Is that where your school fits it?"

"Yes," he said again; "to give them pride. Where there is no pride there is no self-worth, and without self-worth there can be no joy. The Fifth World is humanity with neither aspiration nor faith."

AT ST MARY'S in the evening, George and Russell discussed the sprinkler system which kept the garden soft. Cypress and other trees loomed dark in the grey air; and the earth smelled cool and of moisture. Russell had made this or that adjustment to the system, to which George responded in his emphatic way: "Well done. Excellent."

We went into the church. The interior was a richness of icons, some of them sacred, others profoundly human. One of the first churches north of the Vaal, George said quietly, standing beside me in the aisle. I caught a sense of the church having passed through time: the rigour of the diggings was not excluded here; and then the church had fallen into Boer hands during the Anglo-Boer War; and its members had died in both world wars. All this and more had been written in the stones, so that the church itself was a monument to life, the walls and the pews with their small brass plates redolent of humanity. It suddenly occurred to me that this is what George had meant when he had referred to the magic of my old school; and I saw that this same magic, the magic of tradition, was what he sought to nurture in the unyielding dust of Longlands. I watched him walking up the aisle now, at Russell's request, and I knew it to be his innermost belief that without a tradition tied to place and the passage of time the human psyche falters and finally falls backwards

into the Fifth World pit. Was George's God a part of his sense of
tradition or was tradition George's God? Strangely then, in the richness of the church, it hardly seemed to matter.

"Russell wants to test the buzzer," George said from the front.
"He's rigged this up to buzz outside, so the church bell in the garden
can be rung at the right time during communion. An ingenious chap."
He pushed at an unseen button a few times.

Russell came back into the church. "It's working," he said, smiling
in his diffident way.

"Excellent," said George.

We went together to what must have been the old rectory, now
the parish offices, although a small alcove still contained a single bed.
George stood beside an old-fashioned refrigerator. "I like to have a
little watering hole in every corner of my parish," he said, offering
us a drink. A large map of South Africa had been fixed to a wall of
the room in which we sipped our whiskies. My eye was drawn to
the northern curve of the Limpopo, seeming an infinite distance away
now, standing as I was in Barkly West with my old teacher, and then
sliding down the browns and yellows and greens of the changing
topography to Agulhas, all the way down to the southernmost sea.

"Why South Africa?" George said, also looking at the map. "Why
did my father choose this out of all the colonial possibilities?"

I told him that my father had also chosen it.

"Ours is not to reason why, eh?" he responded, taking a healthy
mouthful of his whisky.

When Russell had gone, George asked me to excuse him for a
moment. He needed to make a few telephone calls. I went outside
and stood in darkness, looking at the shapes of trees where they
blotted out the stars. The Fifth World: a place without icons where
the void of consciousness contained only pain, unremitting pain,
soothed momentarily by the pursuance of altered states perhaps, yet
aggravated by the drunkenness of despair. But could humanity turn
in upon itself completely? Would it not always reach up from mud
and dust to the star of God to assuage the pain and fill the vacuum?
Now George was saying that the star of God resided in the constel-
lation of human-wrought tradition. Reaching up to the star of humankind to be drawn from the pain of being alone? In reality I heard
him say to someone on the telephone: "Come to the church and find
peace. Wait for me here." Come to the place where God and human
tradition merge. Find peace in this specific place. Find a sense of
permanence in all the shifting impermanence and change of life.

They would discover my name on a plastic-protected page when they finally demolished the KHS library. Impermanence and permanence: the two poles of George's equilibrium. Perhaps I had sensed them even as a boy. No wonder he became my secret mentor, bringing to me a sense of the potency and contradictions of human life and will.

When we got back to his home in Kimberley where I had left my car, George's wife was already in bed. I lingered for a moment – indeed, we had a nightcap together – but I could see that he was tired after the day. He walked me to the door. I thanked him for his company, and he smiled. "It's nice to have seen you again after all this time," he said, grasping my hand. "God bless you," he added simply. I looked into his wise and confident eyes, and then I turned without making a reply, but with a sudden gratefulness for George, both in my youth and now.

13

HOPING FOR FLOWERS

A NEW road, this time to Hopetown and beyond, brought with it a new preoccupation. It emerged like a cloud above the flat horizon, and it had at its centre an ancient theme: how to respond to the threat of demise. To fight was one thing. Doing so for God and nation against the forces of evil, like the harsh-voiced Colonel in Lichtenburg, did possess a certain logic: the sons of the frontier republics standing firm on their bloodied earth. But to return, more or less, to where the trekkers' wagons had begun? This was the response I faced now, and it seemed slightly unreal and delusive, like the huge cumulus formations which billowed with promise halfway across the sky on some afternoons, but brought no rain.

Hardly 40 kilometres south of Kimberley, the twin villages of Ritchie and Modder River brought signs of habitation momentarily to the roadside. Somewhere here, according to a map I had bought, a new international border post would need to be erected. One would leave South Africa and enter an autonomous country. To judge by the map, this new country would look like a deepish bite, taken from the west, into the southern African apple. The tentative boundaries included the southern third of Namibia which, of course, had once been South Africa's fifth province with seats in the central Parliament. Even assuming that these ambitions had now been abandoned, the new state would nevertheless command a continuous coastline from the mouth of the Orange River to Saldanha Bay, and would extend inland to more or less where I was driving now. Around 350 000 square kilometres, or slightly less than one third of South Africa's current surface area. This, it was hoped, would be the white Afrikaners' Volkstaat, their very own promised land which they would share with no one. Perhaps it would be called Orania.

The idea had found its rationale in separate development thinking. In spite of the euphemisms, the black homelands had been created to clear the rest of the country of an unwanted black presence. For a time this had seemed to provide a solution, leaving the rest of South Africa as the Volkstaat. But by the mid-1980s, the apparatus designed to keep black people in their homelands – at least those surplus to labour requirements – had collapsed, and black people streamed in their millions to the major cities. For the Afrikaner purists, this was far from satisfactory; and one segment of the purists began to use the separate development euphemisms to plead their own cause. The Afrikaners, this segment said, were the only people not to have been given their own homeland where they could govern themselves and pursue their own culture and traditions. Events in the 1990s – the unbanning of the ANC, the dismantling of apartheid and talk of the re-incorporation of the homelands, and the realisation that South Africa would soon be governed by a black-majority government – lent a certain pathos to their pleas. Partition was essential, they said. How otherwise could the Afrikaners survive in a country where they would comprise considerably less than 10 per cent of the population? A homeland they must have. Give us Orania, they said. Move into Orania to strengthen our claim, they urged their own people; do everything possible to keep alive the flame of true Akrikanerdom. Otherwise face the tragedy of cultural extinction.

It was a relatively empty tract of country which they had chosen. When the great migrations of Iron Age people from Central Africa occurred in the first centuries after Christ, they had filled up the Transvaal and the eastern seaboard of South Africa, but had never seriously penetrated what was now being claimed as the Volkstaat. The reason was simply that for the most part the country was an aridness of semi-desert. When the Europeans began their slow expansion from the Cape Peninsula, they encountered only the Stone Age Khoisan. It was to be over a century and about 800 kilometres later that the first clashes with black tribes began on the eastern frontier. But the eastern frontier was not included in Orania. Orania had been the hinterland more than the frontier, and the wandering Dutch farmers had been free to roam the semi-desert of the Great

Karoo with their flocks of sheep and goats. Indeed, they had disappeared into it for over a century.

Perhaps these considerations could form the basis for some historical claim to the country. But it seemed more likely that the borders had been sketched primarily to avoid all contact with concentrations of black people and with any of South Africa's major cities, which in any case, from an Afrikaner purist's point of view, were now irretrievably blackened by the process of urbanisation. A hinterland still, then, this which they claimed: a country of vast empty spaces and isolated country towns. Like Hopetown, spread out before me on the desolate earth. Or like Graaff-Reinet, which I would visit as I travelled further south, a town made famous as one of the main starting points of the Great Trek. There could be found in this a sense of the Afrikaner coming back to his own, even perhaps a glimpse of a subconscious yearning to return in Orania to the agricultural idyll of his pre-industrialised past. Orania, the hinterland, yet carrying on its northern and eastern edges South Africa's greatest river.

I crossed this river, the Orange, to reach Hopetown. Not much of a spectacle: muddy water flowing sluggishly between low banks occasionally marked with greener trees. Not much of a town: scattered shops attracting groups of black and coloured customers along a wide main street which ended in a grassy circle upon which a few small monuments had been erected.

One of them commemorated the members of the Hopetown community during the first 100 years: 1854 to 1954. When the wandering Dutch farmers, the Boers, had wandered even to the banks of the Orange and a loose community of them had settled there, they finally sought a focal point at which to build a church and village where a trading store might provide them with the few essentials they could not produce themselves. Humble beginnings for a humble town, sunk into itself and in repose even on that bright and windy Saturday morning. It is true that in the late 1860s the first diamonds, including the Star of Africa, were found around Hopetown, but the town soon settled back into oblivion. The neat suburban houses stared blankly out at me from around the grassy circle.

Another monument, a simple tapering monolith pointing upwards from a brick plinth, stood in remembrance of the "inestimable value" of the Dutch Bible: 1652 to 1933. From the first permanent settlement of Europeans on the southern tip of Africa, in other words, to the year when an Afrikaans translation had become available. For nearly three centuries it had served them in their isolation and then in the turmoil of their defeat and subsequent impoverishment. Yet it was in the isolation of the 18th and early 19th centuries that their deepest sensibilities had been shaped: they were Calvinist in outlook; they were under God's protection in a harsh land; they had God's mark upon them; they were His elect. An easy step from there to being the chosen people honoured by a special covenant with God, an essential part of which was that they would not be denied their promised land. If they had ultimately failed to find this land by exodus, then they would do so by returning to their semi-desert source. The myths of a people in travail once more: oppressed by fears of extinction, haunted by the failure of their myths to sustain them. Seeking new ones now, as calamity loomed, to give their lives meaning and their collective future some hope.

A sudden disturbance in the main street: the screams of women and a donkey cart lurching to one side outside a supermarket; the grappling men in a space inside a sudden crowd, raw faces grimacing as they fought; then others leaping in to separate them; the crowd jabbering; women in curlers, black and brown and yellow faces staring in, sleeves against noses, flapping shirts, the sly eyes of youth sliding across my own; then everyone melting away at the sight of a police van which had turned a block or two away.

People walked on the pavements and the verges of the roads carrying plastic bags from the supermarket. They all walked in the same direction. I followed them to their township some distance from the white village which, it seemed to me, was nevertheless dependent on their custom. But the black and coloured shoppers lived out here on the flat veld, a few pepper trees, branches blowing out like pennants in the wind. Unpaved streets lined with rows of identical structures, small box houses built of concrete blocks and slanting asbestos sheets, one row of them painted mustard, another terracotta, still another a dirty olive green. Dust and rocks in the street, people streaming back from town with their groceries, unkempt children carrying water containers. And the small gardens untidy, although sometimes an attempt had been made, a few deciduous fruit trees now losing their leaves, the occasional patch of brown grass. But above all the sense was of litter and poverty. Another Longlands. A drunk man with a pocket of oranges over his shoulder. A crumbling church, the plaster of which had been patched and repatched. Washing blowing in the wind. Thin dogs with tails habitually between their legs. Young women walking with men on bicycles riding hopefully in tow. Other men drinking in the yard of what looked like a shebeen, watching as I passed but declining to return my greeting. Attached to the houses sometimes were lean-tos and shanties, all lived in, everything thick with life and the struggle to survive. And the wind lifted shoals of litter into the air and sent plastic and paper flying across open spaces and sometimes high into the air like kites. And then the township ended in a welter of shacks and wrecked cars lying in various states of decay, a tawny-skinned woman suckling her baby among them.

This juxtaposition of town and township was not unique to Hopetown. It existed everywhere. For every town in the proposed white homeland, as indeed for every town in the country, there existed at least one township for people who were not white, places for people who worked in town, or clung to the hope of work. Yet ironically it was the people of the townships, impoverished and entrapped as they might be, who very often maintained the economic viability of the towns themselves.

But would these people, I asked myself as I watched children scrambling in the mud at a communal tap, be wanted in a pure white homeland? For any value in themselves they certainly would not: these blacks and half-breeds. For the rands and cents in their ragged pockets? Probably not for that either. I thought of the enormity of the cost of creating the black homelands, the forced removals, the anger and humiliation, the consequences of which would haunt the country for decades to come. What plans, delivered by fearful ethnic urges, for social engineering here?

THE NAME Orania had not been plucked out of the air. To the south-east of Hopetown a settlement of that name had existed for several decades. Originally established as a construction village for people working on the irrigation canals emanating from the big Orange River dams upstream, Orania had stood more or less vacant once the canals were complete. Then the whole place had been bought by an organisation called the Afrikaner Freedom Foundation and was now being developed as a prototype of a Volkstaat town. As a young white man whom I had picked up on the windy road from Hopetown put it: "It's only for whites. It's the Boerestaat. No blacks here."

I turned off the tar and drove in through open gates and past a notice which pointed out that Orania was now private property. Did the young man live in the town? "No," he said; "I'm visiting friends. Yes, they are getting on well here. I'm helping them to paint the house."

My first sense of Orania was of emptiness and neglect; concrete streets with weeds growing between the slabs; prefabricated houses set in dusty yards; a few mature trees, but otherwise an encroachment of weeds. The young man directed me to a house with sheets pinned across the windows. He clambered out and I drove on alone, heading in the direction of the river. I had read in a pamphlet that Orania was developing a leisure and holiday resort, but I took a wrong turning somewhere and found myself in a farmyard of sorts, a few cows standing to one side. "You're wanting to come out at the caravan park," a man standing next to a bakkie said in Afrikaans. I looked for something in his eyes, but found only a guarded politeness as he redirected me.

The resort – an ablution block and one or two bungalows under thick trees – had been built at a place where the bank of the river was steep and inaccessible, access to the water being barred by a high fence. On the sloping ground of the resort, grass had been planted and a few fireplaces built. But the place was empty save for a car with a Kimberley registration, doors open and a radio playing. A white couple lay together on the grass close by. But they sat up when I got out of my own car, seeming uncomfortable and on their guard. The wind blew quite violently in the trees, and a slight sound of lapping water could be heard sometimes from the river, brown and hurried at the bottom of the steep bank. The bungalows were locked and empty.

All at once, the whole thing seemed absurd. The emptiness, the wind, the inaccessibility of the river; and the Kimberley couple, 160 kilometres from home, slightly outraged or frightened by my presence it seemed, as if I might be a detective hired by a suspicious spouse. I drove back to the concrete streets of the town.

All-weather tennis courts with no players. No one in sight in the windy streets. The surface of the courts had crumbled in patches; weeds twined up in the fences between; and the net in one of the courts had collapsed and lay in a tangle of rotting neglect. High above me I noticed that the long vapour trail of an unseen aircraft had split the sky, as if it was a sign. Not far from the courts, two concrete foundation slabs and a rusted lorry without wheels had long ago been given to the rankness of weeds.

A sign on a building on top of a low outcrop said: Grotto Restaurant. I drove towards it, going over a concrete furrow, quite dry, and with "1968" stamped out on the side of the bridge, and then up

a curving concrete roadway to the summit of the outcrop. A community hall of sorts with the entrance to the restaurant on the side
which overlooked the town. But here, at the entrance to the hall,
little sign of life. Off the concrete driveway, a braai area overlooked
a sweep of country to the north, but the brick-built fireplace had
broken down, and a metal apparatus for roasting whole sheep on a
spit was also broken, and recent beer cans and a few wine bottles
had been thrown about.

I looked out across the country, all the way down to the low and
stony hills which marked the river's course. Stone Age people had
lived in those hills all along the river for thousands of years. Here
it would have been the San, the small-framed Bushmen as they had
been called, but they were easily driven away by the slow expansion
of the Dutch farmers, or as easily assimilated into subservience and
servitude. The San's time had passed; yet already there was a feeling
of dereliction about the time with which their's had been replaced.
The vapour trail still hung in the air, a sign from another reality,
another world.

Broken glass littered the wide front steps of the community hall.
I peered through the doors and saw bales of straw in the foyer, a few
gem squashes arranged on one of them. The remains of a harvest
thanksgiving, I thought, a religious service or perhaps a party, with
wine glasses and overturned bottles surrounding a solitary pumpkin.

On the other side of the building, the Grotto Restaurant was in
ruin. The sign had once been lit, no doubt to beckon construction
workers and their wives, but now a tangle of wiring hung down
against the wall. Broken windows. The door without a handle, its
plywood cracked and delaminating. And in front of the door a profusion of bent nails rusting against the concrete, and some rotting
pieces of timber to one side, and little piles of bricks. The wind blew
with an uncaring force, but the vapour trail still split the sky.

While the tangled wires from the sign scratched against the wall
behind me, I looked down at the desolate town. There were the tennis
courts, and close by a clubhouse, the remains of a garden, an empty
swimming pool and a single battered cone of thatch giving shade to
a table built around the central support. The town seemed utterly
deserted, not even a single vehicle moving on the concrete of the
streets, but then I saw two figures in the dusty yard of what looked
like a church. A plain enough building, also prefabricated, but with
something of a tower.

Two young men, I discovered when I had driven down: one in his early thirties with an enormous stomach, the other much younger. I talked to them over the fence of the church yard in which, I now noticed, grass had been planted and water sprinklers installed.

"Ja," the man with the stomach said cheerfully; "things are slowly getting done here."

The younger one told me that his father had recently died, that his mother was already dead, and that he had no family. His father had been a farmer in the Eastern Cape and the young man was now waiting for a lawyer to settle his father's debts and to see what would be left over for him.

"But I like it here. We do our own work," he said, his somewhat foolish face crowned with a shock of black hair which invaded his forehead. "We don't need the kaffirs here," he added with a smile.

The older man explained that as a punishment for not attending church the previous Sunday, he was working at the church on this windy Saturday afternoon. He said they were renovating the building. Here, and over there, some of the boards were lifting, and the timber beneath them had been eaten by termites.

"We'll replace these bad bits, and then we'll repaint," he said; "ag, I don't mind the kaffirs too much. I'm from the Transvaal. I'm just helping here. I'm helping people to rebuild. What we do with the houses is we leave the prefab frame and build brick on the outside. Like that one over there."

He pointed to a face-brick bungalow a little way down the street. "Not everyone can afford that though. Some of the people are poor, man. But the houses are cheap. And even cheaper in the old swartgebied. Ja, that's over there. It's like another town, but it's all part of Orania. But now we must go on," he said, turning to the church. "This is going to be a big work."

The younger one said with a grin: "I'm sure we will be on pension before this city is complete."

I drove towards the swartgebied, an Afrikaans word meaning black area, and used to describe those townships which invariably clung to the edges of the country towns. Orania had been no exception and, like so many other towns, its township had been tucked away behind a ridge, out of sight of the main settlement. The roadways were unpaved. I went in among the small houses, originally designed for black and coloured construction workers, but now with white people living in them. I saw the faces sometimes. In the yards: the rubble; the piles of wood for burning in the stoves; the broken cars;

a young woman with immense hips, her child sitting in the sand outside her tiny prefab.

Poor whites. Like the landless farmers streaming to the cities in the first decades of the century; like the men who had built the Vaalharts Irrigation Scheme, like the families who had settled on the first small farms there. Again now: Afrikaners caught in the jaws of rapid social change and economic recession, coming to Orania in preference to the church-administered soup kitchens in the cities, espousing the concept of a white homeland as a way out of their urban misery. Perhaps espousing it with relish and enthusiasm. White independence in the dirt roads and the poor-white faces and broken windows of the uninhabited prefabs and the dilapidated fences and the disorder and litter of this desolate and wind-torn world. And then an almost absurd incongruity: the sight of a boy of perhaps 12 years old driving a shining BMW slowly along a rock-strewn roadway, waving quite sedately to me as I passed.

I returned to the church to establish the time of the service in the morning, then I headed south-east once more, following the river upstream. The country had taken on the quality of the Great Karoo: the plain stretched away as flat as it had been since Mmabatho and Mafikeng, but now studded with abrupt hills. And around the river the country was broken, the hills and ridges high, the muddy water winding through; and then I had a sight, from a distance of 30 kilometres, of the towering wall of a dam curving from one steep hillside to another.

The P K le Roux dam, one of two huge structures built on the river in the 1970s and combining to form the heart of the Orange River Project. The other dam was the Hendrik Verwoerd, 130 kilo-metres still further upstream. Together, the two dams were capable of storing nearly 9 000 million cubic metres of water.

Driving up into the hills surrounding the Le Roux dam, I could see the irrigation canals dark with water, and I saw fields of maize alongside them grown to full height, pale golden fields stretching away between the harsh rock koppies. The wall had been built to a height of over a hundred metres and curving into the water that it trapped. Up in the hills I found a village called Vanderkloof, and in the village a hotel. In the early evening, I sat high up on the terrace of the hotel, looking down at the dam, the water shining against the wall and stretching back. The wind had calmed and the sky went red with the setting of the sun, and the water reflected such radiance. And I suddenly saw the simplicity and yet the sadness of the idea:

this dream of a white piece of Africa, of an Africa without Africans or half-breeds. Only the purity of the Volkstaat, here, at the old river, source of their survival in the arid semi-desert which they were claiming as their home.

I had read in one of their booklets that the Orange River Project, which they had been careful to include in their boundaries, was like a young bride ready to give herself to a nation in need, and in so doing to provide that nation with life and with a future. More mother than young bride perhaps, this ancient river. But the steel and concrete thrown across its course: this was the underpinning which rendered viable the dream of a white homeland.

As the man behind the hotel bar put it when I asked him what he thought of Orania: "Good luck to them," he said in an amiable tone; "they're hoping to make the desert flower, so I say good luck to them."

I WENT to church in Orania in the morning. A bright hot day; and I stood to one side watching as the congregation assembled. I saw small groups walking on the concrete roads towards the church. Others arrived by car. They stood outside the entrance to the prefabricated building for a few moments, colourful in their Sunday clothes, some of the women in hats, men holding Bibles, groomed children restrained, and in carry-cots a few babies who had perhaps been born in Orania.

A man came forward to greet me. He said his name was Van Rensburg. I explained that I was passing through. "You are most welcome here," he said, shaking my hand warmly. He had a distinguished look: well dressed, greying hair and his grey-blue eyes showed strong and steady. I asked what denomination the church was. "The denominations rotate," he replied; "we all worship together here. But, come, we must go in. I am preaching today."

The interior of the hall was unadorned, not even a white-clothed table with a cross upon it as in the improvised church at the school in Longlands. Only a plain wooden lectern, upon which Mr Van Rensburg placed his Bible and papers; and the rows of plastic chairs; and at the back a woman with an electronic keyboard which she plugged in and played, providing a tremulous direction for the singing of the hymns. I stood, for the first one, without a hymnbook. Seeing this, Mr Van Rensburg asked a child in the front row to offer me hers. She approached me with a shy and lovely smile.

Both Bible readings were taken from the Book of Revelation. The first concerned the struggle between the dragon and the woman who gave birth to a man child. The dragon wanted to devour it, but the child was caught up to God's throne. So the dragon, which was the devil, turned his anger against the woman who fled to the wilderness where God had prepared a place; but even so the dragon persecuted her. The second reading concerned the two beasts, the first rising from the sea, the second from the earth. They both worshipped and personified the dragon. They had great followings and great powers, given by the dragon, and they were used by the dragon as his agents of persecution. The reading ended with this insight regarding the beast out of the earth: let him that has understanding count the number of the beast, for it is the number of a man, and his number is 666.

More singing now, a plaintive spectrum of voices pulled on by reedy notes from the electric keyboard, while in the aisle an oblivious child applied wax crayon quite vigorously to a new page of his colouring-in book.

Easy to tell that Mr Van Rensburg was not a professional preacher. Unschooled in the dramatic pause or the value of variations in tone and volume, he delivered his sermon in a straightforward voice, partly reading it from his papers on the lectern. Yet he showed no nervousness or hesitation; indeed, he struck me as a figure of poise and some authority in his community.

He said that we were standing on the threshold of a new and terrible world. It was a world characterised by a steep rise in the antichristian powers, and by a profound struggle between Christian and anti-christian. For the devil was no longer content to allow the struggle between him and God to be played out only in the hearts of men and women. The devil had now created the Antichrist and the false prophets, and these forces would use their power to unite the world against us, the believers. The Antichrist would also control the world economy, and the masses would be swept up in ecstasy by the false prophets who appeared on radio and television, and in magazines and newspapers. We were already living in the terrible new world, the world of the Antichrist and the false prophets. There were black messiahs for the masses. And all these Bantu messiahs and all their massed followers wished to sweep God's true children aside. But, Mr Van Rensburg said, the good news was that God is still in overall control.

The congregation sat in pliant and patient attitudes: good news or bad, all was somehow sanctified, and placed apart, by the simplicity of their worship: church was church and had to be attended. The small boy had fallen asleep, sprawled across his wax crayons; and an elderly woman in earrings and a gold chain at her throat, sat with her eyes closed, although from time to time she opened them, perhaps to make sure that Mr Van Rensburg had not completed his sermon without her knowledge.

But the sermon continued for a few moments still. Standing before them in his neat suit, Mr Van Rensberg said that God would use His power and His love to protect us, the true believers. As He had done for the mother of the man child, God had prepared a place for us in the wilderness. But until it had been secured, this place in the wilderness, we must not be swept up by the lure of the Antichrist or the dazzle of the false prophets. We must stand firm. There were even more difficult times ahead than those which had passed. Therefore we should strengthen our faith in the true God. Ahead lay suffering and struggle. But, if we kept our faith against all the odds, God would not allow His true children to falter or break. We would not be overcome by the bearer of the three sixes, Mr van Rensburg declared in his calm and straightforward voice; and then he spoke for some time about the wonderful perfection of the sevens and how they tended to fall, in the Book of Revelation, into several series of three. But the sixes, he concluded; they were the mark of evil, and in the end would bring nothing but collapse and calamity.

Outside in the sunlight, as the congregation began to disperse, I told Mr Van Rensburg that I was interested in learning more about Orania and the ideas behind it. He smiled at me in his warm and distinguished way. "This will be a pleasure. Come to my home. You have a car? Follow me when I leave."

WE SAT in his garden and talked. His house had been provided with a face-brick shell in the manner which the fat man in the church yard had described to me the previous day. Mature trees stood in the garden. No doubt they had been planted by the construction workers a quarter of a century ago, and beneath them new grass was taking root. Dappled shade on face brick, then, the scent of moisture and the sight of pomegranates hanging in the trees next door as we sat at an outdoor table, drinking coffee. I remarked on the peacefulness of the garden, and Mr Van Rensburg smiled. "Yes, and we've done it all ourselves."

People had started moving into Orania just over a year before my visit, he told me. "When we got here there was nothing. The buildings were derelict. The grass and weeds were this high. At the moment there are three hundred and sixty people in Orania. Eighty children in our school. Now people are coming here with their businesses. It is all going much better than we had ever hoped."

A dentist now practised in Orania, as did a doctor. The community was raising money to establish a small hospital to be installed in a building which would be perfect for that purpose. A town board and 12 town officials saw to the day-to-day running of the town. Everything, even refuse removal and the operation of the sewerage system, was performed by whites. The only time black or coloured people entered Orania, he told me, was when they came from Kimberley to deliver and install various pieces of equipment, like stoves and refrigerators and air-conditioning.

I asked him to explain the notion of the Volkstaat as a whole. Were the boundaries on my map accurate?

"They are suggestions only," he said; "we are careful not to say that we alone have decided on the boundaries. To have moved here – and people are moving in all over the Volkstaat – we have made sacrifices. We have left behind many of our monuments and our cultural places. But we have come because we believe this is a reasonable way to give us the right to govern ourselves. Many Afrikaners are saying: we will fight. But I ask these people: for what? You can't shoot them all. We don't want to fight, and we say that this Volkstaat here is a viable alternative to fighting."

"How many people live in this proposed Volkstaat?"

"There are already over two hundred thousand whites."

"And other races?"

He looked at me with his steady, steel-coloured eyes. "One of the advantages of the proposed area is that fewer people would need to be moved here than anywhere else in South Africa."

But did he have actual numbers?

He nodded: "According to the last census, one hundred and twenty thousand blacks and half a million coloureds."

I listened to a group of small birds chirping busily in one of the trees in his peaceful garden. His earlier words came back to me: you can't shoot them all. The air was hot, and it wafted up the pleasing smell of green and water. I said: "Aren't the coloureds often referred to as brown Afrikaners? There is the common language."

"Yes," he said. He pursed his lips. "Yes," he said again, and there was a faint hint of plaintiveness in his voice for a moment; "But we want our own place. The truth is that the races don't mix. Look at Los Angeles: just the other day the race riots, the burning and looting and fifty dead in two days. Much worse is still to come in South Africa."

"How will you get the people, those who are not white, to move away?"

"The Volkstaat will not be a welfare state. We will not pay out pensions. And there will be no jobs for them."

"Then surely you will have a profound social problem on your hands right from the beginning."

"Look," he said; "There were five hundred coloureds living here when we bought the town. We told them we wanted to do our own work. They left peacefully. They have now all gone."

As I looked at this man, distinguished, relaxed in his own garden, I thought momentarily of the tawny-skinned woman suckling her baby among overturned cars. But this man before me was firm in his convictions, calm in his ability to see the greater good. We too have suffered – I could imagine him saying it – we too are making our sacrifices for the sake of peace. "Of course, Orania, the name, was chosen by the Department of Water Affairs for their construction town. But we like it. Perhaps later it will be the name for the whole country. South Africa divided into Orania and Azania," he said with a quiet laugh.

But wasn't all the talk these days about a unitary South Africa, I asked, with even the independent homelands re-incorporated?

"That's exactly the problem," he replied; "if those powers that are negotiating this new so-called unity say no to us, we will say to them: then you will never have peace. The races can't mix peacefully. Where has it ever happened? Certainly not in Los Angeles. Certainly not in Western Europe with their Arabs and North Africans."

We spoke for a while about conditions in Orania Town. Generally people were working well together, but there had been one or two expulsions. "A few people have not been interested in the Volkstaat. They come because they're poor and unemployed, and because there's work here. Then they drink too much and cause trouble.

"We don't lock our cars or garages here," he went on. "A little while ago, we held a dance in the town hall to raise money for our hospital. When we came out, one of the cars was missing. We found it later at Orange River Station not far from Hopetown. It had been stolen by one of our own workers. He's in jail now. He won't be coming back.

"I know people say there is a ban on alcohol here. But that's not true. What is true is that we have no bottle store. We buy in from Hopetown. But we frown on abuse. Yes, of course there was alcohol at our fund-raising dance."

Mr Van Rensburg told me that the whites-only principle was not based on racism. "A nation must do its own dirty work," he said. I remarked that this was a dramatic shift from the traditional Afrikaner attitude. He agreed, but he said it was a shift that must be made. He quoted modern Israel's first prime minister, David Ben-Gurion, as saying that a nation which did not do its own dirty work was a nation in the process of committing suicide.

I spoke to him about the Orange River Project, and he said, yes, it would definitely be the "growth point" of the Afrikaner nation. We looked at his booklets. In one of them it said that all great civilisations had developed beside rivers: the Tigris, the Euphrates, the Nile, and also the Rhine, the Seine and the Thames. Modern Israel had thrived from the waters of the Jordan and the sea of Galilee. Now it was the turn of the Orange. After 5 000 million litres had been used for industrial and household use in future towns and cities, there would remain sufficient to irrigate over a quarter of a million hectares of semi-desert. It had been the Khoisan people who had named this wilderness the Karoo, "the place of great dryness", but, Mr Van Rensburg's booklets claimed, given a little water the Karoo opened like a flower garden.

If all this was so, I said, why had the irrigation potential of the two great dams not been realised long ago? Mr Van Rensburg had a ready answer: "Because the government's attention has been diverted to other things. Like liberalising the country, and in so doing giving it away."

As I prepared to go, I asked him about the sermon he had preached. He had spoken about the black or Bantu messiahs who, in leading the black masses, wished to sweep God's true children aside. Was the inference that these messiahs were manifestations of the Antichrist?

Mr Van Rensburg shook his head. "I was not inferring that. But the black masses are expecting freedom; they are looking to an earthly leader who will bring them to their political freedom. That is their expectation, not the coming of Christ."

Yet a sense of being swept away by the black masses persisted. In spite of his firm handshake and the steel-coloured confidence of his smile as we said goodbye, I felt him to be a man caught up in the problem of how to live in these latter days, and in his sense of Africans like a swarm of locusts upon the land. I felt him also to be a man caught up in a sort of theological loneliness, almost an entrapment.

When the largest Afrikaner church had already admitted that attempts to justify apartheid were nothing less than heresy, had indeed rejected apartheid outright, and seemed to be sailing foursquare into the storms of a racially undifferentiated South Africa, what was there left for many Afrikaners but a profound crisis of belief? Somehow they must recreate themselves and their relationship to God. They must build new myths in which to find a context for their faith. And they must pull these new myths about them, almost like blankets, to bring at least a little warmth to their struggle for survival, and a little salve to the pain of lives stretched for significance, and beset once more by the pit of material impoverishment and the Fifth World on one side, and by the perfidious morass of liberalism on the other.

I drove down towards the Hendrik Verwoerd Dam, and as I did so I thought about the myths. For more than three quarters of a century the Afrikaners believed that their forefathers had, like the children of Israel, trekked away from bondage in search of their promised land. And they had found it. But now, as the 20th Century ebbed away, and as the loss of their Canaan loomed, some Afrikaner eyes turned backward to the wilderness from whence they came. The wilderness of semi-desert was potent with myth. Like the present-day Israelis now, they had come home to do their own dirty work, as Ben-Gurion urged, and to fill the desert with productive flowers. They had their Jordan. They were yet like God's chosen people, his true children.

Once embarked upon this fertile stream the pace could only quicken. Perhaps they were in actuality God's chosen people. Perhaps they were Israel itself. The ten lost tribes struggling for their purity against the tainted seed of Cain and the powers of the Antichrist. They were Israel in their southern wilderness beyond the rivers of Cush, where God had placed them after delivering them from the Assyrian captivity, and to whom He would return, appearing in a golden sunrise upon the banks of the Orange perhaps, to lead them through His millennial glory, and then at last to take His bruised but steadfast children home.

Were these the delusions of a psyche not long ago clutched with the arrogance of absolute power? Was this a glimpse into the darkness of a people essentially misfitted into Africa, struggling now for their own earth, even for this barren piece?

THE PLEASURE resort at the Hendrik Verwoerd Dam: prefabricated bungalows with rust-red conical roofs; paved streets; a golf course with fairways which zigzagged back to the beginning; bright blue swimming pool; tennis courts upon which black guests played a rumbustious game. And beyond the green and sprinkled lawns, a gathering of yachts at anchor in a natural cove; no boats upon the wider waters that I could see. The level of the dam was low, yet the water stretched away for many kilometres into the distance, the shore presenting a rugged succession of bays and promontories, and in the middle of the slightly ruffled surface a large brown koppie rearing out. The scene quite silent, except for the rapid ticking of the sprinklers, the sound of ball against racket, the occasional voice. The dam wall was an immense grey structure, curving for nearly a kilometre across the valley; and forests of pylons on the stony hills beyond, marching out from the hydro-electric generators below the wall, the wires between them describing perfect arcs and sometimes blazing in the sun.

I went through a doorway and down some stairs into the darkness of the wall. My guide, a big man named Danie, was strapping on a miner's light. He gave me some statistics: the biggest dam in the country; 360 square kilometres of water surface when the dam is full; the wall 914 metres long; 88 metres off the river bed, 27 metres wide at the top where the roadway curved across, 64 metres wide at the base; nearly two million cubic metres of concrete; 11 kilometres of tunnels inside the wall, and 360 steps to the bottom. We began to descend.

Danie showed me many things. Here was a high hall which contained the pneumatic apparatus to control the flood gates, the huge steel arms of the gates reaching nearly to the ceiling. "If you open these to more than one thousand cubic metres a second," he said, pointing to a gauge, "you could cause a bit of a flood downstream." On a lower level: the gates themselves, closed, water seeping from one of the seals. Danie told me the dam had taken five years to build, the construction teams working 24-hour shifts seven days a week. And here were huge motors and generators which could provide the dam with operating power in the event of a failure of the general electricity supply. Down deeper now into the bowels of the wall, the

air heavy in a perpetual twilight. The river outlets: five-metre dia-
meter steel pipes barging through above our heads. Danie showed
me the rubber seals. "Expansion joints," he explained. "When the
dam is full, the wall leans downstream to the tune of six millimetres.
Without the joints the pipes would burst." All along the passageways
in which we walked, he pointed out the instruments installed to
measure the movement of the wall, plumb-lines passing through a
system of calibrated sights from which fine readings could be taken.
Then it was down by ladders, Danie's light fluttering on raw concrete,
right down to the rocks of the river bed. The air felt cool. Apart
from black water lying in pools in the rocks sometimes, the rocks
themselves and the concrete appeared quite dry. "We are now standing forty-seven metres below the water level of the dam," he said
pleasantly; "and ten metres below the surface of the downstream
pool." I said: "It must be quite terrifying in the wall when there's a
flood." Danie shook his head. "It's the safest place to be. There's
another thirty metres of steel and concrete in the foundations below
us here." I asked whether it was noisy during a flood. "Oh, yes, you
can hear the water going through the wall. I was here in the 1988
flood. The place comes alive."

I was standing inside the beating heart of the Orania dream then,
but it seemed a futile place to be. I felt a sudden uneasiness, as if the
wall would crush me. I wanted icons, the solace of tradition, not this
slithering coercion of another myth. I remembered voices.

The voice of the engineer from whom I had gained permission to
come into the wall. "Very effective as flood control, but agriculturally
the whole idea has been a bit of a flop. The problem with putting
water on the Karoo is that there is a very rapid build-up of salts, and
the minerals are quickly leached away. This has been the experience.
Water isn't all you need to make the Karoo blossom," he had said
with a smile; "it's semi-desert. It's designed as semi-desert. And it'll
probably remain that way."

But the Israelis managed, I argued. "Yes, but it's a matter of size
and efficiency," someone said: "you could fit Israel into Orania at
least fifteen times, yet Israeli production is many times higher even
than projected figures for maximum irrigation from the Orange."

"Israel's water-use efficiency stands at around 95 per cent," a hy-
drologist told me. "South Africa's is not much more than 70 per
cent. To use water for irrigation in a dry climate, especially flood or
overhead-spray irrigation, is a very inefficient use of water. Evaporation is extremely high, and this aids the development of salinity.

The Israelis use a finely controlled drip-irrigation method, obviously expensive but possible over relatively small areas. The Karoo? A quarter of a million hectares of scientifically irrigated semi-desert? Probably impossible. The Karoo is sheep country, and should remain as such."

These rumblings in the dark intestines of the wall. A sudden sense of pain and sadness. I wanted to come up for air. We climbed the ladders and the steps, turning on innumerable landings, then climbing again. Illusions and false beliefs, false hopes; illusions crushed; and even the hope of flowers largely forlorn. Then I stepped out once more into the searing brilliance of the day.

14

NOMADS

THE GREAT Karoo provided me, above all, with a feeling of vast
yet strangely finite space. It carried not much of the endlessness of
the great reaches of the Northern Cape, that sense of a world with
no edges and no form. In the Karoo, the huge landscapes seemed
stamped with the idea of passage. Perhaps this was so because in
primeval times the place had been a lake; but more likely the abrupt
hills which characterised each vista brought to me the idea of specific
but invisible routes. The hills – the Karoo koppies – were steep-
sided, free-standing, filled with bush and boulders, and topped with
hard dolerite crowns as flat sometimes as if they had been drawn
with a ruler. These hills served as route markers, the great spaces so
defined, and the combination of space and hills insinuating an unmistakable imperative for movement. Here are routes: we must move
along them so that in the end we are delivered to other places. Places
beyond. The Karoo is like this: a visual manifestation of an endlessly
repeated longing for what lay beyond.

But on the surface, a melancholy and silence, the immutability of
landscape, the vaulted sky. Yes, and the windmills and the gatherings
of sheep; and the autumn colours of the planted trees, those near the
homesteads, the rusts and yellows, and those along the dry water-
courses with their grey rocks and drifts of sand.

Driving through these northern fringes of the Great Karoo on the
way to Colesberg, I came across a group of people who appeared to

213

be squatting by the roadside. Certainly some low hovels, no more than table height, had been erected. A few two-wheel carts were drawn onto the verges, and onto the banks of a nearby river, and donkeys grazed on what tufts of scrub they could find. The people were yellow-skinned and dressed in ragged clothes: they lay under the carts; a few fished in the pools of water which the river contained; others sat by the roadside, watching as I passed. Those faces which I saw seemed compact, some of them wizened. Then I crossed the river by a concrete bridge and drove once more into open country, with only the koppies and the occasional homestead by which to chart my progress across this empty space.

Colesberg, an old town, dating from the early 1830s, had been built among a rash of stony hills. The largest of them, Coleskop or Tooverberg, showing symmetrical and flat-topped from all sides, had been an important marker for early European travellers. The Colesberg hills themselves were littered with Stone Age artifacts. A good-looking man named Mike, an academic from Pretoria who was doing some research around the town, told me this. Evidence of San settlements everywhere, he said, many of them dating back to before Christ. But above that now, the quiet streets of a country town, the flat fronts of typical Karoo houses which lined them. I remembered Paul Kruger's house on the farm Boekenhoutfontein in the Western Transvaal. Plenty of prototypes here: the plainness of central door with shuttered windows on either side, the roofs hidden behind facades sometimes rather starkly decorated with horizontal mouldings along the top. The gardens at the back of some of the houses lapped against and merged into the rocks and succulents abounding on the steep hillsides.

The wooden floor of my hotel room creaked when I moved across it. From the open window I could see the lights of the traffic on the main road, and I heard the roar and blast of big trucks as they by-passed the town. It was the Great North Road again, the first time since Naboomspruit. Over a thousand kilometres, even by this most direct road, from Beit Bridge now; and Colesberg lay in repose and enfolded within its darkened hills.

THE FOLLOWING morning, out of some curiosity, I returned the way I had come, to the bridge where those ragged people had been squatting, but I found the site deserted. No hovels, no carts or donkeys, no people. Nothing, except the cold ash of a few scattered fires.

"Yes," Mike said with a smile; "the karretjie-mense. The gypsies of the Great Karoo."

The karretjie-mense: the people of the little carts. Those two-wheel carts I had seen, small boxes built up over old motor vehicle axles, pneumatic tyres, two donkeys harnessed to the shaft, the driver and his companions sitting on a seat behind, the cart carrying everything they owned; and also, often tucked between the base of the cart and the axle, the tin and timber out of which they would erect their tiny dwellings when the need arose.

"They're all over the Karoo," Mike told me. "They earn their living by shearing sheep, or any out-of-season odd jobs on the farms. But shearing is their speciality. They call themselves sker-bestuurders, shearing managers. They are in competition these days with organised teams of black shearers, but the teams are more expensive, and they're untidy shearers, frequently nicking the sheep with their electric clippers. The karretjie-mense use hand clippers; they're slower, doing only about twenty-five sheep each a day; but most farmers would agree they are the best shearers."

We sat talking in the front room of his Colesberg lodgings, an old cottage with thick walls and a ceiling made from reeds like slim bamboo. Books on gypsies lay open on the coffee table, and in one corner of the room an untidy heap of clothes he had collected for distribution among the karretjie-mense.

Mike told me something about the various social strata among the coloureds in that part of the Karoo. At the top of the heap stood the Cape coloured, more refined than the others, invariably displaying the Malay strain of the manumitted slave. Beneath them came the so-called Colesberg coloureds, with a distinct Khoikhoi ancestry. And at the bottom of the heap were the karretjie-mense.

"I'd like to think they are the direct descendants of the hunter-gatherer San people of the Karoo," he said. "It's enthralling to watch them fishing in the same river – where you first saw them – as their ancestors probably fished two and a half thousand years ago. That's the sort of carbon-dating results researchers have been getting here."

Although no longer youthful, Mike had a firmly-made and rugged face – a strong nose, clear eyes, lines of resolve about the mouth – and his hair had been cut into a slightly shaggy style. A mature film-actor look, I thought, but he possessed a candour and also an honesty as an academic which blended well.

"That's what I think could possibly be established, at any rate," he told me.

The evidence was in three forms. Archaeologically, the area was rich in San sites, rock paintings and stone tools from the late Stone

Age period. The written evidence was of thousands of San having occupied the Colesberg region; of so-called Bushmen hunts in which hundreds were killed by white farmers, the children being taken onto the farms as labour. He had also talked to old farming people whose grandparents had made the distinction between wild and tame Bushmen. The tame ones seemed to be the offspring of the captured children. Domesticated hunter-gatherers, but with their nomadic instincts not yet eradicated.

"This all fits into a feasible background for the karretjie-mense. They live on the farms when they're shearing or digging furrows or whatever, then they go back on the road. Permanence of abode seems impossible for them. They're afraid of giving up their independence. They don't want the responsibility that goes with home ownership, and in any case couldn't afford it.

"They live extremely hard lives. They frequently camp for months under their own carts. Very few have proper identity documents; they speak only a form of Afrikaans; they're illiterate, which they admit by saying that they wear stone spectacles; they have no religion in the Western sense; there is no formal marriage, or very rarely; and their children often go naked for the first few years, in spite of the extremes of heat and cold here.

"And yet," he said, and his quiet enthusiasm had invaded his eyes, "they're wonderful people. An incredible sense of humour, a great appetite for gossip. They maintain a positive perspective on life even under the most pressing hardship, and they seem to accept as inevitable their position at the bottom of the social heap. It has taken me a long time to get them to call me anything but Baas. Now they call me by a name.

"Their own names are interesting. No family or surnames. Just a single, often quite fanciful, label. I know an Arnoster and a Januarie, a Steenbok and a Geduld, a Sors and a Springbok."

I asked if he could discover any remnants of what was known about the old San religious system: a ritual which appeared to have been centred upon dancing and trance and healing, and often the capture and preservation of images encountered in the altered state of trance.

He shook his head. "The closest thing to the trance dance these days is their weekend wine and dagga bouts. They drink and smoke themselves insensible."

Yet they had not been untouched by the world around them, and their perceptions were changing. A farmer's wife had started a school for karretjie-mense children whom she fetched in a bakkie for a week at a time. The children were made to wash their hands, and then they spent the rest of their first day at school looking at and showing each other their clean hands. But with education had come a certain friction between the generations: the younger people were now expressing some criticism of the habitual drunkenness and lack of personal hygiene of parents who never bathed, but would occasionally go into the river. Aspirations were also changing. On their first day at school, the children had been asked what they wanted to become when they were adults. A typical reply for a girl was: kitchen maid. A few months later, however, the same girl had said she would like to be a nurse. Over a similar period, a young boy's horizon had expanded from digging ditches to driving a truck.

I accompanied Mike and a small group of interested people to a Stone Age site on the river where I had first seen the Karoo gypsies camped. We drove over rough fields on the back of a farmer's truck. Then we climbed a low hill towards the rock at the summit. Mike kept pointing out sharp pieces of flint-like stone, and even a few crude stone implements, which were scattered everywhere on the hillside. "This looks like a factory site," he said, "where they would actually have made quantities of tools and arrow-heads. Their reject rate was probably very high."

I walked for a moment beside an elderly English-speaking woman who told me she had not long ago retired to Colesberg and was enjoying every minute of it. I asked her what gave the Karoo its special quality. "The people," she said immediately; "also the light, the landscape, the clarity of the air. But especially the people. So friendly, so down-to-earth." A few moments later, as if to illustrate their practicality, I heard her tell the story of the young Afrikaner woman who had come to town specifically to look for a husband. She had worked at the local museum for a while, causing male visiting figures to rocket. (People laughed pleasantly as they climbed.) Her first boyfriend had been extremely handsome, but in the end had proved unsuitable. There 'had been a divorce in his family, and he also liked to drink with the boys occasionally. "But her new fella seems perfect," the elderly woman said; "He's reasonable to look at. He's wealthy. And he doesn't drink. Mind you, she's a really delectable catch: from a wealthy family herself, and very, very attractive."

At the summit of the hill we came to a shallow cave, more a sheltered place beneath an overhang of rock; and on the walls, the faded art. Interested faces crowded round, and the questions came steadily at Mike. Professor, why has it faded so fast? Professor, how many people would have lived in a shelter like this? How long ago? One old farmer was interested in everything, his intelligent face alert beneath the cloth cap he wore. Professor, he said, what are these marks cut into the rock? Perhaps a calendar or a tally? The marks were vertical lines enclosed in a rough rectangle, a few circles and stars. Mike spoke about the trance dance, and the patterns which everyone could see on the insides of their own eyelids when hot or feverish or in an altered state. "They're called phosphenes," he said, "and we think that this is what the San were trying to recreate when they made their geometric engravings. Yes, almost certainly, they had a religious significance."

A young woman who lived on the farm we were visiting and who had acted as our guide, now led the way to another cave, smaller and deeper, which she had recently discovered. "The honeymoon suite," someone suggested. The laughter and the voices drifted on the clear air of the hill. Again there were geometric patterns cut into the rock. Mike was explaining the nomadic lifestyle of the San, staying in one place for a spell, then moving on, perhaps returning later, but always moving on.

The farmer in the cloth cap said to me: "There is only time to think when one is old. That's the sadness. But I am semi-retired now, and I am thinking. I am also reading poetry. It is very beautiful, I think."

He was a man with an erect back and with the air of being fit and active still. He looked at me with his lively eyes. "I am an Afrikaner," he said, "but I am reading the English poets. It has made me think of the age of everything. Then I come into my own veld, like now, and I think of how all this sediment was laid down. Millions of years. Then how it was all eroded away, except for the koppies. Millions of years. And how the little Bushmanne lived here before us. Everything so slow. It is a story still being written. What is our impatience compared with such a story?

"This age of Africa and all the impatience on it," he said, then added with a sudden urgency, as if the memory had inevitably encroached upon his line of thought: "I saw on television a shocking thing. Children, like animals, rushing on the bags of food. Tearing them with their hands. Somalia, I think. Mass starvation. Man, there are terrible times coming in Africa."

I looked down at the river and at the shape of the land in clear sunlight. This vista of harsh earth lying silent under an enormity of sky. These terrible times. All at once I remembered Sidney again, Sidney in the back of the car as we drove over the Soutpansberg. Living in the terrible times of another decline. Resources used up. Perhaps we were standing on the edge of cataclysm. Yet the smaller dramas could not stop unfolding. It was a mark of the complexity of the human adventure now, this simultaneous unfolding of independent dramas which would sometimes interlock and sometimes collide. These smaller dramas: like the karretjie-mense schoolboy whose ambition had expanded. While I walked on the stony hillside with the Afrikaner farmer who was reading the English poets and thinking about time and catastrophe, I thought of that schoolboy: a compact yellow child with dreams of blasting up and down the Great North Road, a nomad still.

TO EXPERIENCE the Karoo is to draw close to a fundamental human contradiction. Those twin longings for rootedness and liberation seem implicit in the sweeping landscapes themselves: the sense of silent space into which the homesteads have become embedded; and at the same time that awareness of invisible pathways, each view as it unfolds rich with the promise of escape. The peace and the insatiable restlessness which these studded plains evoke is like a deep religious urge. You are drawn to think of elemental things, the problem of consciousness and pain, the problem of what could assuage the sense of void; and you feel that a deity could be very close.

The small towns seemed to float upon the surface of this ancient lake, a mundanity of supermarkets and churches. I was driving slowly down to Nieu Bethesda, a small Karoo village in which a lonely woman had left what I thought might be a monument to this close and omnipresent deity. Meanwhile, the tiny towns. Noupoort, with its blackened railway yards and a bleakness in its streets. Middelburg, heaps of rubbish burning on the eastern edges of the town and the unrelenting ping and bark of electronic games in the cafe where I ate some lunch.

Outside Middelburg, an agricultural research station: large woolly sheep in pens, the smell of dust as they ran past, the oily feeling of their coats when it was parted to show the fineness of the crinkled fibres. The pleasant young researchers talked about genetics and cross breeding and food supplements, about the five million Merinos and three million black-faced Dorpers and more than a million Angoras which grazed on the plains of the Great Karoo where the drought had already killed up to 30 per cent of the scanty vegetation. Then, by contrast, one of the young researchers had confided to me that he had found a girl in Middelburg and had married her three months ago. I remarked that the South African writer, Olive Schreiner, had also married in Middelburg. The young man smiled shyly.

These were the realities, the harshness of drought and the sudden glimpse of human happiness, which floated on the surface of a lake whose bed is sedimentation kilometres thick and filled with fossils. Ancient creatures underfoot; and a persisting sense of deity above.

I remembered, as I travelled further, a scene from Schreiner's most famous book. A young boy named Waldo is tending sheep on the far side of a Karoo koppie. He builds a small alter upon which he places his lunch. He then prays to the deity he believes to be close to send down fire to consume his sacrifice. He is longing for a sign. He bows himself to pray three times through the fierce heat of the afternoon, but no fire comes. Only the fat from the lamb chop has melted in the sun. Waldo finally turns with bitterness in his youthful heart and a feeling of profound rejection. The sense of deity is false, he feels; probably there is no God.

In the late afternoon, I found myself driving into an area of some old upheaval. The koppies joined forces to become ranges of high hills, the ragged cliffs of their crowns enlivened by the setting sun. The surface of the plain undulated in slow waves now, and the mountains were bleak yet voluptuous mounds, treeless, with a brownness of ground-cover and stones spread evenly over their massive slopes. Sheep stood in yellow sunlight, casting long shadows, and all the black faces pointed in the same direction as if the flock itself was engaged in a slow migration, following its own invisible route. And the surprise of homesteads tucked into the hills, the autumn-turning trees as small outcrops of exotic life in this brown-filled wilderness of space and time. And the grey of dusk. And a plantation of already leafless poplars, quite stark in a narrow valley. And then a deep green gathering of cypress trees, a white farmhouse, terracotta roof, out-buildings, a glimpse of Cape Dutch gable; and then the endless rising and falling of the land went on towards the night.

I was thinking of Schreiner and her character Waldo again. Schreiner had written of him, and Lyndall his accomplice in doubt, while working in the 1870s as a governess on a farm on the south-eastern fringes of the Karoo. "That most miserable of all the stony holes on the face of the earth", she had called the farm, and yet the Karoo had lured her all her life, giving her a "sense of perfect freedom and wild exhilaration"; and she was finally put to rest in a sarcophagus built on a lonely hilltop there.

Waldo and Lyndall, burning with a hunger for life, had struggled against the isolation of their African farm. They had grown up together under a torrent of ignorance and oppression, but they had their stars. Their manifold griefs are counterpoised with Waldo's dreams and Lyndall's iron will. They read insatiably from a box of books in an attic. Waldo meets a stranger with an allegory concerning the elusive nature of truth. But above all, they doubt. They are, like their creator, embryonic 19th Century freethinkers embedded in the Karoo. They struggle towards the pathways which will take them physically beyond the bondage of its boundaries. As young people, they both leave. But in the end Waldo is drawn back and he returns unwittingly to grief. Lyndall, he learns, has never fully recovered from the birth and almost immediate death of an illegitimate child, and now she herself is dead. He turns from this news in great pain. He dreams of her, first as a child and then as a young woman whom he had always loved. He awakes in anguish, and he is tormented by the stars, their brilliance and immensity, and the knowledge that Lyndall is nowhere, not even in all the shining space of the Karoo night. He cries for solace from the old deity then, but again there is no reply. He finally finds peace in the continuum of life itself: the fragility and impermanence of the individual embraced within this broader flow.

Wonderful to ponder these things under the great sweep and silvered dust of a star-crammed sky. I sat on an upturned box outside a cabin in the middle of the Karoo nowhere. I sat in an astonishing clarity of cool darkness, looking into dusty light. The sweep of life itself as deity, close and omnipresent, even closer in these restless places with their simultaneous sense of home and transit. I was alone in the place of the nomads. There were ancient dragons sleeping underneath my feet, their bones of stone; and the sky above me was a vault of jumbled crowns.

NIEU BETHESDA lay at the opening out of a narrow valley which began as a cliff-sided gorge cut between high hills. The view from the top was of a dry river and ploughed fields in a narrow strip along its farther bank. The road descended steeply, and crossed the river via a concrete causeway. In the valley, the morning sunshine had not yet reached the bases of the westward-facing hills, but it had reached the poplars which stood half naked and in brilliant yellows against the darkened slopes beyond. I drove through an avenue of trees, leaves spinning down and lying in drifts upon the dappled tarmac of the road. The sunlight slanted through, deepening the warmth and colour of the autumn time. And then the village began.

A grey and white church, venerable and modestly tall; dusty streets in a grid; a few scattered shops, all the buildings showing a dusty white behind dusty hedges sometimes; brass bars gleaming in the dim interior of the post office; coloured people walking in the streets, and one or two parked cars.

I saw outside a general dealer's store a small cart with pneumatic tyres, the harnessed donkeys drooping and motionless. A ragged couple sat on the seat, the woman's doek coming low down on her yellow forehead, the man's wizened cheeks hollowed as he sucked a small brown-paper cigarette held between thumb and index finger. I passed close to where they sat. For a second, the eyes of the man engaged my own. His eyes were little more than slits in the wrinkled face, yet I saw a dancing brightness there. His fingernails were chipped and black with dirt. A breeze snatched away a wisp of exhaled smoke; and I suddenly wondered what was in that head of his with its tight peppercorn hair and quizzical forehead. Not even an echo of the old times of the dancing by the fire? The women clapping and singing in joy and warm good humour, the men in trance sometimes, going through earth and air to God, and sitting small and humbled in the centre of their altered state, then slowly returning to the skin of their bodies once more to make their mysterious marks upon the rocks, those emblems of deity and the great beyond.

I walked in the quiet streets of Nieu Bethesda until I came to more emblems: the cage of cement-made owls on the front veranda of Helen Martins' house. The owls stare out with big glass eyes; one has its wings unfurled, but more in a gesture of protection than menace. After her death, the house became a museum. The interior is a shrine of glass and light: lamps and candles everywhere, mirrors in various shapes, and all the walls and ceilings painstakingly clad in crushed glass of many colours. But it is in the back garden that Martins' most gripping emblems reside. The first impression is of a great surge forward: camels and pilgrims on their way to the east. It is a garden crammed with hundreds of sculptures and dense with jumbled meanings.

Martins was born, in the closing years of the 19th Century, in the Nieu Bethesda house she was later to transform. She trained as a teacher in Graaff-Reinet, 50 kilometres to the south. After a failed marriage to a Karoo farmer, she taught English and did a few other jobs before returning to Nieu Bethesda in the early 1930s to care first for her ailing mother and then her cantankerous father. She tried marriage again, this time to a furniture restorer, but it lasted no longer than a few months. When her father finally died in 1945, Martins, now approaching 50, was at last free to pursue her own life. She began with a few structural alterations to the house, and a few tentative sculptures made to her specifications by various odd-job men. She became increasingly reclusive and increasingly obsessed with her creative activities. An eccentric, people called her. She worked as if time was against her, spending most of her small pension on materials. She engaged the services of a talented coloured man named Koos Malgas, and the full flowering of her vision began. Towards the end, however, arthritis and encroaching blindness sent her into deep depression. During the winter of 1976 she ended her own life by drinking caustic soda. She was 78 years old.

I stood among the camels and the pilgrims caught as they were in the act of surging forward. On every side and in every corner were other images: a replica of the village church, temples built of glass bottles, archways, murals, a dozen Mona Lisas, graceful women beckoning to ponds, figures which danced, which sat, which lay, a proliferation of animals and birds, and sun and moon and stars cut out of tin swaying on their wire supports, and from every perch an owl looked down. A chaos of life from a lonely mind; a feast for the interpreters.

But my mind had swung back to Olive Schreiner, to the grief of Waldo which had found solace only in some broader sense of life. The collective life of bird and beast and human kind, but for Schreiner especially humanity and its capacity to dream. "Age succeeds age, and dream succeeds dream," she wrote, and it was this endless succession which formed the fundamental deity and the rationale for individual life. "Without dreams and phantoms man cannot exist." The trance dance we must have. That was the thought, here, among the manifestation of Helen Martins' sense of dream and phantom.

A sudden gust of wind rattled the tin stars. I looked up into the face of her gifted assistant, Koos Malgas, who stood before me in blue overalls and knitted cap. His face showed age, but it was compact and interested in my presence. He told me he had worked happily with Miss Helen, but that she was strange, never going to church and refusing even to listen to the radio.

"Perhaps this was her church," I said in Afrikaans.

"Yes," Koos Malgas replied, looking thoughtfully around him; "I suppose it was."

I asked him if he had understood all the things he had made for her. He nodded casually enough. He pointed to some small camels seated outside the model of a church, the whole scene strewn with crushed glass. "A Christmas card," he said. "The glass is the snow. The camels were always from the cards."

We stood silent for a moment, the wind raising slight dust among the host of sculptures.

Then Koos Malgas said: "She wanted to keep a camel, but I said this wasn't a camel's place and that it would get sick here. She loved the camels. And she loved the owls. She kept some owls once, but they died. Then she made me make this statue over here."

He indicated a creature with the legs and body of a camel surmounted by an owl's head and wings. "So she could have both together in one animal," Koos Malgas explained. The figure of a naked woman stood on the creature's back, her hands raised as if to shield her eyes from bright light. "She put that on later," he said; "yes, I think it is herself."

He showed me another collection of figures all facing to the west. "They worship the sun when it goes down, to say thank you for the day that has just passed." Then he wandered off among the dreams he had helped to render stable in cement.

I stayed in the garden for a long time, in the wind, the stars clattering and swaying, the dust sifting between the throng. The treeless hills ringed the quiet town like walls. The garden was alive. The camels surged forward, urgent upon their pathway. The owls stared down, wise and peaceful in their rootedness. The Karoo wind blew. And I saw Helen Martins herself, this restless nomad of the spirit. She stood upon her phantom dreams, hands raised in supplication as she moved towards the source of the enduring constant of collective life.

15

FULL CIRCLE

NOT FAR beyond the northern edge of Graaff-Reinet stands a solid-looking monument to the Voortrekkers, more especially to those of them who left on their northern adventures from this isolated town. I stopped to look at it on a hot and blowing afternoon. Above a base of blocks of rough-hewn stone, a wagon wheel is represented in relief against a mass of shaped concrete which itself serves as a plinth out of which rises the top half of a man, looking steadfastly to the north and holding the barrel of his muzzle-loader upright against his chest. The monument spoke of stolid conviction and a deadly seriousness of purpose as the wind buffetted its flat sides. It spoke, also, in a tone of vague threat. But perhaps this quality was less in the sunlit paleness of the imposing edifice itself, and more in the inscription: black metal lettering mounted slightly proud of the stone. Afrikaans words which talked about a wheel rolling over our world, a wheel that for you and for me is unstoppable.

I lingered in the shade which the monument cast. A few pepper trees had been planted about it, their berries bright red and their foliage swept back like knotted hair in the wind. Nothing of the town could be seen. It lay lower down, behind the shoulder of a hill. But closer at hand I could see the top of rugby posts which I knew belonged to the ungrassed playing field of a school in Graaff-Reinet's black township. But the thought of unstoppable wheels rolling forward stayed with me; the sense of a process which could not be tampered with. And yet, at least in some hearts, the wheels were returning to the wilderness of Orania now. The wagons were coming home. But what home was this, this proud monument and town, with barefoot black boys scoring points beneath the soaring posts? I felt myself to be in a contradictory place. The wind moaned in the telephone wires at the side of the road; and I saw long unravelled lengths of magnetic tape, tangled in thorn bushes and flashing along the ground when the stiff branches swayed. But no music in this dry and windy place: only a vague odour sometimes, as of something dead, spiking the turbulent air.

Graaff-Reinet was established in 1786, and, as most people with whom I spoke pointed out, is the fourth oldest town in South Africa after Cape Town, Stellenbosch and Swellendam. It's early years were characterized by frequent quarrelling, lawlessness and insurrection. Now, however, the streets seemed peaceful enough, filled with old buildings, shady trees and a slightly preoccupied consciousness of the dignity of its age. An aura of self-adoration perhaps, or at least self-absorption. I read rich words in a publicity brochure: "Graaff-Reinet – Gem of the Karoo – Oasis in the Desert – Jewel of the Karoo – our beloved town is known by many names . . ." It lay in a horseshoe of the Sunday's River, surrounded by harsh and majestic hills.

It reminded me in some ways of a well-preserved old lady in silver spectacles and jewels: the curve and swirl of Cape Dutch gables behind the autumn leaves; the old lamp standards and cobbled courtyards; the revamped slave quarters, complete with green brass bell, and the dark green louvred shutters; and horse-drawn carriages, drivers in top hats, to complete the picture. The gentility of it all. Whole streets of national monuments, the plaques worn on the white facades like brooches. A hotel housed in a building which was first designed in 1804: chandeliers inside and the gleam of antique furniture. A Gothic-looking church, the tower and spire of which dominated the orderly skyline of the town. And museums and famous houses where the attendants, for the most part middle-aged white women, asked if you preferred to be spoken to in English or Afrikaans and then informed you, in the appropriate language and with a nonchalant discretion, of the entrance fee.

Yet still that odour of fetidness, perhaps of death, assailed my nostrils from time to time. It wafted through my hotel window, long after the wind had died away; and the water in the taps was hard with lime.

"Many Graaff-Reinet gardens have been destroyed by the drought," a man attached to the town's publicity association told me; "and some of our oldest trees are in danger. Mind you, all through its long history the town has had water problems. Allocations; rationing in times of drought; even widespread water theft, neighbours stealing from each other; and all sorts of schemes."

The scheme which interested me now was the dam which had been built across the Sundays River in the 1920s. Its water had always been shared between the town and an agricultural irrigation scheme further downstream, but the constant wrangling between these parties had become irrelevant. The dam was empty. The water in the town's taps now came from municipal-owned boreholes.

"Waterborne sewerage was introduced twenty years ago," the publicity man said; "this increased consumption. The population has also grown; and now we've got the drought. Did you know Graaff-Reinet is one of the few towns left in South Africa which still has open water furrows. But they've been empty for over a year now. People have sunk private boreholes, and this has hammered the water table. Our lovely trees will die if we don't get rain soon."

It seemed an irony: this elegant and well-preserved old lady in secret suffering from dehydration. What use the jewels and brooches now? What use the efforts to attract more tourists to taste the brackish water and to see the expiring trees? What use the self-adoring smiles and the gentility, when all the time the mind was feverish with thirst? And this exacerbating factor: population growth, particularly among the coloureds. The mind slips back to nightmare and Eugene Marais.

"An absolutely delightful town. A joy to live in. Except . . ." A woman with elaborate spectacles speaking to me at the entrance to a famous house. "Except for the water. Our dam, my dear, as dry as a bone. Boreholes. But you know what boreholes are like." She made a strange intermittent sucking noise with her mouth to indicate the unreliability of such a supply. "A few last spurts, and then nothing. So that's the problem here. Water. They wanted to bring water all the way down from the Hendrik Verwoerd Dam on the Orange. But the cost! All those hills to tunnel through, you see. So we live with borehole water, and with the smell."

I said I was interested in hearing more about the Graaff-Reinet smell.

She laughed, her eyes twinkling with mirth. "It's quite simple, my dear. As the level in the dam went down, the fish got trapped. They took a lot of them elsewhere. Then they gave the remainder to the non-whites. The non-whites did a brisk trade, selling them to other non-whites. But there were a lot of fish still left. Thousands of barbel flapping in the mud for days, and then they died. When I first smelt it, I blamed the dogs. Then I made people check their shoes before they came into the house. I checked my own. But whatever I did, I couldn't get rid of it. Then I heard other people complaining, and we put two and three together and came up with dead fish. It's a terrible smell. When the wind is right, it's an absolute stench," she said, savouring the English word.

More than an irony: the well-preserved old lady ostentatiously displaying her gems while trying to hide from the world at large her thirst and her bad odour. Something furtive here beneath the haughty grace and fine respectability: a sense of shame perhaps. I thought of this as I stood on a high vantage point and gazed down at the town in its most lavish setting of majestic hills and the endless plains of the Karoo beyond.

I had driven out to see the dam. It proved to be as people said: nothing more than cracked mud spreading out in a flat expanse. The wall had been built at the head of a narrow valley where the banks of the river were high and rocky. Someone had told me that more than 60 per cent of the dam's capacity had been choked with silt. Easy enough to see this, with the level of the dry mud at least ten metres higher than the river bed on the downstream side of the wall. On the far side of the mud expanse, among pepper trees and half hidden by a low rise, I could just make out the distant shape of the monument to the unstoppable wheel. It struck me suddenly as being part of the town's ostentation, yet like everything else caught in the stench of rotting fish. But eventually the fish would turn to dust rather than into fossils like the monsters beneath them.

I remembered a visit I had made to one of Graaff-Reinet's museums. The attendant told me about the metamorphosed remains of animals which had lived in the Karoo lakes more than 250 million years ago. She urged me quite severely to look at these things. I did so, and found among the exhibits a representation of a beast called Pareiasaur, a bulky and grotesque animal with a barrel-shaped body up to three metres long, thick legs, and a huge lumpy head. During the middle Permian Period, the Pareiasaurs had roamed about this part of the Karoo while the great lakes receded and the sediment settled. They had finally died out in the Triassic Period which followed. All this I read on neatly printed cards. I read, too, that quite often these strange beasts, which weighed up to a ton, had been fossilized standing upright. They would sink slowly into the mud while munching their favourite marshland greenery. They would in this way, standing upright, disappear into oblivion. I recalled the top half of the man as if emerging from the Voortrekker Monument. Perhaps, rather, he was sinking into it. It was a brutal thought, yet it rendered the idea of an unstoppable wheel at once trite and tragic. Too self-absorbed to ward off ruin.

Not far beyond the dam, I turned off onto a concrete track which took me steeply to a vantage point high in the hills to the west of Graaff-Reinet. The town had grown beyond the confines of the Sundays' horseshoe, yet the original grid of streets remained, still lush with trees, and the pale grey church was clearly visible. So too were the black and coloured townships which stood a little distance from the eastern edges of the town. I looked for rugby posts, but my view was too distant to see such detail. The townships were built around the base of a hill called Lokasiekop, dense housing in a largely treeless belt of sloping ground.

Somewhere in there, I knew, was the birthplace of Robert Sobukwe, father of the Pan-Africanist Congress. Somewhere in there, too, his grave. When the funeral procession had begun, the feet of thousands raising dust in the steep streets of the oldest township, dark green shutters had been pulled across the windows of Graaff-Reinet. A furtiveness in those closed houses with their brooches on. And the memory of this perhaps adding to the sense of shame.

AN ELDERLY man named Roly Kingwell showed me newspaper cuttings. We sat in a high-ceilinged room of his house not far from the centre of town. The house had struck me as seeming too small for all the furniture it contained, as if he had recently moved there from another place. Almost immediately after I had introduced myself, he produced the cuttings. One of the articles had been written by Roly himself for the Graaff-Reinet Advertiser.

Newspapers and television, the article said, had highlighted the sensational side of the funeral of Robert Sobukwe on 11 March 1978, but had given little attention to the dignified behaviour of those on the dais or the real and sincere tributes by numbers of speakers. The unfortunate political incident which lasted for about 30 minutes, when a prominent homeland leader and other politicians (considered to be working within the state's system of separate development) were insulted and endangered by young people in the crowd, did not tell the whole story. The real story was about the tributes themselves:

Sobukwe had integrity and a love for people both black and white . . .
never a word of bitterness . . . this great son of Africa . . . a man who
believed, in spite of what happened to him, that he was created in
the image of the living God . . .

Another article quoted Roly, who was one of the approximately
5 000 people to attend the funeral service at the Graaff-Reinet
showgrounds, as saying that the vast majority had come to pay tribute
to a man who had suffered for his convictions.

"We were living on the farm then," Roly said to me; "but we
drove in for the funeral. Because I believed him to be a fine man.
He was a Christian man: his political message was not of hatred and
intolerance. People were advised not to take their cars to the
showgrounds. We didn't hear this and drove directly there. But nothing happened to our car."

Roly smiled slightly as he recalled these things. A man in his middle
eighties, he had told me when I first arrived; he had some difficulty
with his hearing, leaning towards me when I spoke, but his mind
and eyes were alert.

"The whole town was locked up," he said, still with the slight
smile playing about his lips. "I wrote the article to show white people
that the funeral wasn't just another example of Africans making
trouble."

Roly had known many Africans involved in politics. "One man
spent nine years on Robben Island. But there was no case. There had
been some miscarriage of justice. But the man had never expressed
any bitterness," Roly said; "he was a real Christian."

I remarked that Sobukwe had also spent some years on Robben
Island.

"That's right," Roly responded; "First, he spent three years in
prison, then six years on the Island, then he was banned and kept
under house arrest in Kimberley until he died."

I said that he, Roly, was well-informed. Again the slight smile. I
asked him how he had become involved in African affairs. He regarded me for a moment, his eyes unblinking. Then he replied with
a candour and simplicity which immediately gained my respect.

"When I was on the farm, still as a youngish man, I had a change
of heart. I suddenly saw that they were human beings. Then I wanted
to rise above my own prejudice and reaction. I wanted to respond
instead of just reacting. I started making contact with black welfare
societies, and I met a lot of people."

After retiring and moving into town, he said, he had become involved with African child welfare in the townships. "We have a very nice crèche which I would like to show you." When I expressed interest, he walked purposefully from the room, his tread still firm, and returned with a peaked cap pulled squarely onto his head.

We drove through shaded streets and then straight into the oldest township. Within a kilometre we had entered this different world: small houses the colour of dust, sometimes crumbling in disrepair; smoke snatched from chimneys by the breeze; thorn bushes standing on bare earth; people walking on rutted roads and winding pathways as they ascended the hillside; and the unresponding eyes of men and women resting sometimes on my own.

The crèche, for the children of working mothers, had found a home in an old church hall. Sixty-five small children sitting on the floor and eating lunch – baked beans and other vegetables – from an assortment of tin and plastic plates. A contented clatter of spoons; those open mouths receiving; the whites of eyes as small faces looked solemnly up at me, the stranger. Roly stood to one side with his slight smile. He introduced me to the women in charge. One of them took my hand in both her own, a gesture of warmth and unguarded generosity. Some of the children had risen, empty plates clutched in their hands. I engaged the attention of one small boy in neat clothes; he returned my greeting with the shy glimmer of a smile and an inaudible mouthing of one of his own.

Robert Sobukwe, here, in the old Graaff-Reinet township. Growing up in the 1920s and 1930s, reading books discarded by the town's library and by the white family for whom his mother worked as a domestic. Although he was an outstanding student, his schooling was interrupted by lack of funds, and then by a brush with tuberculosis, and he had already turned 23 when he finally entered university. Here, his political awareness rapidly developed. During his second year, he took as one of his subjects Native Administration which involved a detailed study of the laws and regulations by which black people in South Africa were systematically restricted. He examined in this way the bones and sinews of black oppression. Although he joined the ANC, his deepest political response was more sharply Africanist, and this finally led to the establishment under his leadership of the Pan-Africanist Congress in 1959. "We claim Africa for the Africans," he wrote at about this time; "the ANC claims South Africa for all." His idea of Black Consciousness was based on the belief that Africans must first think of themselves as people before they could demand to be treated as people. Only after this equality had been won could a just and non-racial democracy be achieved.

But how to break the stranglehold, both internal and external, of oppression? The PAC's first campaign was aimed at improving the status, and thereby the self-image, of Africans. The call, through stickers and other means, was for the courteous treatment of black people. The second campaign cut much closer to the core. It focused on one of the most humiliating oppressions in the daily lives of Africans: the so-called pass laws which required the carrying of identity documents at all times. Hundreds of thousands of black people were being convicted and imprisoned each year for offences under these laws. Numerous calls to abolish the system, which had been instituted in the first place to control the movement of black people, particularly in the cities, had been ignored. The PAC's plan was both simple and non-violent: Africans should leave their identity documents at home and deliberately court arrest, wave after wave of peaceful and disciplined offenders, until the prisons bulged and the factories fell silent.

On the day of the start of the campaign in March 1960, Sobukwe and other PAC leaders walked to the main Soweto police station and asked to be arrested. Sobukwe was 35 years old, and it was to be his last day of freedom. But the plan was working: all over the Witwatersrand and beyond, crowds were assembling outside police stations. And then in the early afternoon, at Sharpeville, the police opened fire. The crucial shift from passive protest to active confrontation was made, and South Africa's long and bloody transformation had begun.

Roly was talking to me. We stood in a steeply rising township street. His eyes were alert, thoughtful. He said: "We have to find common values with these people if we are to live successfully together. We need a common morality, a common code of conduct."

"Do you think Robert Sobukwe's values would be a good place to start?"

The slight smile played about his mouth. "Absolutely," he said; "non-violence; democracy; self-reliance; the value of life; the worth of the individual."

I looked up the street with its litter of stones and rubbish. Was it down this way that the procession had come, those thousands of feet, the coffin borne in its midst? Since early morning cars and buses had arrived, bringing thousands of mourners to the small township. Now the singing, the slogans, the salutes. Down into Graaff-Reinet on a

Saturday morning, the shops and shutters closed, only police and traffic officers standing their ground as the procession moved through. The crowd sang, "We shall kill the dogs", and the traffic officers stood silent. Some whites had ventured onto their verandas to watch. The crowd shouted abuse; a few mouths pursed and spat. In this way they bore their hero, or perhaps no more than a trigger for their rage, to the showgrounds.

A sense of desertion there now: the modest grandstand empty, a cricket pitch protected by metal fencing in the centre of the oval space, weeds growing up freely among the sparse and struggling grass of the outfield, and a lone black man levelling out a piece of broken ground with a shovel. Geraniums flowered in a row of brick-built tubs in front of the grandstand. But in 1978: the dust and the bellows of anger; the jeers and screamed insults from a section of the crowd. The homeland leader and the sell-outs must leave. White liberals, even personal friends of Sobukwe, were cursed. The homeland leader was kicked and shoved and spat upon as he tried to leave. Shots rang out. Silence now, but the knowledge of those moments seemed to pervade the restless air. I thought of Roly in the grandstand, this Karoo farmer who had undergone a change of heart, witnessing such rage and hatred. Perhaps he too had been reviled, perceived for that frenzied time not as an old man come to pay respect to one whose values he admired, but simply as the colour of oppressor. All the more remarkable that he should have written what he had, and so gently: the unfortunate incident was not the whole story; the tributes to a courageous man were also part of it. Yet was there doubt behind that slightly smiling mouth, those alert old eyes? Had all that screaming rage and hatred left him with a sense of chasm between his values and this appetite for vengeance now? I did not ask him. But I thought of unstoppable wheels as I turned instead in the direction of Robert Sobukwe's grave.

SURPRISING HOW many people in Graaff-Reinet did not know, or would not tell me, where the grave was to be found. The publicity man looked at me with veiled eyes. "I suppose it's in their cemetery," he said. But where was the cemetery? He produced some maps of the town, but no cemeteries were marked upon them. I drove out into the dusty townships and asked a group of young men outside a shop. They shrugged their shoulders. At breakfast in the hotel one morning, a cheerful man who sold and serviced office equipment from his base in Port Elizabeth asked me about my line of business.

I told him I was looking for Robert Sobukwe's grave. "Who the hell is Robert what's-his-name?" he asked. I explained briefly. "Oh, God," the man said, waving his fork in a dismissive way; "the PAC. A nasty lot. Anti-white, you know. The one-settler-one-bullet brigade."

Other voices were generally more helpful, although still vague about the final resting place of one of Graaff-Reinet's most able sons. "He had a degree in economics from London, I believe," said one. Another said: "There was a big march in 1990 as well, after their organisations were unbanned. They called it a peace march. We all drove up into the hills and watched. But it was after all quite peaceful and they did no damage." After closing an office window against the smell of rotting fish, a thoughtful voice said: "Yes, there have been some killings, some house burnings. People who are working in the racially separate local authorities are the victims. Amalgamation is what the blacks and coloureds want. But the white council has recently voted to retain the status quo. They are very conservative. But what can you expect?" And a practical voice, clipped and businesslike: "What we need more than anything here is industry. But industry we can't have. No water. The coloured population, especially, is increasing rapidly. People losing their jobs in the cities and coming home. High unemployment. Depressed living conditions. Major alcohol problems. Robert Sobukwe's grave? Personally, I've never seen it. But it's bound to be out there somewhere."

I drove out there into the townships once more, finding streets of newer houses, broken cars in yards, donkey carts, coloured women at a communal tap. The day was overcast and a wind swept over the low houses, raising some dust. Grey sky; a brownness of earth and dwellings and children hopping in a succession of circles and squares scratched in the sand. I stopped outside a church, the front doors of which stood open. Inside, a woman with a bucket said: "No, the Reverend is not here. He is probably still by the house." From the front steps of the church she directed me.

In this manner, in a neat house built on sloping ground in a township called Kroonvale, I met the Reverend Hafkie of the Congregational Church. A pale-skinned man, middle aged, wearing a terracotta suit and a striped tie. He regarded me with a sort of weary suspicion, yet in the end his dealings with me were polite, although in a fairly formal way.

"Sobukwe was a personal friend," he said. "Yes, I was at the funeral. My choir was the only one allowed to sing. Yes, I am willing to take you to the grave."

But for a few moments we talked in his study which was like a basement underneath the high front section of his house. Papers and books lay everywhere. A small computer, printer and photocopier stood to one side. He indicated that I should sit down. I asked who had made the decision to allow his choir to sing. Didn't I know, he replied, that the Pan-Africanist youth had controlled the whole funeral, even down to the order of service and who would speak?

He sat looking across an untidy desk at me. We spoke about the political awareness of people in the townships. The blacks were highly politicized, he said; the coloureds less so, but certainly more than they had been a decade previously. He told me that he himself had been detained for long periods, first in 1976/77 and then again ten years later. There was a weariness about his half-closed eyes, his minimal gestures, and I sensed some bitterness, but lying far back.

"Why were you detained?"

He half laughed, his expression holding a slight undertone of derision for a moment. "You'll need to ask the various governments of the day that question. I was detained without trial."

Then he stood up abruptly and said: "I think we must go to the grave. I have an appointment in less than an hour."

As we drove along unpaved streets, turning frequently and climbing to a sloping shoulder of the hillside, I directed his thoughts once more to the funeral. What, from his point of view, had been the white response?

He sat silent for a moment, his half-closed eyes gazing ahead through the windscreen. "They were fear-stricken," he said finally. "And not a word was spoken afterwards. No sympathy, no outrage. It had nothing to do with them: that was their attitude."

The burial ground was hardly recognisable; I might have driven past it had not Reverend Hafkie told me to stop. No cypress trees or wreaths. Simply an unfenced expanse of slightly sloping ground, a few thorn bushes, some dust swirling through. The ground was lumpy, and I had a sudden memory of the devastation of some of the river diggings close to Barkly West. But the digging here had been of different intent. We walked in silence between hundreds of mounds, some simply of earth, others clad with the brown stones of the veld. Many of the graves were unmarked; others had crooked wooden crosses, broken crosses, fallen crosses. A few of the graves we passed were pitifully small. On others, hand-written inscriptions had been misspelt. Over the whole expanse, only a few headstones slanted from the desolate earth. But we had stopped before one of them, and Reverend Hafkie indicated with a small gesture of the hand that we had arrived.

A stone of grey and black marble, the inscription contained within an outline of the African continent. In loving memory of my beloved husband, Mangaliso Robert Sobukwe; and adored father to his four children. Husband, father, man, and leader. "True leadership –" his own words had been inscribed "– demands complete subjugation of self, absolute honesty, integrity and uprightness of character, courage and fearlessness, and above all a consuming love for one's people." He lay among them now, these nameless ones in the lumpy earth.

I looked up at the grey and gusting day. The wind scraped in a thorn tree close at hand. The dust sifted through. I could see the same hills as could be seen from the genteel white town. And here in the burial place I could see the flowerless mounds of stones and earth and the confusion of the wooden crosses. Reverend Hafkie stood in silence by the grave, his terracotta suit tugged by wind, his half-closed eyes gazing away. And then slowly, wearily, he turned his eyes to me. We looked at each other for a moment, as though in some unstated acknowledgement of the grave and the memory between us.

"Thank you for bringing me here," I said.

"Why did you want to see it?"

I hesitated. The question was painfully direct. "Because I think it has a great deal to do with all of us."

He looked at me for a moment longer. I wondered if there was not some sadness in his weary eyes then. He turned away. I looked once more at the grave, this modest monument to one of the founders of the country's transformation. Like a blood-stained wheel, this transformation too had rolled relentless, and was rolling still, over all the places I had seen.

16

IN A NARROW VALLEY

THERE IS an impressive turbulence of mountains on the southern edges of the Great Karoo. After the massive plains and a road which has no turnings for more than a hundred kilometres, these mountains assault the senses. They are contorted and bald and suggestive of immense power. The road at last twists into them, this chaos of bent and tilted strata and ravines filled with boulders. In some places, the cliffs are sheer for hundreds of metres, the strata almost perpendicular, and the summits serrated; in other places, it is as if old sedimentary layers have been uprooted and flung against the main body of the mountains where they have lain like towering wreckage for millions of years. The plains are irretrievably disturbed now, and the feeling, even as the road bends through rock, is of a gradual descent.

Especially after Willowmore did the descent become pronounced and unmistakable. I was coming down off the huge plateau at last. I had stopped for a while in Willowmore, a small town to the left of the road lying peaceful in the slanting rays of the afternoon sun. Two young coloured women, faces vivid with make-up, sold me a cool-drink which I drank in the shop. Where was meneer going? they asked me in a friendly way.

"How far is it to Oudtshoorn?"

"We don't know how far, meneer. But we know how long. We go to parties there."

"How long?"

"Two hours. One and a half. It depends on how fast meneer is," the younger of the two said with an ambiguous smile.

"Do you think I can get there before dark?"

"Maybe," she replied, touching her bright red lips with the tip of an equally vivid fingernail.

But the darkness came quickly as I continued. Indeed, I drove down into it, so that the lingering sunlight lay high above me on the hills and then on the mountains which reared on either side. To the left, a big grey wall, buttressed and solid; to the right, black peaks much closer at hand, and the sky beyond was brilliant yet dark with clouds, like fire and smoke up there. I turned off the tar to De Rust and Oudtshoorn, the car rattling on stones and corrugations, and drove into a maze of hills, hundreds of hills becalmed between the mountain ranges, and rolling away until the furthest of them were caught in the vagueness of a gauze-like grey. It was in this way that I entered the narrow valley of the Little Karoo, the place of caves and feathers and profound isolation.

I drove in a deep twilight far beneath the crimson of the dying day. The mountains on either side were shadowed walls, and the valley between was all mystery and closing darkness. In the beam of my headlights, I saw dust surging from the roadway suddenly, and once, against a paler skyline, a row of trees racked by wind. And in the darkness a splattering of rain came down, flung against my windscreen mixed with dust. Rain. My windscreen wet for the first time since that fine spray of mist had gathered as I drove over the Soutpansberg on the Great North Road, the memory so distant now, a country's length away.

Wind and rain, and then in the darkness a cluster of lights. I drove in among the lights. It was the village of De Rust. I went no further. Gauze doors at the hotel entrance banging in the wind. A coloured woman with a creased and stoical face booked me in and showed me to my room. I remarked upon the weather. "Yes," she said in her stoical way; "it's the Cape's winter weather that is coming to us now."

I came down from my room and went into the bar which seemed like a haven inside the wind and splattering of rain and intense darkness of the valley. I sat in the small light of the bar and the blue of a television screen offered blurred representations of the day's events. After serving me, the barman returned to reading an Afrikaans magazine. I was the only customer on a Friday night.

AN IMMEDIATE impression of Oudtshoorn, main town of the Little Karoo and a short drive from my hotel in De Rust, was that it had tourism on its mind. Brash signs enlivened the streets, clamouring to serve the visitor's various appetites. This way to the Cango Crocodile Ranch and various ostrich show farms; that way to the Feather Inn and the Caves Motel; first left to Ostrich International, for the finest in ladies' and gents' fashions; straight on for Cango Angore, South Africa's first Angora rabbit show farm. And the tourists came, several hundreds of thousands of them each year. Luxury coaches swinging slowly through intersections; groups of Japanese people tangled in their photographic paraphernalia, and Americans in floral shirts. They came primarily to see the caves, and at the same time they were ensnared by the lure of ancient birds and reptiles, curios and scones for tea at the Hot Croc Cafe, all "the excitement of Africa" as one brochure expressed it.

As I wandered through the streets of Oudtshoorn, seeing many rooms to let and boarding houses, I came unexpectedly upon the hospital, and to one side of the newer block an old building made of roughly dressed grey stones, with patients and coloured nurses sitting on the wide veranda. I paused for a few moments in the garden here, remembering a famous South African short story. The grey building with its two wings had been built in 1899 as Oudtshoorn's first hospital with room for just over 30 beds.

At the Oudtshoorn museum, before I could ask about the short story, a woman said: "Our central theme here is the ostrich." Easy enough to grasp, since the main hall was given over entirely to this strange creature of the vicious kick and small brain shooting out instinct. The ostrich in history: feathers as fans for the Assyrians, as decoration for the Egyptians, as plumage in the helmets of the Greeks and Romans, as ornamentation on the Coptic cross of Ethiopia. Some Arabian tribes, I learned, believed the ostrich to be a reincarnation of the devil. Another display dealt with the ostrich feather in heraldry. And of course the role played by the ostrich, both through its skin and feathers, in the world of fashion: the hats, the stoles, the shoes and handbags, and even an old photograph of dancing girls which reminded me of the feather-clad Shebas at Sun City.

And then in one of the corridors of the museum I found what I was looking for: a display of books and photographs dealing with the writer, Pauline Smith, who had been born in Oudtshoorn in 1882, daughter of an English doctor then practising in the town and outlying areas. Although she left for England when she was 12 years old, only twice to return for brief visits, her short stories and single novel set in the Little Karoo provide a sharply focused view of the austerity and isolation of the people, for the most part poor and landless Afrikaners, embedded in this narrow valley. One of her stories had been partially set in the grey stone hospital I had seen earlier.

But for the moment I wanted to play the tourist, and with this in mind I drove a short distance to one of the ostrich show farms. The valley had widened, but the two mountain ranges – the Outeniquas in the south and the Swartberg in the north – were clearly visible and provided a sense of definite containment. A few luxury coaches stood under the trees of the farmyard. I joined a group which was immediately whisked away on a tour by a talkative young man named John.

Smooth and glib and faintly absurd, this tour of the show farm. Look at this ostrich chariot; the mayor of Oudtshoorn rode in it on a special occasion and said afterwards, "never again". You see, folks, ostriches don't work together, and they only stopped running with the mayor in the chariot 1,5 kilometres after they were supposed to. Interesting fact: the birds can run at speeds of up to 80 kilometres an hour over short distances. We went into a shed and looked at piles of feathers and skins, and then at an old wooden incubator, water-heated, with dozens of drawers for the eggs. Interesting facts: one egg weighs about 1,5 kilograms and takes 90 minutes to hard boil; the world record for eating a hard-boiled ostrich egg, which is equivalent to 24 chicken eggs, is 6 minutes and 40 seconds. Some people in the party expressed jocular distaste. Then we crowded against a fence to look at the ostriches, the females in their grey feathers, the males in black and white. The long necks, small heads turned sideways to look at us. A few of the tourists held lucerne pellets in their open palms, and the necks curved down over the fence. Interesting fact: the males do a courtship dance in front of the female and mating takes place in a crouched position. John assembled his tourists at one point on the farm and showed them, in the rugged skyline of the Swartberg, the profile of the gentle giant whom he said was lying on his back, resting, after having drunk up all the water in the high-sided trough of the Little Karoo. Then we wandered off to see an ostrich sitting on her eggs, while the male strutted in the background. Interesting facts: the eggs take 42 days to hatch, with the female sitting on them by day and the male by night. John chased the female away to allow tourists to be photographed while standing on the eggs to illustrate their strength. He carried a thorny branch in case the male attacked and started kicking. He explained about the lethal nature of the ostrich kick. The best defence was a thorn bush because the thorns are seen by the ostrich as a threat to its eyes. If no thorns were to hand, another defence was to lie down, but if you happened to be bald you could find your head being sat upon for 42 days. Laughter. In a smallish enclosure filled with straw, the tourists shrieked as they tried to ride the ostriches. Cameras clicked once more. "Do they mind being ridden?" an American woman asked with some concern. John shrugged. "Who knows?" he said. Then we watched some ostrich races, the dressed-up coloured jockeys clowning in that sterile way of endless repetition.

"Don't you get tired of this?" I asked John.

"Sometimes," he admitted; "but one does vary what one says, and it depends very much on who's in the party."

I persevered as tourist. In the afternoon, I drove into the foothills of the Swartberg, the road twisting between cliffs sometimes, until I came to a sign: "Welcome to the world-famous Cango Caves". Ample space for parking. A building standing against a steep hillside: curio shops, a bank for drawing money, a cafeteria of sorts. Directions to the ticket office were in four languages, including Japanese.

"You are too late for the tour," a man said, looking at me through the small glass window.

"I don't really want a tour," I replied.

"Well, you can't go in without a tour."

I turned to go.

"But you could catch up with the tour that's just started," he called after me.

It hardly seemed worth the effort, but I made it. I climbed the steps to the entrance where bored guides played with a tennis ball. One of them hurried me inside. A narrow passage gave way to a huge cavity, the ceiling of which soared away. Artfully lit dripstone formations, some of them huge and fantastical, like the set for a film depicting other worlds. Then we reached the tour. The glib voice of the guide pointing out Old Nick and the Angel's Wing; then changing the lights to reveal new shapes, directing the eyes of the tourists with the beam of a powerful torch. The air smelled heavy and warm. We walked deeper into the cave to look at the Bridal Chamber and the bottle of champagne. Later, in the Drum Room, the guide turned out the lights and we stood in utter darkness while he talked of scorpions and spiders. His voice changed effortlessly from English to Afrikaans and back again. Then we went on to further wonders.

But the caves seemed weary with all the lights and electric cables, all the footsteps and stares; and all the glories seemed to have been worn smooth, their beauty jaded and withdrawn, yet sumptuous still in an aloof and distant way. They reminded me, these well-trod caves, of ornamented tombs waiting to close again, to close forever against all that moist breath and touching, and to be left, at last and as before, in peace.

I drove slowly back to my hotel in De Rust: the place, as I translated it, of rest and safety. In daylight, it was a small village over which the Swartberg towered in dark and forbidding rock. Strange how the landscape would inevitably shape the inner terrain of those who lived within it. A place of sanctuary within the mountain ranges. I remembered the plains of the Great Karoo, the restlessness and need for movement they evoked. But here, in the narrow valley, the sense of rest and safety.

Pauline Smith's characters Juriaan van Royen and his wife Deltje had lived all their lives on a little shelf of hired land halfway up the side of their Aangenaam (pleasant) valley hard by the Outeniqua mountain range. Their house was of mud and thatch, and the living-room floor was made of peach-pips, exactly like the pips in the floor of the old Kruger house at Boekenhoutfontein. Although poor and childless, they had lived a life of simple joy and love in their valley. Now, in their old age, a mystery had come to haunt their lives: a terrible pain in Deltje's side. At first a medicine from the Jewish shop in the village had seemed to help, but then the attacks grew worse. At about this time Juriaan heard from a flamboyant transport rider about the new hospital which had just been built in Oudtshoorn where miracle cures were conducted on a daily basis. Juriaan's heart had been filled with hope. For his tiny wife he made a nest of pillows and blankets in the cart, inspanned his two oxen, and set off on the long journey to the hospital. But there were no miracle cures as the exaggerating transport rider had led them to believe. Worst of all, the old couple were separated, Deltje being taken to a ward, Juriaan being allowed to outspan his oxen in the veld which surrounded the hospital in those days. He stood humbly before the doctor. A cure for Deltje's pain was impossible; alleviation would take time. The old man's simple expectation was crushed, and he felt that his God had withdrawn. For long days and nights he waited in an anguish of separation and longing. For Deltje, too, as her pain and weakness increased, the longing intensified, overflowing into a physical thirst. Not this brackish water of Oudtshoorn, but their own water of the mountain stream. Not the incomprehensible routines of the hospital, but their small shelf of land in the valley. At last Juriaan could stand it no longer. One night, he inspanned the oxen and made the nest of blankets and pillows in the back of the cart. Then he crept into the hospital and said to Deltje: "Come now, in my arms will I carry you out to the cart, and back to the Aangenaam valley we will go." So it was thus, with their faces turned for home, that they found contentment. The tiny woman was surely dying, yet Juriaan's heart had regained its warmth, and he knew that his God was no longer withdrawn.

THAT EVENING, in the street outside the hotel, there welled up suddenly the shouted chant of "Viva, Viva". I thought the revolution might have come to this place of rest and safety; but I found, when I went down, only some boisterous white rugby players who, on their way back to Oudtshoorn, had invaded the bar. They accosted me in their slightly aggressive but jocular way. When they heard me speak, they called me the English tourist. Some sat on the counter, their feet on the stools. They had won their game and they kept bursting into song. The coloured barman, who acknowledged me with a slight grin when I entered, had no time for his Afrikaans magazine tonight. With an impassive face, he lined up the drinks which the rugby players ordered. Soon they were bashing on the counter with their fists, and the singing grew loud. Then came the challenges and the chants of "down, down, down". A stool was pulled away, and one of them went staggering backwards across the bar-room floor. Guf-faws. A moment of tension, of stiffening aggression, then the singing continued louder than before.

"Buy the English tourist a drink." I raised my hand to decline. A big fist grabbed my shirt. A big face with a ginger moustache said into mine: "Don't insult me, you clever fucking Englishman." I said with a laugh that under such circumstances I would accept his offer. The big face grinned drunkenly at me.

In slow motion, then, the business came to its climax: the breaking of glasses, the young men staggering about, the recriminations, a night-watchman in a khaki greatcoat standing guard behind the bar, the repeated crash and clatter of the gauze doors, and then the shouts outside, the sudden timbre of rage, the blood on the steps of the hotel and on the pavement beyond, coloured youths snarling and swaying with aggression, a mini-bus jerking forward and swerving in the road.

Suddenly the hotel was full of excited people. What had happened? White scum, someone said, wide-eyed; they were kicking those youngsters, and then a knife had flashed. Unbelievable, a middle-aged white woman said; the youngsters were minding their own business; I could see that as I came down the road.

The night-watchman, with a creased face and eyes like slits, smiled at me and said: "It's the drinking. I have held on until forty-three. For two years now I have not touched a drink."

A bald man with a round face and gentle eyes stood at my elbow. "We need to learn how to respect other people," he said earnestly to me; "I know those rugby men: when they get drunk they want to swear at the coloureds. It's not necessary. We have to live together. We have to learn to respect each other."

The middle-aged white woman had brought her nine-year-old son into the bar. "My laatlammetjie," she said, my late lamb, meaning that the child had been an afterthought, an unexpected addition to her family. The boy drank cool-drinks while his mother tackled double brandies.

The slit-eyed man in the greatcoat smiled at me again. "The Lord helped me," he said; "I don't drink any longer, meneer."

"I can't believe what's just happened," the middle-aged white woman said with some agitation; "and now I've lost my keys. Have you seen my keys, sir?"

The barman looked at me with a slight grimace and a shake of his head. He fiddled with the controls of the television set, and then brought the laatlammetjie another glass of orange cool-drink.

The bar had filled with dark faces, settling now, and soon quite silent at the tables, for the most part coloured people who sat without drinks and with a sort of patience in their expressions as the middle-aged woman fussed after her keys and the late night film began.

AT LEAST ten years before the founding of Oudtshoorn in 1847, a few wandering white farmers had discovered a way into the Gamkaskloof, a profoundly isolated valley in the very centre of the Swartberg range. Over a century later, their descendants still lived there. Their valley, by then, had for some reason become known as The Hell. A road was built into The Hell for the first time in 1962, but only in the 1980s did the last of them leave this ultimate in mountain sanctuaries. Being interested in valleys, the lure and encasement of them and their impact on the inner terrain, I set out in search of the Gamkaskloof a few mornings after the late night film.

In the bracing air of early winter, I drove through hills which lifted me towards the Swartberg mountains. I saw people in their yards, seeking out the sun against the eastward facing walls of their labourers' cottages; and I saw school children in bundles of clothes on the verges of the stony road. Here were ostriches in narrow strips of green lucerne which grew along the banks of small dry streams. Once or twice the sight of farmhouses and barns standing inside their groves of trees. Then it was into the stark wild foothills, aloes flowering among rocks on either side of the ascending road, their lustrous orange spikes reaching upward like the representation of flames.

Quite by chance I had discovered a woman in Oudtshoorn who knew a lot about the Gamkaskloof. I had been looking at the town's "feather palaces", the stylish and elaborate dwellings and townhouses made possible by the considerable wealth which came to the Little Karoo through the ostrich feather booms of 1865 to 1881 and more especially from 1900 to the start of the First World War. It was at the Townhouse Museum, a sumptuous home built in 1909, that I met Mrs Kotze, the Gamkaskloof expert.

I found her in the curator's office, working on some pages of a bulky manuscript. She looked at me with lively eyes. "My book on Gamkaskloof," she said; "I'm not a writer, but I was encouraged to do it by a previous curator of the main museum. 'We must have a properly researched book, and you must do it,' he said. So I've been working on it for nearly five years." But she proved to be quite secretive. She said, although with an engaging laugh, that she had been instructed to give out no information as this would spoil the book's chances of publication. She nevertheless showed me some photographs of herself holding a tape measure across a dilapidated window. "We've measured everything in the valley, documented everything," she said, tapping the heaped pages of her manuscript.

I told her what I knew: that in the 1830s some farmers had found their way in. Perhaps they were looking for greener pastures for their animals. Perhaps they followed their animals in. Why had they chosen to live in a valley accessible only on foot? You entered either by way of precipitous ravines which carried a river clean through the Swartberg from the Great Karoo in the north to the Little Karoo in the south, or in the north-west corner via a ladder of wooden stakes driven into a cliff by Stone Age people long before. But why settle there? Perhaps because the valley was well watered and fertile. And almost certainly for reasons similar to those which had engendered the Great Trek: to escape British rule and British taxes.

"How am I getting on?" I asked.

Mrs Kotze smiled encouragingly.

I said I was interested in the idea of escape, of seeking a refuge, of hiding among inaccessible rocks, even as our ancestors had done. I told her of Makapan's instinctive flight to caves. I asked her what she thought. I asked her about the impact of the isolation which must come as a corollary to refuge.

She told me that during the Anglo-Boer War the inhabitants of Gamkaskloof had been discovered by a Commando, and that already then they were an anachronism, dressed in clothing made of goat skins, speaking an outlandish Dutch, knowing little of the turbulent events then sweeping the rest of the country, and with broods of half-wild children eating goats' meat and wild honey. All this I could read elsewhere, she said, glancing at her manuscript. Well into the 20th Century, wild men from the valley would occasionally come to town with their pack donkeys, selling leather and fresh produce, buying soap and paraffin and primus stoves. They stared in disbelief at cars and electricity. A school and doctors had only arrived in the valley during the 1920s, and perhaps it was then that the deepest isolation had begun to crumble. But the process had taken another half-century to complete, and it had certainly been accelerated by the construction of the road.

I asked if the valley people's religion had survived. Had they built their own church? "Oh, it survived all right," Mrs Kotze said; "But they never built a church. A minister would go in several times a year for weddings and baptisms. They had their old Dutch bibles which they still used well into this century."

"Perhaps the valley was church enough," I suggested.

"Yes, that's a thought. And now," she said with a lively smile, "I must not tell you too much. Are you going to see the valley? You must. It's wonderful, and the road is not too bad."

But the road alarmed me sometimes with its lonely exposure as it wound through high country of an utterly uncompromising wildness. First it had been up the sheer face of the Swartberg on a gravel road the outer edge of which was often supported by walls built of stone. The strata of the mountain pointed skyward, and the erosion of the softer layers had left the hard ribs vulnerable, and in many places the ribs had broken and crashed down, so that the lower slopes were littered with slabs and huge boulders. The road cuts into cliffs, the gradients steep, the turns too tight for any but the lowest gear; and as I climbed, the whole valley of the Little Karoo lay far below; even to the Outeniquas a hundred kilometres to the south I could see its spread. As I neared the summit, the road struck me as being an impertinence, as if these high places should not be penetrated with the laboured grinding of machines. And then the summit, nearly 1 500 metres above the floor of the valley: no birds, no sound of insects sawing with their legs; only a cold wind blowing through the silence of the heights.

Then, just beyond the summit on the northern side, the tyres of my car skidding slightly on loose stones, I turned off the main pass as it began its descent to the Great Karoo in the north, and took the road to Gamkaskloof.

Driving westwards along the top of the mountain then. Long reed-like grass, heavy with seed, surrounded the road; and proteas and aloes bloomed sometimes among the banks of smaller flowers. Up to the left, the bald summit of the Swartberg; to the right the mountain crags continued, broken by the tops of steep ravines. I drove above the beginnings of the ravines, and small water courses, marked by vegetation of a darker green, led unerringly towards them. As the kilometres fell behind, it seemed to me that I travelled into the turbulent bosom of the mountain: at one moment cliffs reared above the track, at the next a dizzy drop invited my plunge into the ravines of the north. The earth, here inside the mountain, has been violently torn up. Thick slabs of rock lay in a cascading heap, like books thrown carelessly together and gone to the mildew of thin vegetation now, the covers curling up. And I was in amongst them, descending towards The Hell. The books were half buried, jutting out of the belly of the mountain, and small valleys had been gouged out of the sloping covers, running towards me and then turning in deep holes to gush out into the bigger ravines falling to the north. How could the scale and violence of such sights lead to sanctuary? And yet they did. The road began to ascend, caught in its meandering between cliff and chasm, but both diminishing in size and threat as I climbed, and then over a ridge, it seemed at the summit of the world, and the sanctuary of Gamkaskloof lay 500 metres below a precipice at my feet.

A long green slash in the mountain top, surrounded on both sides and at each end by the huge folding of the Swartberg range. I stepped close to the precipice and saw how the road had been cut into its steepness, zig-zagging towards the floor of the valley. I drove slowly down, the bonnet of the car veering into empty space sometimes as I turned the sharp corners of the zig-zags.

The floor of the valley was narrow, only a few hundred metres across in some places, and the walls were steep, inescapable, seeming by their presence to deliver a soft and soothing sense of interment. I remembered reading a typed document once which said that no one knew why the valley had become known as The Hell: if the Biblical hell was described as being like Gamkaskloof, the document went on, people would really have nothing to worry about. I sensed a contradiction now: this yearning for the peace of sanctuary at odds with other yearnings. The contradiction was The Hell; and that is why when the road was built the people began to scramble out. And now the narrow Gamkaskloof was empty once again.

Yet houses still lay scattered in the bush all along the valley floor. Derelict mud structures crumbling away, thatch in isolated tufts, roof timbers caved in, stones pressed into the mud as ornamentation around small windows with neither frames nor glass. Everything measured and recorded by Mrs Kotze. Houses in smothering isolation, yet with signs sometimes of the cause of that isolation's decline: a battered old lorry and, later on, a big American sedan from the late 1950s, one of those low drooping models with tail fins and elaborate rear lights, but without wheels now, marooned in weeds.

I stopped at a small cemetery, surrounded by a broken fence. The silence rushed into my ears, and the isolation pressed down upon me like a weight. JEM Marais: born in 1922, died just before his or her 20th birthday. Also A du Toit: born July 1939, died November 1948. And here was another Marais, perhaps a sibling of JEM who had been born in 1919 and died in 1982. "Rest Softly." This is what Deltje's grave would have looked like, I suddenly thought, with Juriaan kneeling by the stones. But Deltje's would not have been marked, for who would have marked it for the unlettered Juriaan? The inscriptions here in the narrowest of valleys had been scratched by hand into slabs of cement or onto the rough stones of the mountain valley. But sometimes the inscriptions, often with Biblical verses, had been written on paper protected behind glass. Where the glass had broken, the paper had withered to nothing. And the little vases were empty, often overturned, and the mounds were covered with dusty stones and weeds. They had lived and died in The Hell, their sanctuary. Those contradictory forces, staunched only by death. The fading away of memory and pain alike, I thought as I stood among the rough graves and the childlike lettering of those inscriptions which

yet remained. I stood with the silence and the isolation rushing down
upon me.

IN LADISMITH I met a woman to whom I said: "Do you think
there is a fundamental contradiction in all of us? On the one hand,
there is that gnawing pain of consciousness and the resultant drives:
a drive for significance, a constant developing of systems, ideologies,
religions to render the irrelevance of individual human consciousness
less painful, even to cover it up and to say that consciousness brings
no pain but triumph through this or that idea and belief. On the
other hand, there is a simultaneous longing for all this striving to
cease, a longing for peace rather than the strenuousness of belief, a
longing for quiet rather than the rigours of doubt and denial. A desire,
in short, to hide in a valley of safety and rest. What do you think?"

Ladismith was a bleak little town built underneath a now cloud-
swathed Swartberg range. I had woken chilled and groping for another blanket in the night. At breakfast the following morning, I said
as much to the young English-speaking woman who ran the restaurant where I was the only customer. "Oh, not so cold yet," she said
pleasantly from the till; "the real winter's still to come. Snow on the
mountain. Those really biting winds." She shivered at the prospect.

She nevertheless already wore a shapeless knitted sweater which
accentuated the slight heaviness of her frame. I judged her to be in
her late twenties. She had an open face with a small but clearly defined
mouth, and her expression showed an easy self-confidence.

Had she been in Ladismith long? "Oh, for nearly four years now.
I'm originally from Cape Town." And did she like living in Ladismith? "Yes," she said; "it's not unpleasant. But sometimes it can
become quite isolated. Let's face it, it's an isolated place."

I busied myself with bacon and grilled tomato. The young woman
said: "My name's Fiona, by the way," and then told me about the
appetite for gossip in Ladismith, the lack of privacy on the telephone
with its manual exchange, and about a pregnant schoolgirl who had
been hidden away by her parents and no one ever saw her baby.

"Classic small town stuff," she said. "I taught in school here for
a while when we first arrived. I taught Pauline Smith to the standard
nines. It amazed me how accurate Smith was, and still is, about so
many people in the Little Karoo."

I remarked that an underlying quality in most of Smith's work
appeared to be the isolation of the Little Karoo, and also its impact

on the psyche of her simple characters. "But tell me what you think of the isolation. How does it strike you?"

She smiled at me from the till. "It's very easy to find. On one level it's really great. It's peace and quiet. On another level, it's like death. The Little Karoo as high-sided coffin. Look," she said, "let me grab some coffee and come and join you for a moment."

She sat at my table and lit a cigarette. I asked her why, if she was a teacher, she was working in a restaurant. "Oh, we decided to give it a try. We own it. I do this part, and my man does the cooking. I've taught in Cape Town and then for a while in Mmabatho – you know, the capital of Bop – and I'll probably teach again. But at the moment, this is quite a lot of fun."

She tilted her head back to exhale.

"Why like death?" I asked her.

"Maybe it's because we need a challenge," Fiona said.

It was then that I told her, using in part the terminology of Eugene Marais, about what must be the most central and most unresolvable human contradiction: searching simultaneously for significance, and for sanctuary from the relentlessness of such a search. What did she think?

She looked at me for some time. Then she said with a thoughtfulness and candour which seemed to demand respect: "Perhaps in many ways peace – you know, coming to terms with the dilemma of life – can only be achieved by acknowledging one's irrelevance and admitting one's essential isolation."

"Then what is left?"

"Just life, I think," Fiona said.

TRAVELLING FURTHER west, I gave a lift to a youth with pale ginger hair, quite curly, and pale blue eyes, quite vacant looking or perhaps preoccupied. He clambered in clutching a blue travelling bag with dirty white straps. He thanked me and said his name was Bartie, and then sat silent, looking ahead at the unfolding road. After a while, however, our conversation began.

I asked if he was a student.

"No," Bartie replied; "I'm still at school."

"Which school?"

"I'm at the technical school in Oudtshoorn."

After a short pause, I asked what he was doing there.

"I'm in standard ten," he replied; "I'm doing the motor mechanic's course."

"What other subjects? For example, do you also do English and Afrikaans."

"Yes, those two, and technical drawing."

"Do you do a bit of English and Afrikaans literature?"

"Yes," Bartie said; "we have prescribed books."

Was he studying Pauline Smith who had been born in Oudtshoorn? Bartie shook his head. Or perhaps Langenhoven, the Afrikaans poet, who had been born just down the road? But Bartie had not heard of Langenhoven.

I asked for the names of some of his prescribed books.

Bartie frowned in his blank way and said: "They have all sorts of funny names."

After a moment he asked me: "Why are you driving in third gear?"

"I'm not," I said; "I'm driving in fifth."

"There is no fifth," he said, indicating the gear lever.

But I changed down to show him. I said the manufacturers had perhaps run out of levers marked with a fifth gear when they had assembled my car. Bartie nodded.

I asked if he could remember the names of some of the authors of his prescribed books. But he could not.

He said: "I want to be a mechanic in the air force."

We spoke about his mechanic's course. Yes, he did diesel engines; yes, he did petrol engines. "Well," I said, "if you join the air force you might have the opportunity of learning about jet engines as well."

He looked at me in his blank way, his lips parted, but offered no rejoinder.

I asked him then where he was going. Should he not be in school?

"Yes, it is school time," Bartie replied; "but I have asked for a week off school because I must help on the farm."

His father's rented farm lay further west. The trouble was that his father was in hospital. What was wrong? "Something to do with his lungs and heart," Bartie said in a suddenly tightened voice.

Then, as a distraction, he pointed to the bottom of the dashboard. "What's that small light for? Why isn't it on?"

I explained about the alarm and immobiliser."

Bartie asked if he could light a cigarette, and opened his window slightly to release the smoke. I got an inkling of his loneliness as I listened to the sharp sound of his inhalations.

"Is your mother still alive?"

He shook his head, his face impassive. "But I have a sister. She is alone on the farm."

"How old is she?"

"My sister is 15 years old."

He smoked in silence then, and in a discomfort which filled the small space of the car with an intimation of some secret pain.

Bartie was 18 years old, and I left him standing with his blue bag on the forecourt of a filling station not far from the end of the Little Karoo, and not too far from his father's rented farm. I drove on alone. This valley of sanctuary and isolation bore me forward. And finally the valley released me. The road descended through rock-strewn places and through the twisting of a narrow ravine. Then I emerged into broader country once again, this time the gently sloping landscapes of the south-west Cape.

17

AT LAST THE EDGE

WHEN I passed into a denseness of soft rain, I knew that my journey was complete. The continuity of dust and sunlight was at last broken by this winter rainfall place, this Cape weather which had crept all the way up to De Rust one night, splashing my windscreen with a brief shower. Now my car streamed in this sodden piece of Mediterranean climate tacked onto the bottom of a sub-continent tortured with drought. There were other discontinuities.

There was a consciousness of style and beauty, here, which largely had been absent from those harsher places on the slow and crooked pathway of my journey. Survival had been overlaid with some finesse in this damp grey world, and struggle replaced by opulence and grace.

The rich interiors of restaurants: candlelight on glass and flowers; antiques and delicate cuisine. Slightly jarring to recall the crude smells of cooking in the smoke and chaos of Moria now, Jake's eyebrows pale with dust, his hand guiding me forward through that potent throng. The hands of the woman at the next table, elegantly ringed; and pearls at her ageing throat. It seemed to me she was wining and dining her daughters, young women with shining hair and clearly articulated voices. "Mummy, that's absurd," said one, with a polite frown; "you know I can't expect him to pick up the tab." The grace even of these differing perceptions. The style. No stench of latrines here, as the waiter replenished their glasses, holding the bottle in a white napkin.

Antique restorations and a bric-a-bac shop in a street lined with oak trees. The shop reminded me immediately of the house of Petrus Uijs on the dry side of the Soutpansberg. Collectables, but generally more refined than Petrus' diverse preoccupations. Things for the cottage and townhouse here, old brass, old wood; and also hand-made leather sandals and bags, fine Indian-print scarves seeming already worn out, embroidered purses, and a little corner redolent of hessian and straw in which were displayed chutneys and unusual jams and other delicacies, normally with doilies wrapped over the lids of the glass bottles. I remembered old Petrus Uijs, all sinew and muscle and the military beret, and the black boy in the back of the bakkie whose knee had been ripped away from the bone when he fell onto a fence. Behind the counter of the bric-a-bac shop, a serene-looking young woman in jeans and sweater answered my question about the rain which drifted down beyond the windows. "Oh, yes, this is Cape weather all right. But I don't think it'll go on for very long. Maybe three or four days." She smiled gently. "No, that's not long. Some-times we have this sort of weather for three weeks without a break."

Driving through this weather, the country flat, the suddenness of the Cape mountains unseen, and the weather bringing down a softness from a soft and undefined sky. And here were racehorses in their paddocks; and there a row of trees all wraith-like in the mist; and laughing coloured labourers walking on the verge, their yellow water-proofs shining in the rain; and restaurants and discotheques sign-posted in the green country. I passed a field which seemed to bulge with lush grass, sprinklers arching through the drizzle. The sump-tuousness of meadows and trees, and dark ploughed fields, and staked vineyards coloured warm, the gnarled stems of the vines black in the wet. And later the clouds lifted a little, and I could see steep moun-tains partially unveiled, the mist like scanty lace across the cliffs; and I saw white homesteads, always Cape Dutch now, peering out from trees, or standing at the ends of avenues of oak, or seen across the vistas of the russet vines. The elegance, the bounty of earth and sky, the husbandry. No place for the thorny thickets of bush encroachment here; nor for the thin rows of grass on Oom Willem's kingdom, the seed piled to picture rails in the living-room, and the thought of men killing for the last remaining drops of water.

I drove in a slow circle through the south-west Cape. I found a narrow road which traversed a mountain. I drove up into dense mist, my headlights revealing only whiteness. I stopped when the road was high and got out and stood in the rain, seeing little but the vague outlines of rocks. But I heard water running everywhere. Individual drops began the symphony; close at hand they joined and trickled; then the gurgle and the splash began, the sound of streams and that urgent sluicing between rocks; and as background to all this the throaty torrent in a ravine below. It was an astonishment of life and moisture. And it was while I stood there in the drenched mountain that the knowledge of my journey coalesced into a burden within me, at once a loss of innocence and an onus to conclude. I drove on.

I came to a bigger town in the pouring rain, hundreds of students walking under identical yellow umbrellas which advertised an insurance company. Old trees graced their campus, and I thought of acacias in a bare school yard: George's school in the Fifth World and the faith in icons. Icons everywhere here; a sense of rootedness and tradition as if immutability went without saying. "We're living in another decline," Sidney had said; "we'll see levelled cities again." Smashed universities, old trees chopped down for fires, historic houses caved in, Cape Dutch gables toppled, pictures in art galleries ripped open.

I looked at large canvases as I sheltered from the rain. With the heavy timber doors closed, the gallery was silent. I stood in a highly polished, empty, and vaguely reverential space, reminiscent of a church.

A sombre-looking triptych by William Kentridge lured me. Panel one: an elegant couple sit in a room with a wild animal; there is a reading lamp and the back view of a nude at the door; the man appears to be asleep, and the woman's expression is resigned. Panel two: the opulence, the style, the vaulted ceiling of the cafe; a man holds a conversation with a rhinoceros; two women dance together; other women wear elbow-length gloves and plunging necklines; a pair of binoculars lies on one of the tables. Panel three: beneath a fish-and-chips sign, a whole street is filled with wrecked and abandoned cars; razor wire adorns the tops of fences; an animal, perhaps a hyena, stands on the roof of a car in the foreground, wearing roller-skates. The whole work has about it a slightly warped perspective and almost no colour at all. This grey vision of stylish decadence, of depravity, and ultimately of nightmare and the sudden crying out of anxiety and alarm.

Penny Siopis offered more colour – indeed, a slightly jarring use of it sometimes – in her rich canvases. Here is a pastel drawing of a hand offering for view a picture which depicts a half-naked woman taking a photograph of a small statue of Venus set among a lavishness of fruit and flowers. Pictures within pictures and a vague sense of self-indulgence. And again here, in oils this time, a table set for a perfect feast in a gloomy room. In the background a tall window admits only a little light, but by it the furniture can be made out, much of it under wraps. The questions rear out: who has prepared this deserted feast, and who will eat it? This profusion of fruit and chocolates and cake and the bright pink succulence of watermelon, all set out among flowers and, again, a small Venus as centrepiece. Such inappropriate abundance, the waste, and again a feeling of private self-indulgences exposed, accentuated by the almost lurid use of pinks and purples and blues. I thought of putrefying smells and the buzzing of flies.

Paintings of psychosis and imminent collapse, these in the silent gallery, glimpses of the inner landscape behind the elegance and style. Always a half-hidden expectation of calamity and doom. Those nightmare visions and no one there to eat the feast.

Outside, the sun had broken through, although moist cloud still lingered as if it would at any moment cover the world once more. Weak sunlight slanted onto the white facades of old and elegant houses, and the facades were dappled sometimes with the broken shade of largely leafless trees. And the yellow umbrellas were furled now, and the students strolled along, or went jogging, or indulged in tracksuit romances under the big wet trees. The students seemed so bright and well scrubbed that it was hard to imagine the inner landscape with its warped perspectives now. And the dappled houses seemed so clean and permanent that any other reality was pushed aside. But another reality, cause of psychosis, was close. Epidemics of tuberculosis, unemployment, alcoholism and above all violence, raged in the beauty of the south-west Cape.

Collapse and desperation. An entire country caught in the coils of upheaval and change. Travelling school children protected by armed parents during the Gazankulu boycotts. A million people on their hands and knees in the dust of Moria, praying for renewal but more profoundly for peace. A moment's silence at a political meeting, a rallying point as well as an act of respect for old people murdered in their homes. Memories of the soldiers of a homeland coup, of torture and brutality; and the enraged youth spitting and kicking at Robert Sobukwe's funeral. Intimations only as I had travelled through, intimations of a land caught in the tremors and estrangements of transition.

My visit to the church-like gallery had brought to me a memory of some of the more elemental things I had seen: Helen Martin's camels, without paranoia, and how I had said to Koos Malgas that perhaps her yard of sculptures was her church; and Jackson Hlungwani with his pointed beard and impassioned eyes. His carved fishes were being eaten by termites, but his mind had been filled with his image of a monumental god, arms outstretched, even as Jackson's had been in his rejection of violence and his great quest for peace. "Where is peace?" he had said to me; "peace is woman, Jackson think."

The lovely contours of them as they danced with their men on the concrete floor of a wineland festival I went to one evening. The slightly arched backs, the swirling earrings, the hair free-flowing and bobbing from shoulder to shoulder sometimes as they turned. Cold in the large metal shed, a warehouse of sorts, where the festival was held. But the crowd had warmed it, and the wine and dancing had warmed the crowd. The aroma of roast chicken floated on the air; the aroma of wine; and a band called Chelzea made the music. I saw a young mother and child, the woman's pursed lips blowing smoke over the tiny bald head. All round the walls of the shed stalls had been erected and were now occupied by various wine makers and dispensers of local cheese and homemade bread. People clustered about the stalls, or sat at tables filled with jollity, or came into the open space in front of the band to dance.

I had spoken to a social worker that morning and she had talked to me about what she called "the psyche of violence". "That is my greatest fear," she said; "more and more now, I see evidence of an element in the communities that revels in violence. It's like a cult which has embraced a lot of people who otherwise appear normal. Young people in particular. At the slightest provocation, this blood-lust is aroused. And then they want to see death, and they jeer and mock at the suffering involved, especially the suffering of a slow and agonising death."

Haunting thoughts for an event as gay as the wineland festival. Yet they hovered within as I thought of Jackson and looked for signs of peace in the women around me. They had dressed up for this special occasion. Even about the girl in a T-shirt which bore the slogan "live and die on the beach" there was a sense that a careful choice had been made. Taken together, there was a vague Frenchness about them: the straight noses, the general smallness of bones, the dark complexions, dark eyes flashing. Descendants of the Huguenots,

no doubt, speaking in English or Afrikaans, an air of slightly countrified worldliness, an air of grace and warmth, and a knowledge, as
subtly discernible as their perfume sometimes, of themselves as women
and how they stood in relation to their men and to their children.
They passed about me in the sort of proximity which a public wine
tasting inevitably engendered: the flash of jewellery at a throat or the
primary colours of a chiffon scarf; the cheeks and eyelashes and lips;
the expressive hands; the boldness of youth, the make-up and the
sparking sexuality; the reassurance of the older women, assurance and
reassurance; and in the eyes enjoyment and excitement, and also
melancholy sometimes and longing. Peace is woman? It seemed to
me that there was something there: perhaps no less than women's
acceptance, and perhaps an unconscious or instinctive one, of the
love within them as impetus for the rolling forward of life itself, this
great adventure. I turned away. I had asked the social worker whether
the psyche of violence she described afflicted only males. She had
shaken her head. "Girls, too. That's the terrible thing."

Yet it was something else Jackson had said which came to me as
I turned south again, and for the last time, seeking a conclusion or
at least a sense of completion to all the complexity which my driving
had revealed. The mountains lay behind me now, and the country
was slow with undulations, a low and gentle landscape. Much of the
land showed brown, ploughed earth lying open to the sky, but sometimes there was a sheen of green, young wheat emerging, and sometimes plump sheep stood in fields of vivid lucerne. Only a few low
outcrops of rock had not been ploughed; they stood like islands in
the stretching away of husbanded land; and the blue road seemed
almost lazy now, swinging and sweeping its way across the undulations and towards the final dying of the land.

Jackson had spoken repeatedly, as if of a universal truth, about the
three levels. In the air, on the ground and under the ground. Mysteries
to me then, but now I understood. It flashed upon me as I drove.
This recurring sense, even from the Limpopo, of things underneath
the ground, ancient things, bones, relics, other worlds and other times
as our foundations; and of things in the air of our consciousness, our
gods, our kings on Mapungubwe hill, our sanctuaries of thought and
worship, all the raw material of faith and doubt and self-delusion;
and we are trapped between with our vacuums and our pain. We are
on the earth, rooted like baobab trees in what lies beneath, our branches
reaching into the turmoil of the stars above us. That is what my
journey had revealed.

Yet there was something more. "Just life," Fiona had said in her Ladismith restaurant; "just life, I think." That shimmering of things which holds such potent beauty and such promises of wounding; the miracles, the brevity, the renewal, the rolling forward. And the concerns of people's lives: the love, the steadfastness, the isolation. The shimmering of things. Like my final landscape here, the flattened earth and a row of trees all twisted and flung backwards by the prevailing winds, as if pointing to Africa; the coarse coastal bush stretching away on whitish sand; the low sky and the wind across the edge of a continent; and the fishermen's cottages of whitewash and thatch between end gables; and then at last the sea.

The road turned around the edges of a small bay, holiday bungalows to one side, rocks and breakers and seagulls to the other. Then the sign: welcome to L'Agulhas, the southernmost town in Africa. The banded lighthouse loomed ahead. I drove on a short rough road until it petered out at rocks.

The last of the rocks of this tempestuous land of mine. White rocks, dark brown when wet, and tinged with a rustiness of lichen. And Africa, from here, was simply a treeless mound: at first the rocks, then a bank of white pebbles, and then this treeless mound with the lighthouse to one side. And the sky lay low and windswept. I turned to watch the waves roll in from ice. I saw bad weather as a wall approaching, and two fishing vessels pitched and tilted as they ran for home before it. The waves rolled in and crashed against the rocks. I stood upon the rocks and thought of those other rocks and the blood-red sunset at the confluence of the Limpopo and the Shashi. My journey lay within me as burden again. Those rocks up there and these down here. And all the dust and upheaval, all the emptiness and teeming of life and human aspiration between. I listened once more to the voices of all the people I had seen. At first I heard only a babble of argument and contradiction, but then the voices seemed to merge, no individual songs or stridencies; they were one voice, humanity's, seeking always to assuage the pain and find significance. Om; I am. And the voice seemed as restless and as searching as the waves which swept between the rocks and then slid back, swept in and then slid back, the ebb and flow of life and breathing.

I stood on the rocks until pellets of cold rain flew into my face. That became my sign: my purpose was complete. The weather closed about me. I turned and went back into the storm-racked land.

N
W E
S

BO

NAMIBIA

Upington

Bar

Orange River

Hopetown

ATLANTIC OCEAN

GREAT KAROO

GAMKASKLOOF
(THE HELL)

SWARTBERG MOUNTAINS

LITTLE KAROO

Willown

Ladismith

Paarl

Swellendam

De Rust

Oudtshoorn

CAPE TOWN

L'Agulhas